TATELINES

by
Loren Tate

Published by
The News-Gazette, Inc.

The News-Gazette

EDITOR AND PUBLISHER — John Foreman
EXECUTIVE EDITOR — John Beck
MANAGING EDITOR — Dan Corkery
SPORTS EDITOR — Jim Rossow
PHOTO EDITOR — Darrell Hoemann
PROJECT MANAGER — Amy Eckert

Front cover photo: John Dixon, The News-Gazette
Cover design and book layout: Joan Millis, The News-Gazette

ISBN: 978-0-9798420-4-7

© 2008 by The News-Gazette, Inc.

All rights reserved. Reproduction or utilization
of this work in any form now known or hereafter
is forbidden without the written permission of
the publisher, except for use in a review.

Printed in the United States of America

The News-Gazette, Inc.
15 Main Street
Champaign, IL 61820
Phone: (217) 351-5252
Fax: (217) 351-5245
www.news-gazette.com

ACKNOWLEDGMENTS

It all began with Darrell Tippett in Monticello, Ill.

After my father, John Loren Tate, died of tuberculosis in Kentucky, mother and her brat moved to Illinois to be closer to her parents in Hoopeston. She met Tip in Urbana, and they were married in time for me to enter the third grade in 1939 at Monticello. Tip loved sports, played and umpired softball, was Scoutmaster, helped initiate Little League, served on the city council and ran the weekly newspaper with a column, "Just a Tip." It was as though we were of the same blood, except for the Scout part. I played sports year-round and, through Tip's influence, enrolled in journalism at the University of Illinois.

Lady Luck played a big part from that point. T.O. White covered Illini baseball for The News-Gazette and knew me as a deep sub. So several years later, when I was calling in Monticello's 1955 Eastern Illinois League results to White on a Monday morning, he told me of a prep coverage job that was opening in Hammond, Ind. It wasn't fair to Tip, who had groomed me to succeed him, but he understood that I couldn't turn down the Hammond Times opportunity when it was offered. After all, while I was debating the move, the publisher raised my pay to $100 a week, and all I had to do was report on high school games.

I became sports editor there in 1963 and, again, got a fortuitous call when Ed O'Neil resigned as sports editor of The News-Gazette. This call came from Lou Baker, my former American Legion baseball coach in Monticello and, by 1966, the linebacker coach under Pete Elliott at Illinois. I was hired almost before anyone else knew the job was open, and just a few months before the infamous "slush fund" scandal struck down the Illini that December.

These are the events that brought me to a position that has changed only slightly since I semi-retired at age 65 in 1996. Along the way, I was sports director at WICD-TV Channel 15 for 11 years and continue to do radio work for WDWS. I still write four columns per week, many of which are included in this book of favorite articles. This book wouldn't have happened without a strong push from publisher John Foreman and sports editor Jim Rossow, who did a lion's share of the editing.

Additional thanks must go to daughters Melinda, Lori and Kathy, and son Travis, who were indoctrinated early with the realization that all important dates — marriages, family events, trips, etc. — were constructed around Illini and Cardinal games.

For the News-Gazette, I have covered 460 Illini football games, more than anyone else has seen (258 were losses). In basketball, the number is something well over 1,200. Like Joe Paterno, I'm taking them one at a time.

— Loren Tate

FOREWORD

For serious followers of the Fighting Illini, Loren Tate needs no introduction. His name is nearly synonymous with the primary subject of the newspaper column he's been writing for four decades.

For all those years, Tate has been a reporter, editor and columnist on what's almost surely The News-Gazette's most important beat. But his work is recognized far beyond the limits of our circulation, beyond even the distant borders of the vast Illini Nation. National broadcasters, flying into Champaign-Urbana to carry a game, are known to seek him out first, often referring to him later in their television comments as "the dean of Big Ten sportswriters." The famed Brent Musburger is fond of calling him "my old friend Loren Tate" and directing a camera at him courtside during Illinois basketball games. When a street in Champaign was designated "Loren Tate Way," ESPN carried footage.

In part, that's because Tate is not "just" an accomplished reporter and writer. His voice is heard over radio station WDWS-AM at least three times a week, and for years he shared the booth as color commentator on all statewide game broadcasts of the Illini Radio Network. He has done local television, transitioned to the Internet and found himself quoted as an expert by other newspapers.

But it's through the pages of The News-Gazette that most people have come to know Loren, and it is from those pages that the following is drawn. Quite simply, Tate has covered it all – big games, big names, big wins, big losses, big news, big scandals. You name it, if it involved the Illini, Tate had the story – usually first and always best. Readers came to love him – or hate him – or alternatively love him and hate him. But they read him still – regularly and religiously.

That's about all a newspaper publisher can ask.

So just start reading this book. You'll be amused, enlightened, occasionally infuriated. But if you care about big-time college athletics, I bet you finish every word, whether you read them 30 years ago, yesterday or never before.

John Foreman
Publisher
The News-Gazette

TABLE OF CONTENTS

Acknowledgments iii
Foreword iv
Table of contents v
Introduction vi
Games 1
Issues 89
Coaches & Administrators 163
Players 203
Miscellaneous 253

INTRODUCTION

It's always about people.

Tradition, history, the past, the future ... they always boil down to the personalities, the achievers, the controversy makers, the trouble makers who create the legacies we remember.

Buildings are important but a revamped, ultra-modern Memorial Stadium would be an empty shell without the ghost of Red Grange and the warriors who have kept it alive. These young athletes have been the essense, the spirit, the memory makers, and with their coaches are the transmitters of the events that take place.

That's why, for me, the people come first in this compilation of columns, followed by the issues that highlight the decades, and finally the contests themselves.

The toughest part is where to start after 42 years and more than 10,000 Tatelines columns. Where do you turn between J.C. Caroline and Arrelious Benn, between Harry Combes and Dee Brown?

How do you decide between the triumphs and the notorious activitiy, the character and the characters?

The story line begins when a 34-year-old novice scribe arrived at The News-Gazette in the autumn of 1966, just missing football greats Jim Grabowski and Dick Butkus and basketball standout Don Freeman, and only four months ahead of the traumatic UI "slush fund."

Tate's version of Illini athletics begins in that distant time, and comes to life in what were once daily columns. But it won't be told chronologically. Rather it will weave back and forth through the athletes, coaches and great rivalries, and through events that often tested the university.

The eight-year reign of football coach Mike White was typical of the larger era with his Rocky Mountain highs and Death Valley lows, the big games won and the bigger games lost.

The story line will veer off to include little-known academic revelations about Jesse Jackson when the one-time presidential candidate, who arrived on campus as an Illini quarterback candidate, was obliged to leave the university for plagiarism. And the lineup will get back on track with in-depth analysis of the Missouri-Illinois baskeball series, the sparkling Final Four runs in 1989 and 2005, and the dash to the Sugar Bowl in 2001.

For better or worse, these columns comprise one man's view at the time these events took place, or perhaps a reflection of them a few years later.

— Loren Tate

GAMES

FIRST OF FIVE COLUMNS ON ILLINI - OHIO STATE FOOTBALL
NOVEMBER 11, 2007

For the first time in more than a half-century, the Illini defeated a No.1-ranked football team and put themselves in position to earn a Rose Bowl trip at the end of a topsy-turvy season.

COLUMBUS, Ohio — Why not Illinois? WHY NOT?

In a long football season marked by coast-to-coast upsets, Ron Zook's Illini pulled off the most significant shocker of all Saturday. And now, after dispatching Ohio State 28-21 with a game-ending, eight-minute march, these gritty Illini, reflecting the unquenchable energy of their leader, possess a triumph that will mark them throughout their careers and their lives.

Not since 1956 had Illinois defeated a top-ranked team, and that long-ago win against Michigan State didn't carry postseason significance. This one guarantees a tie for second in the Big Ten if the Illini defeat Northwestern and could propel this 8-3 team all the way into a Jan. 1 bowl.

And if Zook isn't Big Ten Coach of the Year, who is?

His imprint on this UI program is getting larger every day. Last season, Zook's recruits at Florida deprived Ohio State of the national title. And on Saturday, in the gathering darkness with 105,453 desperate fans roaring and pleading for a rally, the Illini broke Ohio State's 20-game Big Ten win streak and shattered the Buckeye dream.

And yes, Yes, YES, the Illini have an inexplicable tendency to play their best against Ohio State. These were the same old Illini knights felling their favorite dragon. Unbeknownst to anyone in this state, they've won three of the last four in Ohio Stadium and have split the last 18 games in the series.

If you complained about Zook accepting unnecessary penalties at Iowa, bite your tongue. If you were critical when 10 UI infractions spoiled the effort against Michigan, go sit in the corner. If you called for Eddie McGee to replace Juice Williams, don the dunce cap.

A master schemer on this day, Zook gambled twice on fourth down and won. Shortly before halftime, with the score 14-14, it was fourth and 1 at the Ohio State 43, and Rashard Mendenhall bounced outside for a 25-yard romp to set up the go-ahead TD.

More dangerous was a fourth-down call from his own 33 with less than seven minutes to go.

"I knew it was only an inch," Zook said, "and during the timeout, Juice grabbed me and said, 'I can get you 1 inch.' I could see it in his eyes and I said, 'You'd better.' Juice is a tough competitor. People saw in that fourth quarter why he's our starter."

Zook tied his program to Juice two years ago, calling the Chicago Vocational senior from Columbus after a 40-2 loss and promising, "When we return here in two years, it will be different."

There were bumps along the way, just like Zook said there would be. There were times earlier this season when McGee came in out of the bullpen. But Illinois started every new week with Williams No. 1, and Zook never wavered on that.

Not that Williams didn't suffer.

"For a long time, I stopped reading the paper," he said. "I let the negative things get to me. I was down after I took a hit (and was sidelined) in the Missouri game, and after the Western Illinois game, I didn't know if I deserved to be No. 1. But after we lost to Iowa, I said, 'Enough is enough. I'm just going to have fun.'

"Today was very satisfying, with all that noise in the locker room, guys on chairs and water flying everywhere."

It looked like a shootout at 14-14, but the UI defense shut down the Buckeyes for nearly the next 40 minutes. That gave Williams time to build a 28-14 lead with four touchdown passes against a team that had permitted five in 10 previous games. And he managed this stunning effort without a turnover and with one penalty. Illinois netted 260 yards on the ground, just 88 of it by the UI's new all-time single-season rushing leader Mendenhall, against a foe that was giving up 65 rushing yards per game.

And it was Juice, bursting up the middle as Ohio State protected the perimeter, who kept the late clock ticking with clutch 13- and 12-yard third-down runs to run out the clock. Juice was right at home in this hard-hitting encounter.

It was the level of near-perfect football that Zook proclaimed would be required. And he got it from both sides, whether it was J Leman turning in a spectacular 12-tackle game, whether it was an attacking D-line putting pressure on Todd Boeckman or whether it was Dere Hicks, Miami Thomas and Antonio Steele spearing interceptions.

Before the game, two trusted Columbus authorities spoke with concern about the Buckeyes, noting that a favorable schedule and "a weak conference" allowed them to reach No. 1 in a path cleared by shocking upsets elsewhere. And athletic director Ron Guenther, ever the optimist, reminded that Illinois was only three crucial plays from being undefeated.

Maybe these old rivals were closer in ability than some of us realized. And once the dust settled from the game's early breakaways, it became clear that Illinois had the strength up front to take Jim Tressel's club to the limit, that Zook had backups ready to fill in for injured standouts Vontae Davis, Arrelious Benn and Russ Weil, that Illinois had a battle-hardened quarterback whose time had arrived.

"Zook painted the vision for this team," Leman said. "He brought in the talent, and he pushed us through hard, speedy practices. I only had eight wins in my career, and now I have eight wins this season. We got beat on some plays early today, but I had good keys and intuition on what they were doing. I knew their personnel and I read the guards on runs and the tackles on passes. They run a lot of power plays, and we like that.'

Illinois still might have pass defense problems, although 14 interceptions this year is a marked improvement. And Illinois might not be able to play 60 minutes without a turnover next Saturday. But it is obvious, from a pure physical standpoint, that Illinois hasn't been overpowered in a game all season. Zook has successfully meshed the old with the new, the veterans like Leman, Chris Norwell and Martin O'Donnell from the Ron Turner era, with the more highly touted youngsters.

He put them together and got a masterpiece Saturday.

Days later, in watching Illinois control the clock for the last eight-plus minutes, it seemed impossible that Williams would keep coming up with just enough on third down. No wonder Ohio State fans felt "this couldn't be happening." And it occurred that an Illini upset of this nature could only come against Ohio State, which has lost 11 of 23 in the series dating to the magical 17-13 win that led to the UI's previous Rose Bowl trip in 1983. There is something about Ohio State that brings out the best in the Illini.

NOVEMBER 17, 2002

Before instant replay, a debated non-catch by Illini Walter Young in the end zone allowed Ohio State's Buckeyes to survive in overtime and maintain their national championship run.

CHAMPAIGN — Why is it so many football showdowns, epic clashes that fans will debate for generations, hinge on plays that unfold too swiftly for the human eye?

One blink and you missed it. Look at the feet and you overlook the bobble. Follow the ball and you misjudge the feet.

And so it happened again Saturday at Memorial Stadium in this Year of the White-Caned Officials.

Ohio State is still unbeaten and heading toward another shootout with Michigan. But if the Buckeyes lost a first-quarter TD when a diving Craig Krenzel reached the ball over the pylon — three 5-yard penalties followed — the Illini lost an overtime score when Walter Young bobbled and then regrasped the ball before tumbling out of the end zone.

"The ball was not in possession of the player (Young) when he was inbounds," Big Ten referee Dave Witvoet said.

"There is one more reason for instant replay," said UI coach Ron Turner, frustrated and worn down by year-after-year pleas to the Big Ten office.

Illinois, playing its most physical game of the season, saw consecutive end zone calls go against it in overtime. First, Aaron Moorehead went high for a jump ball from Jon Beutjer, and his landing foot came down barely out of bounds. The fact that contact carried him over the line doesn't matter.

Then Young, with Illinois trailing 23-16, ran a fade route to the opposite corner.

"I knew after I juggled it that I had it before I went out of bounds. He (the official) made the call, and that's what he's paid to do," said Young, who like last season is closing fast with 25 catches for 324 yards in his last three games.

"I started to protest, but I knew we had another play (which failed). This one hurts. We felt they couldn't stop us. I told Jon that we had a favorable matchup on my side (against No. 37 Dustin Fox), and he kept going to me (10 completions)."

Truth is, once the Illini survived a first quarter of ineptness and weak punts against a numbing north wind, an Ohio State defense that hadn't given up a second-half touchdown in five games was placed in constant stress.

"We stopped ourselves" is the way Turner put it. And he was right.

The Illini had the Big Ten's premier defenders on their heels with their tongues out on the last eight possessions. Note these consecutive Illini efforts.

— The UI marched 73 yards for a field goal before halftime.

— Boosted by Eugene Wilson's 52-yard punt return, Illinois went ahead 10-6 on Young's 19-yard TD reception.

— With Ohio State reeling, Antoineo Harris committed the game's only turnover after reaching first-down territory inside the Buckeyes' 18.

— Two sacks halted the Illini ahead of John Gockman's 47-yard field goal late in the third quarter.

— Beutjer scrambled 5 yards to the Ohio State 30 in another promising drive, but tackle Tony Pashos was called for a 15-yard penalty after the play, Turner noting: "I saw it, and I didn't think it was a good call. If it's blatant, call it, but in a game like this, let it go. Guys get emotional."

— Illinois returned yet again to the Ohio State 36 where Beutjer recovered his own fumble 5 yards behind the line, just enough for Gockman to miss a 59-yard field goal attempt.

— With 1:04 on the clock, Illinois quickly covered 44 yards to set up Gockman's tying 48-yard field goal.

— Then came the overtime, where one end zone pass was ruled correctly and the other was not.

So, how good are the Buckeyes? Do they belong in the national title game against Miami?

You be the judge. From here, they look like 1,000 other Buckeyes teams, better than some and not as good as others. They made it into Michigan Week via five road wins by an average margin of six points.

Cincinnati was distressed at not beating them. So were Wisconsin and Purdue. Even Northwestern, with 396 yards in total offense, hung in until two late turnovers in a 27-16 result.

But give the Buckeyes credit. The defense rises when it has to, and it survived again with the help of a friendly overtime call that instant replay might have reversed.

Don't look for any outcries outside of Iowa. The league will profit by more than $500,000 per school if both Ohio State and Iowa reach the eight-team Bowl Championship Series. For the Illini, it is a lost season, starting turtle-slow and finishing in a nasty breakup with Lady Luck at home.

I remember thinking, "Wow! The Illini got all the breaks in the 2001 season." They rode Kurt Kittner's clutch passing to the Big Ten football title as rivals encountered quarterback problems repeatedly down the stretch. But the breaks turned the other way in 2002 as a good team tumbled to 5-7, including an overtime loss to the national champions.

NOVEMBER 9, 1980

Dave Wilson awakened the football world to Mike White's aerial game when he shattered NCAA records in a 49-42 loss to Ohio State.

COLUMBUS, Ohio — Mike White had asked his beleaguered athletes to relax and have some fun.

That's exactly what they did Saturday afternoon in Ohio's heartland. And even as they permitted 49 points in the modern game of passball — a cross between soccer and outdoor basketball — they nearly surprised themselves, and narrowly missed joining the Oregons, Georgia Techs, San Jose States, Mississippi States and Arizonas who have rocked the upper structure of Division I football.

"I've been hesitant to express pleasure, even with what David Wilson has done, when we failed to win," said the Illini coach after the Buckeyes' breathless 49-42 victory, "but this was something special. We gained the respect of a fine team, and the respect of their fans. This could be an important cornerstone upon which we can build.

"I'm especially pleased for our players. This gave us a great psychological lift. Sometimes it takes years for a team like Illinois to realize it can play on the same level with an Ohio State. The guys threw their bodies around, got into the swing of things and regained their self-esteem. Now they're looking forward to going to Indiana next week. This game could have some very positive returns even though we lost. We could take off from here."

Turning to Dave Wilson, whose passing heroics have rewritten the Illini, Big Ten and NCAA record books, White said:

"It's unbelievable what he has accomplished in such a short time.

Can you imagine, in 10 games he has set the all-time Illinois career passing record. It's amazing. Back at Cal, Steve Bartkowski and Steve Rivera worked on their act for several years. We operated on the belief that it took two or three years before a passer and a receiver really got to know each other. Dave wasn't even here last summer, and yet he walked in here this fall and started completing passes to everybody. Look at all the different receivers."

Ten teammates caught 43 passes for 621 yards, shattering the all-time NCAA pass-yardage record by 50 yards. He threw bullet turnins, led darting receivers over the middle, threaded the needle on sideliners and lofted bull's-eye bombs. It was an absolutely fantastic performance, one that clearly stamped Wilson as a bonafide NFL prospect. And he did it against a conference-leading defense with three seniors in its deep foursome, two of them 3-year lettermen and NFL candidates in Vince Skillings and Ray Ellis.

"That's what makes it such a tremendous accomplishment," said White. "It came against a quick, aggressive Ohio State defense. He just plain wore them out. Maybe we didn't realize it but we actually had a chance to win with just a couple of breaks. We had momentum and their fans were in shock. It proves that if you have a good pass game, you have a chance against an opponent with better personnel. And let's be honest, Ohio State has exceptional personnel.

"Dave is a remarkable person. He never lets anything bother him. He has great powers of concentration."

Wilson was surrounded by Ohio writers afterward. He was almost nonchalant as he spoke.

"We relaxed and had a good time out there," Wilson said. "I think back to the Michigan game, and with it being televised in my home (California), I was probably pressing. Last week against Minnesota, my mother and girl friend came to see the game and I tensed up again. I was more relaxed today."

As always, the query came about his eligibility status and his pending case. Again he replied directly:

"That's past and it's not on my mind so much anymore. Still, little things come up and certain people from other schools have to get their two cents in. I don't worry about it"

One who knows something of the UI athletic program and its finances offered an eye-popping opinion of what the White-Wilson combination has meant to the UI this fall.

"Illinois hadn't won a home game in two years and attendance dropped sharply in Gary Moeller's third year," noted our informant. "It went from 43,000 for Michigan to 41,000 for Ohio State and finally 30,000 for Indiana, and the outlook for 1980 was extremely bleak.

Based on what has happened, I'd estimate the changeover to White and the performances of Wilson has been worth nearly $1 million to Illinois this fall. Without Wilson, I'm not certain who, if anyone, Illinois would have beaten."

For the only time I can remember, a rival crowd stood and cheered the losing Illini after the game. For me, this signaled a breakthrough for a White operation that brought the fans back and surged forward to register five straight winning seasons and a perfect Big Ten season in 1983.

OCTOBER 29, 1967

First-year Illini coach Jim Valek enjoyed his finest hour in a 17-13 defeat of Ohio State. His tenure, however, was short-lived in the post-slush fund era as the Illini won just one game in 1968 and 1969.

COLUMBUS, Ohio — Did you notice the picture on Page 1 of Dave Jackson diving high over the pile for the game-winning touchdown against Ohio State?

That was no spur-of-the-moment thing. Coach Jim Valek installed that special leaping play in practice last week after the Illini failed in so many short-yardage situations against the huge Notre Dame line. It paid off twice in the winning drive. Jackson dove for 3 yards on a fourth-and-2 situation at the Buckeye 28, then dove those final few inches into the end zone.

"You should be able to make something on that play every time," said Valek, noting that defensive linemen have to charge low to keep from being blocked out and hardly have time to react to a scoring missile with the quickness of Jackson.

In practicing the maneuver last week, Valek lined up four freshmen just past the line of scrimmage to catch Jackson in the air, thus preventing possible injury. The first few times he tried it, Jackson didn't really leap too high. Then as he gained confidence in the idea (and for the fact the freshmen would catch him), he dove high over the line.

There wasn't anyone there to provide Jackson a soft landing Saturday but that didn't bother him.

"I just wanted to win," he said and he did everything possible with his 19 carries for 78 yards and two TDs. The young speedster has shown no tendency to fumble and is running with greater confidence all the time, indicating that Illinois may have that long-distance threat it has been looking for. And you can't help but wonder how Illinois might have fared against Minnesota if he hadn't been injured trying to block on the opening kickoff. Valek had built his offense around Jackson for the Minnesota game, just as he did for Saturday's game.

Used primarily as a flanker before, Jackson was moved to a set position behind the quarterback and provided a 1-2 threat with fullback Rich Johnson.

Johnson didn't have a big day (nine carries for 29 yards) but he was a mighty happy boy when the game ended. He had been the brunt of a practical joke the previous night at the Lincoln Lodge when a mysterious box arrived with his name on it.

It was postmarked Columbus and it had something alive in it. Figuring it was practical joke, the Lodge deskman opened it (ever so slowly ... some thought it might be a rat) and it turned out to be a chicken with a yellow stripe down the back.

A connected note told Rich that this yellow-striped fowl could be the Illini mascot for Saturday.

Johnson and his mates were more amused than mad about the incident, but they were aroused enough to make several references to it following the 17-13 victory. Although the note was signed, "Bucks," no one believed that Ohio State players or officials had anything to do with it.

Dean Volkman had his finest afternoon as an Illini quarterback and much of the credit for his 200-yard day must go to the offensive line.

Dean received superb protection for his passes in the second and fourth quarters (he only threw twice in the other two periods). He was tossed for only one loss all day, and his poise and execution were perfect on the final game-winning march.

"The line blocking has never been greater," said Volkman, the married senior from Evansville who went all the way.

"The nice thing about the final drive was the fact we had plenty of time to mix the running game with passes. Each supplements the other. If there's only a minute or two left, you have to pass and it is plenty hectic. This time, we didn't have to worry too much about the clock."

Woody Hayes, braving the 40ish temperatures in a short-sleeved shirt as usual, took the defeat hard. He was downcast and bitter.

But this writer doesn't hate him for that. It was interesting to hear Louisville's Larry Jordan tell of his experiences with Hayes when he was on Woody's priority recruiting list four years ago.

"Woody got me in his office and he locked me in with him," recalls the Illini senior, who made one particularly hard tackle Saturday.

"He told me I'd better come to Ohio State because his team was going to whip the tails off Illinois in two years. It was really interesting session and I'll admit I was swayed.

"But I came to Illinois and sure enough Ohio State beat us in my sophomore year. Woody came right over to me and reminded me. We have gotten even the last two years but I haven't said anything to him."

Jordan says Hayes mentioned that he "doesn't care what people think of me. Just look at the record." Larry still has a tie given him to wear on a night out in Columbus. Woody saying, "Here, take mine. It is more important for a young guy like you to look sharp than an old guy like me."

But Woody's magic is fading on the football team, and if his prize freshman squad doesn't blossom and make him a winner, the dean of Big 10 coaches could be in trouble. He is 0-3 at home this year and the wolves are starting to howl.

We'll never know for sure, but the scuttlebutt is that UI assistant coach Buck McPhail, a former fullback at Oklahoma, put the chicken in the box and sent it to Johnson to fire up the Illini. It was 15 years before Illinois beat Ohio State again, although the 31-24 thriller in 1968 remains one of my five most memorable Illini losses.

OCTOBER 16, 1983

Illinois defeated every Big Ten team in the fall of 1983. The 10-game win streak got its lift from a mid-October comeback against Ohio State.

CHAMPAIGN — When Illinois received one last chance against Ohio State on Saturday, quarterback Jack Trudeau moved toward the huddle with mixed emotions.

He was puzzled by Ohio State's decision not to try a field goal on fourth-and-4 with 1:48 left, thankful that the defense had held firm at the 17, and hopeful he could move Illinois into field goal range.

"A tie keeps us one full game ahead of the Big Ten's best team," coach Mike White had reminded a day earlier. So, trailing 13-10 and having been dominated throughout the second half by Ohio State's massive bruisers, the UI brain trust was thinking in terms of a wind-assisted field goal.

The five-play series unfolded so suddenly, so shockingly that it took everyone's breath away, including the Buckeyes'. Turnover-troubled Illinois, which hadn't generated an offensive touchdown in the game (Dave Edwards scored on a 49-yard interception return), traveled 83 yards in 37 seconds.

So if the 17-13 victory stands as a tribute to the defense, left black and blue from blockbuster Keith Byars' 168-yard performance, the precision two-minute offense that White brought from the NFL deserves a share of the limelight.

This two-minute operation was a total mystery to a bungling, confused Illini team before White arrived. Most memorable were the wasted timeouts and sideline indecision in narrow losses to Navy (13-12) and Iowa (13-7) in 1979. But that was another era, forgotten in the din of a windy Saturday that, in those riotous concluding minutes, tested 60-year-old Memorial Stadium to its foundation.

In that sudden, decisive strike, these Illini covered 83 yards and changed the course of Illinois football. And regardless of what the polls may indicate, the Illini, not Michigan, are the favorites in the Rose Bowl race because Michigan has yet to face the other Big Ten powers, Iowa and Ohio Sate, and must play Illinois at Illinois.

PLAY ONE: Trudeau is blessed with the excellent trait of not permitting his previous mistakes to bother him.

"No, I didn't even think about those two interceptions," he said. "I knew what had to be done and I concentrated on that."

He picked out Argenta-Oreana's seldom-used Scott Golden, the third wide receiver in Illinois' special passing formation and a senior with seven catches in the first five games. Jack sent him deeper than usual on a previously-unused sideline pattern for a 24-yard gain.

White, who sent in the play, said: "We had been taking the underneath routes. On this one, we moved up to the next level."

PLAY TWO: Identical with play one, good for 22 yards.
"They meant to bump Golden and throw him off his route, but he avoided the cornerback and found a hole in front of the 2-deep zone near the sideline. I figured it would work again if they played the same defense. If they changed, someone else should be open. They didn't change and there was Golden again."

PLAY THREE: Trudeau figured it was time to go to his tight end, Tim Brewster, but the Buckeyes had similar ideas. Looking around, Trudeau saw Golden, who wasn't even supposed to be in the pattern, break into the clear again but his pass deflected off Golden's hands.

"Scott was so shocked to see the ball coming toward him again that I don't think he was prepared for it," said Trudeau.

PLAY FOUR: Trudeau scanned the field for a receiver when he realized that the Buckeyes' containment had broken down.

"When it opened up, I had an angle to the right sideline and I ran as far as I could. I thought I could get us in field goal territory."

Trudeau gained 16 yards before Rowland Tatum banged him out of bounds, placing the ball on the Ohio State 21 and allowing Illinois to hold onto its two timeouts.

The timeouts were critical to the game strategy because if Illinois had used another timeout, Trudeau would not have gambled on the upcoming run. Also, if Ohio State led by six instead of three, the Buckeye defense could have played more conservatively at the 21. The Buckeyes, you see, were desperate with the realization that a tie would kill their Rose Bowl hopes as surely as a loss.

PLAY FIVE: White called for a fullback draw but, at the line of scrimmage, Trudeau caught the movement of the Ohio State safety and anticipated the impending blitz. His audible call was "38 toss," a simple sweep with Thomas Rooks carrying.

"The best place to call a play is at the line of scrimmage," said Trudeau, "because you can see what the defense is doing. That's the strength of our two-minute offense and we work on it a lot. We can call almost every play in our repertoire without a huddle."

Said Rooks: "When I looked at the Ohio State defense, I was hoping Jack would call (an audible) and he did. I was immediately open to the outside and I got great blocking from Jim Juriga and the others. I want to thank them. The execution was great. The only defender I saw was No. 12 (Garcia Lane) and I cut back inside him.

"It was a great feeling, a great victory. We had been frustrated by the fumbles and interceptions, but Coach White had us prepared for them. He said that in a hard-hitting game like this, there were bound to be mistakes and we shouldn't let the ups and downs discourage us."

With that burst, Rooks set off the wildest hometown celebration in nearly two decades. The huge crowd had almost come to accept the inevitability of another hard-fought loss to Ohio State when Illinois erupted 83 yards with only Trudeau, Golden and Rooks touching the football.

It was the first win over Ohio State since 1967 (by the same 17-13 score) and it made heroes of Dave Edwards (two interceptions), Don Thorp (11 tackles) and those gritty defenders who remain the heart and soul of the UI Rose Bowl quest.

"It was the most wonderful victory of my life," said middle linebacker Mike Weingrad, a Columbus (Ohio) native. "I've never been involved in anything like it. Ohio State plays tough football and I'm proud to be on a team that defeated them. The Buckeyes don't give you anything. You have to take it from them."

For me, Julie Rykovich's 98-yard interception return to nip Ohio State on a sloppy field in 1947 will always be my biggest football thrill. Second on the list is Rooks' TD dash, the St. Louisan seemingly headed out of bounds to stop the clock for a tying field goal when he cut back and took it all the way against the Buckeyes.

FIRST OF FOUR COLUMNS ON UI'S 2005 BASKETBALL RUN
JANUARY 26, 2005

A hard-fought basketball triumph at Wisconsin was No. 20 in a row for Bruce Weber's athletes.

MADISON, Wis. — Sometimes skill isn't enough. Sometimes it boils down to courage ... poise ... discipline.

And that's how Illinois severed the nation's longest homecourt winning streak Tuesday night at Wisconsin. Tuesday's 20th consecutive victory, 75-65 against the Badgers, was unlike any other contest this season.

The carnival required 217 media credentials and attracted 18 television stations. A few stragglers from Orange Nation, blessed with bank accounts capable of taking a $300 to $500 hit (for each ticket), were spotted around the Kohl Center. But they were outnumbered by 17,000 deep-throated partisans in a sea of red. It marked the first time all season the top-ranked Illini didn't have extensive vocal support.

And for the first time, the Illini received what could have been a knockout punch in the second half. Lockport's Alando Tucker went berserk with six straight bull's-eyes directly after the break, and the Badgers could smell victory up 56-48.

"They were picking us apart," Illini coach Bruce Weber said. "They had relied on three-pointers in the first half (7 of 13), but they decided to go inside in the second half. We couldn't stop them."

But Wisconsin coach Bo Ryan felt the need to rest star center

Mike Wilkinson and Tucker at the same time. Just that quickly, the Illini defense took a bite out of the hosts, who failed on three straight possessions while Illinois climbed back in on Rich McBride's only three-pointer in the last three games and two free throws each by Deron Williams and Luther Head.

In a flash, it was a tossup game again with more than eight minutes to go. And big sub Jack Ingram, who had turned down some earlier looks from the perimeter, drained two straight treys to ignite a 20-7 run in the last eight minutes.

What we're watching is one of the most remarkable runs in Big Ten history: 16 consecutive Big Ten triumphs and 34 wins in the last 36 games overall.

The Illini did it Tuesday night despite another stretch of weak three-point defense, with interior problems created in part by foul troubles (James Augustine sat out 16 minutes in the first half), and with Dee Brown basically nullified on offense (he was 2 for 9). But in the final furlongs, doubt crept into the Badger huddle. Illinois won the last four minutes 14-1.

"This was a great moment, the most exciting of the year," Weber said. "This is all part of our journey, and we need to smell the roses and keep having fun. These guys enjoy the limelight and the crowd. They rise to the occasion and play their best in the biggest games. They are proud of what they accomplished."

And like the overtime defeat of Iowa, where late defensive stops saved the day, a defense that at times appeared so helpless locked in with the help of some erratic Badger play.

Ingram's production continues to impress — he was effective on both ends — but the Illini have been hampered this month by starters picking up two fouls early and spending long minutes on the bench. This happened to Williams against Northwestern and Iowa and is an ongoing concern in the front line, where neither Augustine nor Roger Powell played more than 26 minutes Tuesday.

It is a tremendous break to have the same starting lineup for 20 consecutive games, but that lineup is shattered frequently by the need to protect regulars in the early minutes.

"Augustine had two fouls in the first four minutes," Weber said. "I wanted to put him back in before halftime, but he is so rambunctious, and I didn't know if I could trust him. They weren't going to Wilkinson at that time, so I just kept him out."

And just when the agile Augustine returned, Tucker erupted. It was another case, as the Illini have seen through the years at Wisconsin, Indiana, Iowa and Purdue, where a former Illinois all-stater has caught fire in coming back against the home state. But Tucker, who sat out last season with a foot injury, is somewhat hobbled again and apparently can't sustain these lethal outbursts. He didn't have a point in nine first-half minutes, scored six baskets in the next 7 1/2 minutes and had one basket thereafter.

If Tucker returns to health, Wisconsin will be difficult to deal with. But the Badgers miss Devin Harris and Boo Wade, not because their guards didn't shoot well but because the offense lost all semblance of discipline when the heat became hottest.

It was happening before our eyes, win after win, and I wondered in the press room: "Do any of us realize just how dominant Deron Williams is becoming as a playmaking guard?" Don't look now but he could become the greatest Illini in the NBA as he keeps growing with the Utah Jazz.

MARCH 7, 2005

Illinois' 29-game winning streak came to an end at Ohio State.

COLUMBUS, Ohio — They're still mighty good, but they're not perfect.

With a magical 30-0 regular season a few seconds away, Bruce Weber's rock stars were felled by the inside power of Terence Dials and a once-in-a-lifetime, 25-point spree by an oft-overlooked redshirt junior from Cincinnati, Matt Sylvester.

The large orange-clad turnout in the sellout crowd (19,200) at Schottenstein Center could only shake their heads and walk away.

Blitzed early by an 11-0 Illini uprising, Ohio State trailed throughout and had just one chance to go ahead. That's when coach Thad Matta elected to go for the jugular with 12 seconds left and his team trailing, 64-62.

"What did we have to lose," said the Hoopeston native, all smiles a year after his Xavier team knocked St. Joseph's from the unbeaten ranks. "When we huddled, I said, 'Gentlemen, we're going for the win.' I've never seen them more excited, and Matt told me he'd make the shot."

Launched from well beyond the arc, Sylvester's three-pointer splashed the net with five seconds remaining. When Roger Powell Jr. couldn't answer from similar distance, several remarkable Illini streaks ended: 25 straight Big Ten wins, 14 consecutive road wins and five straight against Ohio State.

"This was our chance to put Ohio State back on the basketball map," said the massive Dials, who scored 21 points and blocked Powell's layup attempt with a minute to go.

"This feels like a dream," Sylvester said. "The fans and the atmosphere were incredible."

Big Ten all-star teams will be announced soon, and it's likely Illinois will have three members on the first unit: Dee, Deron and Luther Head. But on a day when a modest bench produced major helpers in Jack Ingram and Warren Carter, none of the UI guards played like all-stars Sunday.

"Even if one of them is off, we usually have a couple step forward," Weber said, "but we didn't execute down the stretch today. Except for James (Augustine), we didn't have much offense toward the end."

None of the guards scored after Brown converted one of two free throws to make it 51-39 with 11:34 to go.

Brown scored eight of his team-high 13 points during a dazzling first 5 1/2 minutes when Illinois went on a 16-4 getaway. But ultimately Brown, his energy seemingly dissipating, ran aground in what might be called a delayed Sports Illustrated jinx coupled with heavy "air ball, air ball" jeering after he missed everything with a long shot, following that with another air ball.

Brown claims that "boos pump me up," but this wasn't the case Sunday.

Head, who has struggled to score in recent days, drained three treys in slightly more than three minutes at mid-game but otherwise was quiet, and Williams never got going as he produced a sub-par three assists and two points as fouls limited him to 33 minutes.

After going 29 for 50 from the arc in the two previous games, the Big Ten's most accurate and prolific three-point squad made 5 of 19 treys. Looking back, of Illinois' 23 field goals, 13 were layups or putbacks as poor jump shooting saw the field goal percentage dip to the second-lowest of the season, 38.3.

With three-pointers comprising 38 percent of their shot attempts, it is clear that this average-sized Illini team can't afford this kind of cold-shooting game when the NCAA tournament rolls around.

What does Sunday's loss mean?

They're still the same team, very good but beatable. By keeping their squad intact and healthy, and by mixing speed, ball handling and tenacious defense, they've earned the No. 1 ranking at a time when the Big Ten and the nation are feeling the impact of early NBA departures.

Illinois rose to the difficult challenges at Michigan State and Wisconsin but, since mid-January, mediocre teams like Michigan (57-51), Indiana (60-47), Iowa (73-68 in OT and 75-65) and Ohio State have found ways to defend and break the Illini rhythm.

As Illinois will discover in the near future, there are more Sylvesters out there ready to erupt. There are other centers with power moves comparable to Dials. Illinois, remember, no longer can be evaluated by what happened in November or December. The Wake Forest game is important from a rating standpoint, but it's a full season away. The basketball world has changed since then, and Illinois gets no more games at home. As we've seen by failures elsewhere, the UI's preconference schedule isn't as strong as it appeared at the time. And more recently, Illinois has been the beneficiary of meeting Big Ten teams in the midst of internal and/or injury problems.

Sunday's loss won't be detrimental to the future. It might, as some experts claim, even cause the Illini to be more focused. It's more likely that it won't carry any meaning whatsoever when the NCAA tournament begins.

But first comes the Big Ten shootout in Chicago, where Illinois enters as the only team with considerably more to lose than to gain. Once again, the target on the UI back is large ... just the right size for some underdog playing loose and confident with a "what have we got to lose?" attitude.

Some said the Illini didn't get out on Sylvester fast enough. That's poppycock. You can't stop a 6-foot-7 forward with a high release from launching a trey off a pick from well beyond the arc. Sylvester averaged fewer than one trey per game and was stone cold in the next game. He had his day in the sun. Such are the fortunes.

MARCH 27, 2005

Bruce Weber's Illini made the greatest basketball comeback in school history to defeat Lute Olson's Arizona team, 90-89, and reach the 2005 Final Four.

ROSEMONT — "I still don't know what happened," puzzled a weary but still healthy Luther Head.

"It's all a blur," a drenched Bruce Weber said.

Excuse these numbed participants because this Team of Destiny just got tapped by Lady Luck's wand in the most remarkable basketball game, considering the stakes, in 100 years of Illini history.

What happened was a miracle finish — "Praise the Lord," bellowed Rev. Roger Powell Jr. "He does make miracles" — in a shocking 90-89 overtime triumph that kept the title drive alive.

Even the roaring orangeclads in the Allstate Arena crowd of 16,957 began to lose hope when Arizona stormed ahead 75-60, and the Wildcats had the basketball and a 77-68 lead with 1:30 to go.

Then lightning struck.

Head's steal made it 77-70 with 1:21 showing. In the huddle, the gritty UI players tried to convince each other they still had a chance.

"Coach said, 'If we're going down, let's go down fighting,'" Deron Williams said.

"I said if it's going to be, it will happen," Dee Brown said.

And it happened ... somehow. Williams blasted in for a layup between three Arizona free throws, and Head's three made it 80-75. Suddenly pandemonium reigned as the huge crowd became a cobra around the Wildcats' neck. A mid-court steal allowed Williams to lead Brown for a layup. And still another steal on a tip by Jack Ingram set up Williams for the trey that tied it 80-80.

That's how they caught up, and then they almost broke it open in overtime when the UI's 12th steal shook Head for a breakaway and 90-84 spread.

But what will become known as the greatest game in Illini history, even surpassing the twin victories against Louisville and Syracuse in 1989, didn't end there. Junior Hassan Adams hauled Arizona within one and had the ball at the top of the circle with 10 seconds left. OK, take your hands from your eyes. You can look. Adams couldn't create anything against the rugged Williams and wound up missing badly a rushed shot at the end.

Weber's team, ranked No. 1 for 15 weeks, now has progressed as far in the tournament as any UI team in the past.

So often these dramatic March showdowns end the other way. It all began more than a half-century ago when great UI teams came up two points shy against Kentucky in 1951 and St. John's in 1952. Moving ahead three decades, Lou Henson's strong clubs lost by three to Utah in 1983 and to Kentucky in 1984, by two to Alabama in 1986, by one to Austin Peay in 1987 and, in a devastating rally, by three to Villanova in 1988. The history lesson includes a last-ditch two-pointer to Michigan in the 1989 Final Four and a two-point loss to Dayton in 1990.

All those heart-breakers in a day long past, and more bitter disappointments under Lon Kruger, Bill Self and Weber last season. But if former Illini teams deserved better, Saturday's Illini were blessed. Arizona flat-out dominated Illinois on both ends for 38 minutes. Channing Frye ruled the lane with 24 points, 12 rebounds and six blocks, literally nullifying foul-troubled James Augustine. Williams and Brown struggled through long periods without scoring, Dee putting Illinois ahead 31-25 and then going nearly 24 minutes without a point. Lute Olson's basket-attacking offense ripped through the Illini defense for 21 point-blank baskets on dunks, lay-ins and tip-ins.

There wasn't the slightest indication that Arizona would let up, the Wildcats ruling even as the pregame story line, Salim Stoudamire, went 2 of 13 from the field. New York's Dick Weiss and other big-city scribes were poised to bury Illinois with their computers. They were already writing their leads. Illinois had lost. Illinois wasn't that good in the first place. Illinois hadn't defeated anybody worth note. Illinois couldn't handle a team with a quality big man. Illinois depends too heavily on three-pointers.

Well, they're in the Final Four. The body was temporarily flatlining, and it came back to life. Check for breathing before the burial. You might make a mistake.

Before the rally began, a Chicago Tribune writer made the long trek to the media room to file his story. Oops, better look again. To be honest, with four minutes to go, my only wish was to see the Illini make it close. It never occurred when they were 15 down that they could pull it out. It was a blur for everybody watching.

APRIL 3, 2005

Illinois reached the national championship game for the first time by manhandling Louisville, 72-57.

ST. LOUIS — How do you figure?

In a Halloween-like clash of Illini orange and Louisville black Saturday, three extraordinary Illinois juniors combined for one meaningless field goal in the last 25 minutes of the most important game of their lives.

That's Dee Brown, the "face" of NCAA basketball; Deron Williams, a sure-fire first-rounder in the NBA draft; and James Augustine, the MVP of the Big Ten tournament.

One basket. Plus three free throws. Five points in a Final Four showdown.

And yet there was little doubt as to the outcome. The giant orange-clad fandom in the packed Edward Jones Dome barely broke a sweat. Louisville hung close for 30 minutes and cashed in with barely a whimper, 72-57. The Cardinals managed eight points in the last 10 minutes.

It is one more example of this team's remarkable, sometimes inexplicable sense of sharing, a quality of bubbling chemistry that has carried Bruce Weber's forces into Monday's national championship game against North Carolina.

It is exactly where they belong. They have set the table with a scattershot of heroic performances. Look here and they hit you there.

It was Roger Powell Jr.'s turn Saturday. And Luther Head's.

They grabbed the Cardinals by the throat shortly after intermission and left them dangling. Those two gritty seniors split 40 points down the middle, Powell sitting out 15 minutes in the first half before going on a rampage with 12 of Illinois' first 14 points after the break. It reminded of his sterling finish a year ago when he bagged 22 against Cincinnati and 15 in a season-ending loss to Duke.

Head, meanwhile, drained six three-pointers to match the total of a Louisville team that had lived by the trey.

In the final count, four UI seniors of this supposedly junior-led team produced 53 points, almost enough to whip the Cardinals by themselves.

"Our juniors are great," Weber said, "but I said all along that we'd only go as far as our seniors could take us. They stood up tonight and got us to the championship game."

So Monday, with the miraculous rally against Arizona still ringing in their ears, the Illini will attempt to finish off their spectacular thrill ride. It already is the deepest advancement in UI basketball history, Harry Combes' three Final Four teams losing in the semifinal round, and Lou Henson's Flyin' Illini falling to Michigan in Seattle.

The last three Final Four losses came by an agonizing two points in games that could have turned either way in the closing seconds. Illinoisans have had to live with those disappointments.

Weber's athletes didn't leave any doubt Saturday. After shooting too many three-pointers (19) and drawing too few fouls (five) against Louisville's 2-3 zone in the first half, they conspired to force the ball inside thereafter. After a prayerful intermission, a fresh Powell was ready to take up the challenge. He erupted, even blasting in to dunk his own missed three-pointer. When Head converted Williams' feeds for back-to-back treys, Illinois was on an 11-0 run that had Louisville gasping, 61-49, under the six-minute mark.

The Illini, after shooting 37.5 percent in the first half, cashed 15 of 24 fielders for 62.5 marksmanship thereafter.

No excuses Monday. They have no limping Efrem Winters or ailing Kenny Battle as they reach this chance-of-a-lifetime showdown in the same near-perfect health that they've enjoyed throughout a 37-1 season. They couldn't be in a better mental frame, the entire squad confident that Dee and Deron are poised to break out as they often do after a chilly (5 of 17) performance. And they can count on a strong bench effort from Jack Ingram, who has grown to the point where he is as valuable as a starter.

Like Lute Olson before him, Louisville coach Rick Pitino poured out accolades.

"So many times, you say, 'What if?' when it's over," Pitino said. "You look back on a few key plays that could have changed the outcome. But in this case we had to pitch a perfect game.

"We hung in as long as we could, and then we lost. We had to zone primarily because we had a limited bench inside, and we knew it would be difficult to stop them from penetrating. If we played them 10 times, they'd win eight or nine."

Now comes the matchup the nation has been waiting for. Let the drum roll begin.

I have come to expect NCAA semifinal games to be the best, but the matchups with Louisville strongly favored the Illini, and they dominated without their junior stars' normal production. But I was worried because I knew the refs wouldn't call the back-down charges by North Carolina's Sean May in the title game. Sure enough, the Monday showdown found May bulling his way inside to make 10 of 11 shots. At the same time, Illinois missed 28 treys and Augustine was limited to nine minutes in a 75-70 Tar Heel win. It wasn't fair.

ILLINI THROTTLE MICHIGAN IN TITLE RUN
OCTOBER 30, 1983

Michigan football, ranked No. 8, blocked the streaking Illini in 1983, and this time the UI defense did the trick, 16-6, for the only UI win in the quarter-century between and 1967 and 1992.

CHAMPAIGN — Mighty Illinois shattered the last yoke of Big Ten football subservience here Saturday.

With a legendary, former redhead watching in Central Florida, and a coast-to-coast audience of millions tuning in on CBS-TV, Mike White's athletes completed a miracle October by whipping Michigan at its own game.

The score — 16-6 — tells the story. Michigan was held without a touchdown for only the second time in 72 games. It was the UI's first win in the series since 1966, only the second in a quarter-century and the first over the Wolverines at Memorial Stadium since 1957.

An 80-year-old Red Grange called in the formula by telephone. Blocking and tackling. And as bright sunshine bounced off the green Astroturf, these surging Illini hammered the proud visitors into submission and realized their finest hour in 20 years.

The outcome sent a long-suffering community into delirium. The old town hasn't seen anything like it in 20 years, and that last Rose Bowl-clinching effort took place at Michigan State with the nation in mourning over the death of President John F. Kennedy. By any measuring stick, this one was bigger.

Sophomore safety Craig Swoope, bidding for Midwest defensive honors, spearheaded a gutty unit that for the third time this season refused to allow its goal line to be crossed (Iowa was blanked and Michigan State scored on a pass interception).

"Defense! Defense!" was the cry in the locker room. With Mark Butkus rejoining the fold and linemate Don Thorp turning in another all-conference performance, the Illini never permitted Michigan's well-conceived slants and cutbacks to penetrate their 10-yard line and didn't allow the Wolverines to reach their own 40-yard line in the final one-third of the game (20 minutes).

And the blockers gave Jack Trudeau all the time he needed to complete 21 of 31 passes for 271 yards and two touchdowns.

At the same time, left-footed Chris Sigourney had one of those days a punter dreams about. He repeatedly knocked the Wolverines back on their heels, a hustling coverage downing the ball at the 7-, 2- and 11-yard lines and finally notching a two-point safety when Joe Miles tackled Evan Cooper in the end zone.

It was, as the Los Angeles Times' Bob Oates said, "a game between old and new concepts" — Bo Schembechler representing the old and Mike White the new.

This was never more obvious than in the last two minutes before halftime. Illinois went ahead 7-3 on a string of short passes with 1:50 showing, and Schembechler was given the football on his own 20. Three times he called line plays to nearly eat the clock before Steve

Smith passed into an interception (by Mike Heaven) with :10 showing.

Illinois sought to make use of what little time it had. Trudeau fired downfield to Tim Brewster for a 23-yard gain to the Michigan 32, the alert Brewster bouncing off the turf with a timeout signal just as he did a year ago in the closing seconds at Wisconsin. It put Chris White within field goal range but his 49-yard try lurched low and left.

The point is, while Schembechler's athletes have always appeared out of sync in short-time, long-yardage situations, White and his Illini thrive on them. Michigan had possession for 34.5 of the 60 minutes Saturday, but Illinois made more yardage, 378 to 246, and was again in absolute control throughout the fourth quarter.

Was it a revenge meeting? Yes, by any definition of the word, and Schembechler did not accept the result with grace.

He complained loudly about the officiating — it appeared on TV replays that two Michigan completions were erroneously disallowed — and he griped about crowd noise that jammed Steve Smith's signals. Michigan received only two penalties and he whined about both.

These, it would seem, are "rub-of-the-green" factors that make it tough to win at (as Illinoisans have learned) Wisconsin and Iowa, not to mention Michigan and Ohio State.

Nor has Michigan defensive coordinator Gary Moeller lost any of his bitterness. He refused at game's end to even shake hands with UI aide Brad Childress, an assistant under him during the 1977-78-79 seasons here. Moeller remains furious with Illinois when it really ought to be the other way around. After all, he nearly destroyed the UI football program, chasing away the fandom as he misdirected the team through 13 consecutive home games without a win.

But the fans are back and Illinois is taking aim on a Top 5 rating. This football program has been accused of everything from illegal picks to dirty play to outright cheating, so a little more complaining by Bo and more hatred stemming from Mo merely goes on the growing pile of unsportsmanlike bull feathers.

You see it really doesn't matter any more. Underrated and shamelessly discredited all season, these Illini are going to the Rose Bowl ANYWAY. They're going because they've been able to overcome such mini-disasters as a lost fumble on Michigan's 1-yard line and bounce back. When the chips were down this October, they believed in themselves and not in what their detractors said about them.

Hey, Bo, junior college products have character, too. And they can sure play football, can't they.

Michigan has always pounded Illinois, setting up a long line of great receivers for key touchdowns. But Bo Schembechler was short of receivers in 1983, and the Illini were safe after David Williams raced past the Wolverines for a 46-yard TD reception on the first play of the fourth quarter. This win seemed almost routine to me.

FIRST OF SIX COLUMNS ON FLYING ILLINI
MARCH 22, 1988

Villanova holds the distinction of producing the greatest title-game upset against Georgetown and the most demoralizing basketball triumph over Illinois.

"I've never suffered a loss quite like this. I guess it'll take time for it to really sink in." — Steve Bardo, Illini sophomore

CINCINNATI — Fervent Illini fans hold a variety of expectations for Illini basketball.

Some dream of the team reaching the Sweet 16, others the Final Four. For me, a close follower for considerably more than 40 years, the single wish is that they leave the tournament on the attack, that they lose to a superior team, that they not embarrass themselves.

This is a much more challenging request than you would first imagine.

On Sunday the Illini walked off the court glassy-eyed and stunned. Each witness will have to put his or her tag on it.

My view is conditioned by my feeling that each NCAA game is a crapshoot, and this goes double since the arrival of the three-point shot. For the first time in history, a team can gain a point by fouling even if the free throws are good. And on Sunday the Illini, unable to convert their free throws after building a 56-46 lead with 3:00 showing, became the latest victim of it.

Coach Lou Henson will recover. He spends too much time balancing himself on the high wire to be thrown by any eventuality. He prepared the athletes and put them in a position to win, and that's all he can do.

The truth is, this team shot too poorly for too long a stretch this season to think this weakness might not crop up again under intense tournament pressure.

It's like golf. Fundamental flaws aren't always apparent in routine games or hot streaks. But when the screws are tightened for tournament golf, when each shot grows in importance, look out. For the unsound, fundamentally weak putter, 3-footers begin to look 10 feet long. The better golfers prevail because they were better in the first place.

For the Illini, the unfortunate aspect, again, is that the team will be remembered for its last game. The "big one" got away. It was hanging, right out there on the line, and it slipped the hook.

These Illini bounced back from a similar loss at Ohio State to blitz the Buckeyes, 118-86. They avenged losses to Indiana, Iowa and Michigan. But now there are no more games. Sunday's 66-63 loss to Villanova will provide the inscription for the tombstone.

"This one hurt," said Kenny Battle, "because it affected our future. We could have gone to the third round to play Kentucky."

"We kept encouraging each other and we kept thinking the free throws would drop, but they didn't. On my last one, I thought it was fine when it left my hand, but it bounced off the rim."

Eight UI tosses bounced off the rim in the last 2:45, the Illini getting just three points out of a possible 16 (if they had hit all their one-and-one opportunities).

"That's a hard way to lose, but it happened," said Battle. "We'll have to live with it for awhile, but we have next year to redeem ourselves. Unfortunately, Glynn Blackwell won't get that chance."

There were moments in those closing minutes when the Illini thought they had weathered the storm. Kendall Gill's breakaway three-point point play made it 60-53 with 1:53 to go.

"I thought that iced it," Gill said. "I felt we were in good shape and we'd make our free throws."

But Mark Plansky countered with a three-point bomb within seconds, and the trio of Jens Kujawa, Bardo and Battle went to the line with the score 60-56, all missing. Suddenly, it was an epidemic. Six potential points went down the drain as the game stood scoreless for nearly 50 seconds.

Here, Jens, take the ball and win the game. Or you, Steve. Or you, Kenny. Anybody?

Said Henson: "I never felt comfortable because Villanova has such great shooters, but when your team plays this hard for this long you deserve a break once in awhile. Our problem, I'm afraid is that we wanted it too badly."

Unfortunately for the Illini, the game of basketball is divided into two distinct contests. The first lasts approximately 37 minutes and involves execution and positioning and techniques. It is excellent, flowing entertainment. The last three minutes is a free throw contest. The flow stops. So does the clock. If you're weak on free throws, you'd better build enough of a lead to survive that shortcoming. Or maybe have just a fair share of luck at the end.

"I don't believe in luck," said Henson. "You make your own luck. This was just a case of our shortcomings catching up with us. Remember, when you can't make a free throw, it's like a turnover.

"Villanova did the only thing that a team can do in that situation. Foul! No, I'm not suggesting a change in the rules. There's always too much fouling in the last three minutes, but we've done about all we can with the rules. You have to be able to make your free throws to be successful. We just have to put players on the court who can make them."

With so many quick, young athletes on the squad, Henson is searching for steady shooters to bolster that aspect. Chicagoan Marcus Liberty is already on campus. Jacksonville's 6-5 Andy Kaufmann, an 85-percent free thrower with an even higher percentage in the fourth quarter, is signed.

High on Henson's list is Lake Forest's 6-6 Rob Pelinka, who had runs of 46 and 40 free throws this year. Illinois is still in the chase for Mississippi deadeye Litterial Green and St. Louis Vashon's Sean Tunstall.

Maybe Henson should consider a platoon system. Use the "athletes" for 37 minutes and stick in the free throw shooters for the last three. Now there's a thought to get your mind off LaPhonso Ellis, missed opportunities or whatever agonies it has wandered into.

Call me stunned, speechless. Seeing that little sub drain those treys when the Illini couldn't make a free throw. This was more damaging than the Austin Peay game because this talented team had a real chance to go far in the NCAA tournament. It was the most damaging because the Illini simply blew it, a phrase I have seldom used.

DECEMBER 23, 1988

The Flying Illini were never more lethal than when they scored a record 127 points against Louisiana State shortly before Christmas.

BATON ROUGE, La. — This was a basketball game in the image of the late Pete Maravich, for whom Louisiana State's Assembly Center was named. Maravich was Louisiana's master of the run-and-gun game. He produced baskets by the bushel-full with a flamboyant, racing style.

With a lineup of NBA scouts looking on, Lou Henson put five Illini runner-gunners on the court here Thursday night, and they responded with an astonishing avalanche of points.

No Illini team ever scored more baskets (53). No LSU opponent ever got so many in the Center, or did more damage to the psyche of the Southerners. No Illini team ever matched the point production in the 127-100 triumph.

Yes, you guessed it, Henson wasn't happy about a porous first-half defense that allowed LSU to cling within 10 points, 61-51. But in the end he acknowledged the thoroughness of win No. 9, eight of which have been blowouts. Only once, in Monday's stirring 87-84 defeat of Missouri, has anyone been within shouting distance of the Illini with 10 minutes to go.

Still Henson, anticipating a tough Thursday game with Georgia Tech if the UI handles Tulsa as expected in Honolulu on Wednesday, fretted:

"They got behind our zone press early because we didn't rotate back quickly enough, and we let them penetrate our defense for too many layups," said Henson. "We used to have the reputation as a good defensive team, and I hate to see that slipping away."

Illinois came off 65.5-percent second-half shooting against Missouri to shoot 73.3 percent in the first 32 minutes, at which point Henson began his customary bench-clearing procedure. No Illini regular played more than 25 minutes in what had figured to be a hard-fought contest, the fifth-ranked Illini entering as a mere 5 1/2-point favorite, the same margin by which Missouri was favored over the Illini on Monday.

Lowell Hamilton destroyed LSU's starting center, 6-10 Rich Krajewski, so completely that coach Dale Brown removed Krajewski after three minutes and never put him back in. Kendall Gill was a whirlwind, running free for a career-high 27 points. Nick Anderson ruled the boards with 12 rebounds, nine more than highly touted LSU forward, Ricky Blanton.

Six Illini attained double figures and, while Larry Smith was scoreless, he had eight assists.

"You saw how we got inside early, and that opened the perimeter," said Gill, who measured his long jumpers as though they were free throws. "We traded baskets for awhile, but I figured we'd break out eventually. I was sure it would come, and it did."

Gill had high praise for LSU freshman guard Chris Jackson, a cat-like dribbler with a brilliant jump shot.

"He's the best guard. I've played against," said Gill. "I've had to guard Ken Smith of North Carolina and Rumeal Robinson of Michigan, and a lot of good ones, but he's got the quickest release I've ever seen. I've gone against Michael Jordan, and his release isn't that quick. I blocked one shot on him and I still don't know how I did it."

Jackson fouled out with 8:52 to go, just as Steve Bardo brought Illinois to the 100 mark with two free throws. Whereas the UI reserves have stumbled on other occasions, they kept the point total climbing in this one, and P.J. Bowman broke the UI scoring record with a medium jumper on the team's last possession.

Like everyone else, I was beginning to see the Final Four potential of this Flying Illini team. The Missouri rally three days earlier was spectacular, and the players were still riding high in Louisiana, but it was the red-hot reserves who brought the total to 127.

JANUARY 23, 1989

Crack junior Kendall Gill was injured just as the Illini reached No. 1 in the nation with a 103-92 defeat of Georgia Tech.

CHAMPAIGN — Marcus Liberty played 11 of 50 minutes Sunday. Larry Smith played seven minutes of regulation time, 17 minutes altogether.

Those two will be carrying a much bigger load in the future. The 17-0 Illini, who face eight Big Ten road games in the last 14, will proceed with Kendall Gill as a memory. Gone is the superb 6-foot-4 athlete who was recently honored as the Big Ten Player of the Week, who was named one of Dick Vitale's top five on defense, who ranked No. 11 nationally in three-point shooting, who may have been the most improved basketball player in the country.

"We just have to suck it up and keep going," said coach Lou Henson, recalling setbacks in recent years when Anthony Welch, George Montgomery, Doug Altenberger and Tony Wysinger were sidelined.

"This is not the first time something like this has happened. We'll pretty much have to go with seven guys from here on."

Gill suffered a stress fracture of the fifth metatarsal bone in his left foot in the 40th minute of the UI's 103-92 double-overtime defeat of Georgia Tech on Sunday. A pin was surgically implanted to strengthen the healing process, just as it was done for tailback Keith Jones at the outset of his junior season. Henson said Gill will be out for seven to eight weeks and might be able to return for postseason play.

With Andy Kaufmann gone due to a blood clot, the Illini squad has shrunk to an alarming level. Liberty, Smith and Ervin Small will round out a top seven that includes regulars Steve Bardo, Nick Anderson, Kenny Battle, and Lowell Hamilton. The only other recruited squadman is Parkland transfer P.J. Bowman. Junior college transfer Rodney Jones is available for practice purposes.

But the problem isn't depth as much as losing a player who, with his heady, explosive play, has given Illinois the winning edge.

Still, whatever the future brings, Sunday remains one of the high points in Illini athletics. And Henson paid tribute to his club's spirit in rallying from a 47-31 deficit.

"Our guys put a lot into this game, but what else is new?" said Henson. "They've been doing that all season. Tech almost gave us the knockout punch. But we hung in there.

"We had a problem communicating and executing the offense in the first half. Tech was red-hot and we couldn't hit anything. But we began to move in the second half and you could feel the momentum turn."

Tech coach Bobby Cremins, who has been singing Illinois' praises, said: "We played out hearts out, and I congratulate Illinois. We didn't want to fall on our faces, and I don't think we did. At the end, things got crazy, and we were in serious trouble (with Tom Hammonds and Brian Oliver fouled out) in the second overtime.

"I knew they'd come back in the second half. I love the way this Illinois team plays. They wore us down and they deserved to be No. 1.

"I feel horrible because we had a chance to win it. We were just a rebound and a shot away, and I thought we had the rebound at the end of the first overtime. I saw two blue shirts and I thought we had it, but those guys are so quick and they (Battle) made a great defensive play to tie us up."

Battle said of that play:

"I figured Lowell was on the other side of me...he (McNeil) faked and pumped, and when he came up, I was there. I had my hand on top of the ball and the ref was right there to call it.

Cremins called it "a nightmare," noting the Yellow Jackets lost in similar fashion to Louisville, 67-65, the previous Sunday.

"When I first scheduled this game, I didn't want to come here and I did everything I could to get out of it," said Cremins. "But this is a great team and a great basketball state, and I enjoyed this trip very much."

I commiserated with Henson about the high of reaching No. 1 and the low of losing Gill. With the Big Ten so strong that year, it was obvious the Illini couldn't stay No. 1 without Gill, but we felt confident about the NCAA tournament because we knew he would be back.

MARCH 17, 1989

Still burning from the upset loss to Villanova the year before, the 1989 Flying Illini faced their first severe tourney test against a Ball State team coached by Rick Majerus.

INDIANAPOLIS — I've seen ugly. I've viewed apparel featuring red hogs and red birds.

I've turned my head on red felt hats with a feather, and red cowboy hats that would frighten the bravest Apache.

I've witnessed red V-necks and red turtle necks and red plaid pants.

I was nearly run over by a white Cadillac with red plates, followed closely by a bright red Pinto with white plates.

I've seen the sartorial limits of red, mixed with black, or trimmed with greens, or flowing through all the colors of the rainbow.

And now we find ourselves bombarded from four sides by the red hordes of Louisville, the red hog-callers of Arkansas, the Cardinals of Ball State and the unhappy followers of Indiana University. They have common desire Saturday: defeat Illinois.

No, Indiana's Hoosiers won't be in the Hoosier Dome. But many of their legions will, and they're seeking revenge. They'll be solidly in Ball State's corner when the athletes from Muncie pit their 29-2 record against 28-4 Illinois.

An uproarious sea of red, which brought Thursday's evening session turnout to an NCAA first round record of 37,242, helped lift sagging Ball State out of a 54-47 deficit in the last eight minutes against Pittsburgh.

Had Pitt won, more than 10,000 Illini fans would have had the vocal edge Saturday. But with Ball State in, we're talking about nasty. We're talking about fierce. Ball State has picked up the Indiana flag that was thrown down when the NCAA sent the Big Ten champion Hoosiers, beaten twice by Illinois, packing to Tucson after their fans bought up more than half the Indianapolis tickets.

Don't listen to the experts who say it's a break that Illinois doesn't have to play Pitt. Hey, Pitt coach Paul Evans wants no part of the Illini.

Despite repeated efforts by coach Lou Henson, Evans simply refuses to pay back the game Pitt owes for an Illini trip to Pennsylvania in December 1986.

Ball State is quick and balanced, and has beaten three Big Ten schools — NCAA first-round winner Minnesota (63-57 up there), Purdue (70-56) and Northwestern (77-71). The Cardinals are on a 16-game win streak and are ranked in the Top 20 by AP, UPI, CNN-USA Today and Sports Illustrated.

Ranked defensively in the top five, Ball State has permitted only three players to score 20 against them all season, including Pitt's Jason Matthews (23) Thursday night. Nineteen foes have shot sub-.400 against the tight defense put together by colorful Rick Majerus.

So, we have two rivals at the peak of their game, both expecting to play better after getting the feel of the dome, and both supported by active home crowds.

I agreed with a supremely confident Illini fandom after watching the early-March triumphs at No. 3 Indiana and No. 8 Michigan, with a 118-94 rout of No. 15 Iowa in between. The Big Ten was tops in the country, and Ball State was no match for the Illini, 82-70.

MARCH 25, 1989

Injured Illini fly past Louisville with an exceptional NCAA regional performance.

MINNEAPOLIS — Some fans see the "A" at the top of the column and don't know what it stands for.

Well, today the numbers add up to 22, and they represent teamwork. Assists.

Of 39 Illini field goals against Louisville on Friday, 22 were the direct result of passes that set up those baskets.

On a night of incredible adversity, when the Illini were left without their two seniors, when the free throws wouldn't drop, when Louisville's behemoths were rejecting 13 of their shots, the undaunted Illini kept ripping through the Cardinal defense via both the dribble and the pass.

And coach Denny Crum, who has made six visits to the Final Four in 18 years at Louisville, recognized the Illini as something more than a gang of dunkers.

"You've got to give Illinois credit. They execute in the stretch getting the ball to the open man and shooting in on us," said Crum. "This is one of the best passing teams I've seen. They got the ball to the right man at the right place."

Nick Anderson was frequently the right man. He scored 24 points and was the dominant player on the court.

But don't overlook guards Steve Bardo, Kendall Gill and Larry Smith. While combining for 33 points, they also dished out 15 assists.

These Illini are, if you'll pardon a commercial, considerably more than a gang of athletic dunkers, as they are so often described. They are the products of a thorough coaching effort, unselfish on offense and fiercely competitive on defense.

"It's always hard to defend great athletes who pass the ball. And sometimes, even when we were in defensive position, they were quick enough to shoot over us," said Crum.

"Down the stretch, they turned it up a notch and they outplayed us. That's why they're 30-4 and that's why they haven't lost (22-0) in the games that Kendall Gill has played. They're good players."

Nothing that happened Friday discouraged them ... not the injuries to Kenny Battle and Lowell Hamilton ... not the 13 blocked shots.

Pervis Ellison, who garnered seven of those rejections, said he mentioned the intimidation factor Thursday in hopes the Illini would read it.

"We had a height advantage, and I wanted to contest as many shots as possible. But there was a stretch when Nick Anderson took control of the game. He just shot right over us. He really played well. They got a lot of high-percentage shots by punching it in on us. We blocked some, but we didn't block enough of them."

Anderson, asked to carry a heavier load than usual, admitted he "put more into this game than any other."

The husky Chicagoan shared the spotlight just as he shared in the teamwork: "Marcus (Liberty) really helped us tonight. He got to start and he responded to the coaches' confidence in him. I've played with Marcus for years, and I know his game. All he has to do is play Marcus Liberty's game and he'll be OK."

Prior to the Illini's comeback against Arizona in 2005, I have always paired the 1989 Louisville and Syracuse games in answering the question about Illinois' greatest basketball triumph. That regional tournament in Minneapolis was overrun with pro talent. I often compared it to a Final Four.

MARCH 27, 1989

The Flying Illini qualified for the Final Four with a resounding 89-86 defeat of seventh-ranked Syracuse.

MINNEAPOLIS — The rapidly diminishing "We're Thru With Lou" society canceled its meeting Sunday.

Crippled, embattled Illinois, the team that "can't win the Big One," emerged from another fiery shootout as the only No. 1 seed in the Final Four at Seattle.

They did it on guts, talent and great coaching.

So what's new?

They've fought from behind all season, so a 13-point deficit only made them play harder.

They were staggered by some questionable officiating calls — 10 of ref James Fife's first 13 calls favored Syracuse — but that's par for the course.

They hung on to eliminate Syracuse 89-86 despite physical disabilities and family concerns, just like always.

And in a tournament where a single wild Thursday evening took (1) a three-time champion who has been voted national Coach of the Year, (2) "Michaelangelo of coaching" Dean Smith, (3) 1988 runner-up Billy Tubbs, and (4) the possible 1992 Olympic coach (Lute Olson), the UI's 57-year-old Lou Henson demonstrated he still has a few tricks up his sleeve.

"Lou Can Do," read one of the Illini signs in the Metrodome. And Lou did.

With Lowell Hamilton barely able to go, Henson re-patched a center position that was weakened in the summer by the unexpected departures of Jens Kujawa and Phil Kunz and the inability of junior college transfer Rodney Jones to gain fall eligibility. Worse yet, an estimated 1,000 hours of recruiting on LaPhonso Ellis were wasted.

Marcus Liberty gave it a try but could not equal Friday's sterling fill-in job against Louisville. Ervin Small completed 17 minutes of bumping with just three personal fouls. And a gimpy Hamilton gutted it out for a time.

"The ankle was sore and I had no lateral movement," said Hamilton.

"I couldn't jump and I couldn't do anything offensively. I just tried to play defense the best I could and not get too involved offensively. I wanted to be out there, but it was hard. I was probably only 55 or 60 percent."

Syracuse recognized Hamilton's plight, fouling him in the desperate finish. Lowell hit just 3 of 10 free throws, causing Henson to return briefly to Liberty, who was promptly fouled and also missed.

But no amount of handicaps would stop these athletes in their relentless pursuit of Seattle. There's a fire burning within this squad, and hordes of Minnesota fans in the crowd of 33,496 recognized this as they became vocally involved in the Illini rally.

Down the stretch, game after game, Henson's 14th UI club has played with a fury that no Illini basketball team has ever matched. Nick Anderson, the heart and soul of the 10-game win streak, would jump over the Statue of Liberty if there was a rebound to be contested there. How do you do it, Nick?

"I love to bang with the big guys," said Anderson. "Hey, if you want to tussle, I'll tussle with you. You may get your half, but I gotta have my share.

"I hear Bo (Schembechler) wants Michigan to play Illinois. Well, you can tell him we'll be there. Just make sure he is."

Anderson, who speared an incredible 16 rebounds and scored 26 (but was mistakenly credited with 24), added:

"It all goes back to togetherness. You gotta play team ball and help your buddy. Each guy helps the other one. I scored because the guys got me the ball in scoring position."

Kenny Battle, ineffective Friday, performed as though trainer Rod Cardinal had fitted him with a bionic knee. While Syracuse was heralded for its lob play, Henson reminded the team that Syracuse's zone was vulnerable deep, and Battle sailed into the stratosphere to dunk three lobs in the first 11 minutes. He worked inside the Syracuse defense to convert 12 of 17 shots.

"When Kendall was hurt, we pulled for him. And when I was hurt this week, the guys pulled for me. We're a family," said Battle.

Battle and Hamilton had special words for Cardinal, who had not one but two invalids on his hands, and applied new ice packs to both at 10 p.m., midnight, 2 a.m., 4 a.m. and 7 a.m., hardly the way most people start their Easter Sunday.

And there was Gill, still unbeaten (23-0) this season, blood all over his jersey from a split lip, and shining as yet another product of Cardinal's magical handiwork.

Gill combined 18 points with eight rebounds, five assists and three steals. His spectacular one-handed tip dunk at 2:31 gave Illinois breathing room 83-78. His rebound save on Liberty's missed free throw at :20 let Battle expand an 87-86 lead with two at :15. And his sterling defense held All-America guard Sherman Douglas to one basket in the second half.

This is where Henson leaves his deepest mark: defense. Others talk about it and make an effort at it, but the Illini emphasize it and work at it.

After early-game breakdowns, Henson ordered two guards back to halt Syracuse's blistering fast break, and the UI's stern halfcourt "D" gave the Orangemen fits during the game's final 26 minutes. At times, for all their skills, the Orangemen ran down the clock trying to find an opening.

While Illinois continued to dent the Syracuse defense for point-blank shots, making 20 of 27 (74.1 percent) in the second half and rebounding several of the misses, the losers met increasing resistance.

Down 46-39 at the break, the Illini opened the second half with Anderson's bank and Gill's trey to get back in the thick of it. When they finally forged ahead 72-70 on Anderson's rebound with 6:24 left, the Illini led right to the end.

It's hard not to have feelings favoring Lou Henson. He's the original nice guy. But he caught a lot of heat for past NCAA shortfalls, and my strongest feeling after another heart-stopping win was for him. The Illini were overdue for some breaks, and they got them.

ILLINI LET PRIZE VICTORY SLIP AWAY
NOVEMBER 13, 1994

Penn State's greatest challenge in an undefeated season came at Illinois where the Nittany Lions rallied for a 35-31 victory.

CHAMPAIGN — Within minutes of Saturday's disastrous ending, when the adrenalin and the single-minded focus and his first-ever cortisone shot were wearing off, when his mind and body were returning to normal, 287-pound Illini guard Jonathan Kerr could barely walk.

"I was told what was going to happen, and I accept it," he said before lurching down a stadium hallway.

"This was a game I couldn't miss. But it's tough, these last few weeks. It's getting tougher every time."

Kerr has a sprained ankle but took a shot and played every offensive down in Saturday's 35-31 loss to unbeaten, Rose Bowl-bound Penn State.

In fact, the oft-criticized starting unit of Kerr, Mike Suarez, Derek Allen, Ken Blackman and Chris Koerwitz ... the guys who couldn't create the surge needed for Illinois' running game ... played all the way against the Nittany Lions. And for three solid quarters, they had 72,364 Memorial Stadium fans and a nation of partisans between delirium and shock.

Illinois' failure to pull off the school's most earth-shaking upset since the 1950s doesn't alter the fact that Koerwitz, Blackman, Allen, Suarez and Kerr overcame a myriad of ailments and played the game of their lives in propelling Ty Douthard to 172 yards rushing on 35 plays.

It carried into the third quarter when Douthard and Johnny Johnson (on one scramble) rushed for 58 of 71 yards in a bid that ended with a Chris Richardson field goal. That, unfortunately, was the UI's last legitimate shot as Penn State, growing stronger while the Illini faded, controlled the ball to overcome the UI's 31-21 lead. It was similar to Penn State's rally at Michigan State last year, the Nittany Lions erasing a 37-17 deficit to win, 38-37.

You don't beat a great offensive juggernaut unless you keep scoring, and Illinois did not. And Joe Paterno's gang put their winning

TD across with just 57 seconds showing, thereby not leaving Illinois enough time to counter. Illinois fell to 6-4 with defeats by one point, one yard, one punt return and one last (96-yard) drive.

"We let one get away," said Johnson. "They're good, but we showed that we could play with them.

"We came together as a team today, and we went inside and outside on them. We were right on top of them. We thought we were going to win. That's why we're taking it so hard."

The rugged Douthard had the kind of game a back dreams about. He had just 3 negative yards in 35 trips. His net of 172 was the most by an Illini since Howard Griffith rushed for 263 vs. Northwestern in 1990.

"We converted the third-down plays in the first half but we didn't in the second half. That was the difference," said Douthard, sidestepping the "moral victory" cloak.

"I thought we dictated the way the game would go in the very first series. I saw how the game was going to go, and I could tell I was going to get the ball a lot. The line was blocking and everything was clicking."

On the other side, the defensive zone crumbled as Collins picked apart the UI secondary. The quarterback completed 17 of 21 second-half passes, and all seven in the winning 96-yard drive. The proud UI defense, which was No. 4 in the country going in, didn't even force a fourth-down play in the last two Penn State possessions.

And those five offensive linemen, who could have been sitting on top of the football world, who would have drawn accolades from coast to coast, who could have had the pain of their injuries dulled by a glorious victory, trudged head-down to the locker room in a could-a, would-a mode.

Could-a, would-a, phooey.

I never saw the Illini crowd at a pitch of higher expectation as the underdog Illini created a double-digit lead. But I could see the Illini tiring and there was just enough time left for Collins to direct that final Penn State march. It was a heart-breaker.

PACKERS MEET BEARS IN CHAMPAIGN
OCTOBER 2002

Memorial Stadium draws the national spotlight by hosting the Chicago Bears vs. the Green Bay Packers.

CHAMPAIGN — For heaven's sake, use your head, people. Let the university workers off an hour early. Give them a chance to clear the parking lots before the late-afternoon onslaught.

What we have is the biggest sports event in Champaign-Urbana history. No, it's not Farm Aid or Elvis, but Bears-Packers on Monday Night Football. It is huge ... so huge that we're scratching our heads trying to find something close to the magnitude of tonight's game.

Here's a rundown of 12 previous sports events staged here that had a combination of fervent fan interest, quality teams and national implications. All but two were Illini football or basketball games. We'll mention those first:

(1) Sept. 8, 2002, Bears-Vikings: The first regular season NFL game at Memorial Stadium spotlighted C-U and attracted a packed house, many of whom had difficulty reaching their seats if they entered the wrong side. Still, the stadium was never noisier, and the Bears, coming off a 13-3 season in 2001, displayed more of their close-game magic as they rallied to win 27-23.

(2) June 4, 1977, NCAA track meet: Illinois hosted such a successful, moving championship that NCAA officials brought it back to Memorial Stadium in 1979. Illini stars Craig Virgin and Charlton Ehizuelen contributed to the excitement with second-place finishes, and Doug Laz soared 16 feet, 6 inches to take fourth in the pole vault.

We will now turn back to football, where four unforgettable showdowns meet qualifications:

(1) Oct. 18, 1924, UI-Michigan: An undefeated Illini team drew 21,579 for its last Big Ten home game against Wisconsin in 1923 and 12,599 for Butler one week before the stadium dedication. A hat-wearing sellout crowd of 67,886 turned out for Michigan, and Red Grange splashed the champagne bottle with one of the great performances in college annals. Grange's renown was such that, a year later, he turned pro at season's end and drew previously unheard-of crowds all over the nation.

(2) Sept. 28, 1946, UI-Notre Dame: The Irish claimed national championships in 1943, '46, '47 and '49, and the undefeated squad in 1946 posted a 26-6 victory against a talented UI squad that won the Big Ten and the Rose Bowl. Whereas the Illini drew 14,060 for their previous home game with Iowa in 1945, the September showdown packed in 75,119, the first stadium crowd to surpass 70,000. It was, after all, Notre Dame.

(3) Oct. 29, 1983, UI-Michigan: Mike White's 9-0 Big Ten run, gaining impetus with a 17-13 comeback win against Ohio State, was capped by a 16-6 defeat of the Wolverines, the losers' only Big Ten setback. Ticket scalping was never more feverish as 76,127 crowded in to see two Top 10 teams. The game stands as the UI's only home victory against Michigan since 1957.

(4) Nov. 12, 1994, UI-Penn State: Joe Paterno's Nittany Lions were en route to a 12-0 season, but the stage was set for a major upset as Illinois broke ahead 21-0 and still led 31-21 with eight minutes to go. With the stadium literally steaming with excitement, Kerry Collins led Penn State on a 96-yard march to turn it around in the final minute and win 35-31.

Now to basketball, where the intervals between serious contention have not faced such long periods of separation:

(1) Feb. 20, 1943, UI-Wisconsin: The Badgers, national champs in 1941, stood as the Whiz Kids' primary rival during World War II. But little doubt remained as to the nation's premier quintet when Illinois blanketed the Badgers at home 50-26. The Whiz Kids completed a 12-0 Big Ten season with an average victory margin of 24 points but declined an NCAA tournament bid when Jack Smiley, Ken Menke and Art Mathisen entered the armed services.

(2) Jan. 14, 1952, UI-Indiana: Red Kerr joined the returnees from a Final Four club, and the Illini used a riotous 78-66 Huff Gym victory against the No. 4 Hoosiers to reach No. 1 in the nation and move toward coach Harry Combes' third Big Ten title in four seasons. Archrival Indiana gained revenge a year later and took the NCAA crown.

(3) Jan. 11, 1979, UI-Michigan State: Illinois made the cover of Sports Illustrated after Eddie Johnson's sideline jumper edged Magic Johnson and the top-rated Spartans 57-55 to give the Illini a 15-0 record and a likely No. 1 spot — if they hadn't lost to Ohio State in overtime two days later. Michigan State regained its momentum and took the national title.

(4) March 1, 1987, UI-Indiana: Illinois became the last team to defeat Indiana's national champions, 69-67, as Steve Alford clanged a three-pointer at the end. Indiana was ranked third at the time, and,

of the many high-intensity, bitter-feeling clashes with Indiana during the period, this one stands out.

(5) Jan. 22, 1989, UI-Georgia Tech: In a season where nearly every Flyin' Illini game had national import, the double-OT 103-92 defeat of Tech is spotlighted because it lifted Illinois to No. 1 ahead of a 69-62 loss at Minnesota. Lou Henson's club was undefeated at home as the nation's eyes followed his team into the Final Four.

(6) Feb. 6, 2001, UI-Michigan State: In a shootout between Top 10 quintets, Bill Self's first Illini squad laid it on the Spartans' defending national champions 77-66 before an electric crowd at the Assembly Hall. This was the high moment as Illinois carried its momentum all the way to the Elite Eight.

The Packers and Brett Favre won that day, and I left wondering more about the nature of those crazy Bear fans who littered the south campus with empty beer cans. Yes, this was a much more rowdy crowd than attends Illini games.

FIRST OF TWO COLUMNS ON ILLINI - KENTUCKY SHOWDOWNS
DECEMBER 6, 1966

Harry Combes, in his final season as Illini basketball coach, could smile after a hard-fought victory over Adolph Rupp's Kentuckians.

LEXINGTON, Ky. — The University of Illinois basketball team has shown coach Harry Combes one very important thing.

It is a lot tougher at game time than it is in practice, and this ability to play in competition is something you can't buy or learn.

You either have it or you don't, and if you do you can set back and let the other guys complain as they inevitably will in this wild, emotional game. Overall, Illinois played a sparkling game Monday night, just as the team had in the opener against Butler. The outcries of Adolph Rupp in defeat should not be taken seriously. If Illinois got any breaks in the first half, things evened up after that.

Kentucky was called on 30 fouls to Illinois' 19, but this does not necessarily prove anything. Illinois never trailed in the game, and used holdout tactics which led to Kentucky fouls, especially late in the game.

If Pat Riley is disappointed, he can blame it on his own over-eagerness and the misfortunes of circumstance. He was simply too aggressive under the basket early when the officials were especially watchful for such things. It got rougher and rougher underneath as the game wore on.

In the Illinois dressing room, a jubilant team was still very much in awe of the performance of Wildcat senior guard Lou Dampier, the Indianapolis Southport star who had remarkable 40-point night in trying to make up for the absence of fellow All-American Riley.

"They were in trouble, so naturally everything went to Dampier, he is an amazing shooter," said Combes.

One of the more jubilant of the stars was Rich Jones, a product of Memphis, Tenn.

"It's great to win one in the South," he said with meaning. Kentucky still hasn't had that first Negro basketball player and it's not likely during the reign of Rupp who is 65 and may not retire until he is 70.

Only this year Kentucky gave out 10 basketball scholarships, nailing down No. 1 prep star Mike Casey of Shelby County among seven excellent recruits from the homeland.

"We picked the state clean," said the proud Rupp. "Of the top nine Kentucky, we got seven. It was a great recruiting year."

The two Kentucky didn't get were black. You can draw your own conclusions. Rupp has been too successful for anyone to question. As a matter of fact, he is revered so highly in Lexington that he can do no wrong. His is above the law. He openly defies the fire marshal, putting in end bleachers and permitting standing-room-only sales beyond legal limit. He could park in the middle of Main Street and no policeman would ticket him.

Rupp is a legend in his own time and Kentuckians fight for the right to participate with him. It is a remarkable atmosphere. Stop and think. When was the last time you saw cheerleaders run to console a beaten coach, and fans by the dozens agreeing "it wasn't the coach's fault?"

Did the noise bother any of the players?

"We're used to that kind of stuff," said Rich Jones. "Their zone pretty much cut me off in the second half, and I didn't get as many good shots. They overshifted my way."

Jim Dawson called it a wrapping zone which swarmed all over anyone who got the ball in the corners. The Kentuckians are very fast and aggressive, but the one slow one on the court, 6-8 Ron Dunlap, more than made up for this lack of speed with his rebounding.

He and Deon Flessner especially demonstrated confidence gained through experience. The rest they received in the easy Butler victory helped save them for this master effort. Flessner said his sore leg didn't bother him although Combes took him out once late in the game when he began to wear down.

Combes was sorry he didn't get to use the sophomores more but, under the circumstances, he could not. Of the "big three," Dennis Pace saw the most action at the end, Steve Kuberski played briefly and Dave Scholz did not get in at all.

As a new writer on the scene, I mentioned some of the racism attached to the game but I didn't feel free to write extensively about it until years later. I thought this Illini team might be a Big Ten champion and a Final Four contender, but those possibilities soon ended when the "slush fund" broke later that December.

MARCH 25, 1984

After defeating Villanova and Maryland, Lou Henson's Illini fell to Kentucky in the 1984 NCAA regional at Rupp Arena.

LEXINGTON, Ky. — Just before suppertime Saturday, Kentucky's proud fandom stood as one in the dusk to salute The Good Kids as they flew out of the Commonwealth toward a hero's welcome in Illinois.

The Kentuckians could afford to be gracious. Their high-powered Wildcats won "the battle for Seattle" by a score of 54-51.

But not before Lou Henson's courageous athletes bucked superior talent and the grand tradition of Rupp Arena to come within a single less-than-courageous officiating call of having a shot to tie the game with 14 seconds to go.

It was that close.

From a fundamental standpoint — and the back-slapping Kentucky fans recognized it — the Illini outplayed Kentucky all the way. Bruce Douglas, Doug Altenberger and the gang dug in defensively with as much determination as they have ever shown. The tall, swift Wildcats had not a single fast-break layin nor a dunk in 40 minutes. Think about it.

Offensively, the Illini methodically persisted until they found an open jumper, the exact shot they wanted under the circumstances, unguarded and easily makable.

Ah, but there's the rub. UI shots reverberated around and wouldn't drop. In the first half, when the Illini clung within 24-22, they shot 45 percent (9 of 20) on generally unguarded attempts while Wildcats caressed the home nets at 64.7 percent (11 of 17) on, as they say in the gymnastics, attempts of a high degree of difficulty. There were three flying jumpers by 6-foot-11, 245-pound Melvin Turpin, two Mount-like recoil bombs by Jim Master, a couple of double-clutch, flip-and-hope slopins by Winston Bennett and, to break the tie, a desperation rainbow from the erstwhile three-point range by Dicky Beal with Douglas in his face at :02.

Kentucky, to its credit, upgraded its shot selection later as 7-1 Sam Bowie, with an assist from the officials, broke out of a scoreless first half. When Bowie slammed over the top and sent bodies flying for a rebound goal, the zebras looked away. When he butted and backed straight into a flat-footed Efrem Winters, they mistakenly whistled the foul on sore-ankled Efrem. When Altenberger made a clean steal — "Sam even said to me, 'You got it clean'" said Doug — a phantom foul sent Sam to the line for two of his 11.

But Hank Nichols, who sent Henson leap-frogging off the bench with a five-second call on Illinois' first possession, saved his most hurtful decision for last. This is the same Nichols who, as an Atlantic Coast Conference ref, participated in an NCAA commercial to show what human fellows these refs are.

Human is the right word. In Rupp Arena, with all those rabid Kentuckians threatening your life, you don't take the ball away from the Wildcats in the closing seconds, not even if Beal travels (which he did) or is tied up against the midcourt and the sideline by Douglas and Winters (which he was).

"I knew he traveled," said Douglas. "Then I thought we'd either get a jump ball (Illinois' possession) or a five-second call. I never dreamed they'd call a foul. We had Beal trapped. I didn't foul him. I definitely didn't foul him."

All Beal could say later, after cashing two free throws to expand the 52-50 Wildcat lead and being named MVP in the Mideast Regional, was: "Man, I'm glad we don't have to play those guys again."

Small wonder. In the unselfish world of floorplay, Beal was throughly bested by Douglas, who distributed 11 assists, came up with three steals and blunted the pointman on Kentucky's fast break like a hard-riding cowboy turning a stampeding herd.

But the Quincy sophomore, who nearly brought his season shooting average to .500 with a 37-for-60 finish in the last four Big Ten games, never quite regained his touch in postseason activity. He was 10 for 31 in three playoff games, and he had the open shot from the top of the circle that could have turned a 50-48 Kentucky lead into a deadlock just under the two-minute mark.

When it was over, a distraught Henson shook his head as he saw Illinois with two more field goals despite overall 46 percent shooting to Kentucky's 55.3.

"The thing that's hard to believe is that Kentucky can be that physical and have just two personal fouls in 19 1/2 minutes in the second half," he said. "I don't mean to cry but that foul ratio (8-2 in that span) was critical. It's tough enough to play Kentucky on their own court without letting them shoot 17 free throws to our nine.

"Did Beal travel? Well, again, I don't want to sound like a crybaby, but they've let traveling go throughout the NCAA playoffs. This isn't a criticism, it's just a fact. Check that last play on TV. You can see what happened."

And in the hearts of the blue, Kentuckians knew what had happened on this Saturday afternoon. The system had prevailed. When they constructed the 23,525-seat arena adjacent to the Hyatt Regency complex, they perpetuated both Rupp's name and a high likelihood of continuing success. They've won 16 straight home games this season, holding the number of home losses to 48 over the last 42 years.

This is the world's most lavish amateur basketball program. It once produced an entire U.S. Olympic team. Its worldwide reputation attracts superstar athletes like Germany's 7-foot-4 Gunther Behnke and Brooklyn's Ed Davender who, if mystified by Lexington's Southern twang and love for horses, will quickly learn.

Its players reside in a $750,000 lodge; its radio network is the nation's largest; every game is televised; there are countless publications on the Blue and White.

Still, with just a break here or there, with just a little better shooting or a gutty officiating call, Illinois might have upset Kentucky's applecart. Thus ended a 26-5 season in which Illinois carried every loss to the closing seconds. Senior Quinn Richardson and The Good Kids deserved that mythical Kentucky salute and the hundreds of loyal Illini who met them at the airport.

Efrem Winters was the UI's leading scorer at 15 points per game going into the regional, but was barely able to jump against Kentucky. He had stayed up all night with UI trainer Rod Cardinal working on his ankle injury. Had Winters been healthy, well ... who knows. It seemed the Illini always had something go wrong in the NCAA during the mid-80s.

UI FOOTBALLERS WIN SOME CLOSE ONES
OCTOBER 29, 1982

Mike White's Illini had extreme good fortune in close games in 1982 before losing to Iowa 14-13 and Michigan 16-10, but still reached the Liberty Bowl where they lost to Alabama 21-15. What follows is a history lesson.

IOWA CITY, Iowa — If the Fighting Illini have any emotion left, Mike White will attempt to muster it up Saturday in Iowa City.

In a topsy-turvy Big Ten football race that has seen teams winning and losing in the final seconds every week, the Illini have survived four of the most exciting weekends in modern times with 75 percent success ratio.

Think about it for a moment:

— Beginning at Minnesota, back when the Gophers were undefeated and thinking 7-0 (they've now lost four straight), the Illini overcame a 31 to 11 disadvantage in first downs with a 22-0 fourth quarter deluge of big plays, resulting in a 42-24 triumph.

— Purdue fought back repeatedly in a spectacular shootout, nearly reversing a 38-34 result on a final play when a deflected Scott Campbell pass was actually caught beyond the end zone. It marked the first time Illinois ever won while allowing 34 or more points, and the squad entered the locker room too stunned to celebrate.

— Outplayed on the field and in the statistics, Illinois rallied sharply in the fourth quarter with two TDs to create 21-21 deadlock, only to have Ohio State prevail with a last-ditch march and a tiebreaking field goal with :03 showing.

— No game in recent memory compares to last Saturday at Wisconsin when, in the final minute, Illinois lost it (on a trick bounce-lateral pass play) and won it back, 29-28, on clutch passes by Tony Eason and a 46-yard field goal by Mike Bass.

Now, as the Illini prepare for Saturday's game at Iowa, they stand 6-2 overall and are very possibly within one victory of a postseason bowl berth.

If that should develop, it would be only the fourth UI postseason appearance in school history. But, if those historic game results are true indicators the UI has never been truly dominant even in their Rose Bowl championship years. They advanced with precisely the kind of narrow victories the Illini have been salvaging in recent weeks.

1946

The Illini looked back on a miserable stretch in the 1930s and the weakened war years — the 17-year record was 57-73 (6 ties) — when, in 1946, an enormous outpouring of talent emptied from the military onto the UI campus.

At the end position alone, the Illini were five-deep in standouts like Ike Owens, Sam Zatkoff, Bill Heiss, Jim Valek, Bill Huber, Ray Ciszek, Joe Buscemi and Frank Bauman, while Buddy Young, Art Dufelmeier, Juile Rykovich, Tom Zaborak and Paul Patterson headed the huge core of halfbacks.

Nevertheless, after an early 14-7 Big Ten loss to Indiana that dropped the team to 2-2 overall, Ray Eliot brought them through four consecutive Saturdays as heart-throbbing as the last four.

Repeated Rykovich heroics saved a 27-21 win against Wisconsin. When Don Maechtle's missed conversion left Illinois trailing 21-20, they tossed off all thought of playing for a tie. Rykovich, who starred as a Naval trainee at Notre Dame in 1943, fired a 31-yard halfback pass to Owens to set up the winning TD in the final two minutes.

Then came a surprise 13-9 upset of Michigan. With tackle Lou Agase playing 53 minutes and other regulars wearing down, subs like Valek, Buscemi, Babe Serpico, Jocko Wrenn and Vern Seliger joined forces to protect the lead in the face of Michigan's marches to the 16-, 6- and 8-yard lines in the fourth quarter. The Illini have made few more courageous stands.

The 7-0 win at Iowa was almost routine. Battling toe to toe with the Hawkeyes on a cold day in Iowa City, the Illini sent Ruck Steger rumbling into the end zone in the fourth quarter win it.

That brought on Ohio State and fullback Joe Whisler. The Illini hadn't beaten OSU in a dozen years and it was Buckeye day: wet and 43 degrees. Time after time Whisler hammered goalward in the second half, turning the middle of the field into a quagmire.

Just when it appeared the Illini might not be able to hang on any longer, Buckeye QB George Spencer decided on a piece of trickery, flipping a shallow pass toward Jameson Crane on the right side. A mud-caked Rykovich smelled it out, intercepted and returned 98 yards to save the game, 16-7.

That play was the single most remembered UI play since Red Grange ran wild against Michigan in 1924, and it laid the foundation for an eventual 45-14 Rose Bowl rout of UCLA.

1951

This mobile club, captained by Chuck Studley and featuring South Shore products Tommy O'Connell, Rex Smith, Dan Sabino and Pete Bachouros, stands today as the only undefeated UI team in 55 seasons. But each weekend was a thrill.

First, these defense-oriented Illini reversed a 7-6 loss to Wisconsin the previous year by turning back Harlan Carl and Alan Ameche, 14-10. Ace passer O'Connell was injured and the Badgers were more than doubling first downs as they led 10-7 in the fourth quarter when UI sub Don Engels squirmed free to launch a blind pass. It deflected off Steve Nosek's hands to Smith at the 8-yard line. John Karras banged in from 2 yards and Illinois hung on to win.

No one who attended the 7-0 win against Michigan here will ever forget it. A howling blizzard in 29-degree (and dipping) temperature turned the fans into human icicles. Twice Michigan threatened but could not score. Finally, with the clock rolling under five minutes, O'Connell brought Illinois mushing out of two inches of snow with a wobbly a 23-yard pass to Smith. The same duo worked again for 14 and finally, with 75 seconds left, Smith took an 8-yarder in the end zone to whip the elements and Michigan.

A 0-0 tie with Ohio State saw both clubs blow scoring opportunities, the Buckeyes gaining field position and forcing the UI to punt from its own 1-yard line in the fourth quarter. The bid died, however, when Bob Lenzini pounced on a fumble deep in UI territory, and Ohio State looked back on a bungled field goal try by Heisman Trophy winner Vic Janowicz from the 8-yard line earlier.

Then came a clearcut 3-0 win against Northwestern, the margin coming on Sam Rebecca's first-ever field goal in the second quarter. Again, the UI went to the Rose Bowl and shattered Stanford, 40-7, after Stan Wallace returned an interception to the 12-yard line with Illinois trailing 7-6 in the third quarter.

1963

The Illini were just a year removed from a 15-game losing streak when they rallied around Dick Butkus and Jim Grabowski to chase away the Saturday blues ... and they went to the Rose Bowl without defeating either of the Big Ten's perennial powers, Ohio State and Michigan.

The Illini fought back from a 17-7 deficit to tie Ohio State. Seven Illini turnovers, including a fumbled lateral to Jimmy Warren deep in UI territory, allowed Michigan pull out a 14-8 win in Champaign.

But this muscular team was otherwise perfect, avenging a 45-0 loss to Northwestern the year before by nipping the favored Wildcats, 10-9. The lone Illini touchdown came on a bid of trickery: QB Fred Custardo lateraling to ex-QB Ron Fearn who pegged a 33-yard TD pass to Warren. It was Illinois' first opening-game Big Ten win in 10 years, and it wasn't tucked away until Jim Plankenhorn booted a field goal past the outstretched body of Northwestern's George Burman, who came in unblocked. Actually, Burman ran past the ball.

Illinois was regarded a three-point underdog against Wisconsin but prevailed on (1) an early march aided by roughing-the-kicker penalty and (2) George Donnelly's 24-yard interception return for a score. Illinois was outgained 274-199 and outdowned 17-11, but protected the lead with superb defense.

Finally, with the title on the line, Butkus & Co. grabbed seven turnovers at Michigan State on Thanksgiving Day, and the Illini used two field goals and a Grabowski TD for a 13-0 ticket to the Rose Bowal. It was more of the same in Pasadena, 17-7, over Washington.

The point of this history lesson is that none of the past Illini successes, separated as they were by years of interspersed failure, came easy.

In 1946, 1951 and 1963, the Illini needed several major breaks somewhere along the way, became progressively stronger in November and reached a peak on New Year's Day. That 3-0 Rose Bowl record is particularly significant because it put a winning tradition on a program that has fielded losers in 32 of the previous 52 seasons (since 1930).

Part of the history of Illini football is how they've pulled out so many narrow triumphs in their championship years. The 1982 run to the Liberty Bowl preceded the undefeated Big Ten season a year later.

ILLINI POST BOWL RUNAWAY
DECEMBER 31, 1999

Illinois won its third bowl game in 36 years as quarterback Kurt Kittner led a 63-21 rout of Virginia in the Micronpc.com Bowl.

MIAMI — Ron Turner's Illini wasted money on their bowl trip to Miami.

They paid air flight, lodging and meals for something they absolutely didn't need: a punter.

While senior Neil Rackers wore his right shoe thin with 11 kickoffs and nine extra points, these incredible Illini didn't officially use their ace punter, Steve Fitts, all evening.

OK, you noticed, the red-haired Fitts came in with the intent to punt in the first quarter but Virginia jumped offsides ... and he did stay busy holding for extra points.

But this was an offensive outburst for the ages.

Considering the opponent and the circumstances, it was probably the most impressive outpouring of points in Fighting Illini history ... coming right after Lon Kruger's basketball team put up 107 against Loyola.

That's 170 points by those teams in one day. What other school can say that?

The wonder is that Kurt Kittner & Co. didn't score more than 63 because Virginia never came close to stopping them. This was strictly men vs. the boys, Illinois entering as an underdog (barely) for the ninth time in 12 games, and making a mockery of the oddsmakers for the fifth time, 63-21.

That's 178 points in the last four games, these Illini finishing as the highest-scoring team in school history.

Everyone got in his licks.

Kittner fired two TD passes to set the school record of 24, ran a bootleg for another and caught a TD pass from Brandon Lloyd on the latest Turner trickery. Receivers found gaping holes in the Virginia secondary, Rocky Harvey and Steve Havard combined for 194 yards rushing, and happy Miamian Jameel Cook demonstrated that Ohio State linebackers aren't the only ones who can't cover him in the flat.

They made it look so easy.

And these 63 points came despite two awful officiating calls that would have been reversed by NFL replays ... a goal-line Cavalier interception on which the ball clearly caromed off the turf, and a spectacular punt return by Lloyd that was nullified because the official didn't recognize an Illini rusher was blocked into marginal contact with the Virginia punter.

Like the Illini rally at Michigan, nobody saw this one coming. Virginia had tied for second behind Florida State in the Atlantic Coast Conference and had beaten Georgia Tech and Maryland in a three-game streak at the end of the season.

Illinois asserted itself with a 71-yard opening march, Kittner scoring on one of several UI touchdowns on which the Illini ball carrier skated unchallenged into the end zone. It was 42-7 at halftime, a stunned coach George Welsh suggesting "that was a bad a half as our team has had in many years."

From that point, it was just a case of finishing it off, and trying to bring some meaning to an 8-4 season in which the Illini fell at Indiana and were abused by Michigan State, Minnesota and Penn State.

The only conclusion is that this is a program on the upswing, a program with hot young athletes and a pro-style aerial attack with a flair for the unexpected. Most of all, it is a program now under the firm control of an alert, professional leader.

While we must remind ourselves that Illinois received the Big Ten's lowest-rung bowl berth as the seventh pick, the future looks bright because Turner has virtually his entire offensive unit back in 2000 while Penn State must rebuild its powerhouse defense, Minnesota has serious graduation losses, Wisconsin must reload without Ron Dayne, and it isn't clear whether Ohio State will regain its once-lofty perch.

What we see in the Big Ten is a league which has become dominant across the board, but may not have a clearcut national title contender in 2000. In other words, Illinois could be back in the loop and ready to look Michigan and Ohio State directly in the eye when they come seeking revenge in Champaign next season.

These Illini did everything in their power Thursday to send that message, to demonstrate that the turnaround is real. Enjoy the rush. That's only the third bowl victory for Illinois in 36 years.

When Illinois opened October by losing at Indiana in overtime, and fell a week later to Minnesota 37-7 with only 49,000 showing up, it looked like another dismal season. A miracle 35-29 win at Michigan turned it around, and all of us in the Illini community were astonished at the late-season explosion of touchdowns.

TATE SELECTS ALL-TIME BEST ILLINI
DECEMBER 9, 1998

Following are Tate's 1998 picks as the best Illini basketball players between 1940 and that time.

CHAMPAIGN — If it seems too soon to choose the Fighting Illini's 20th century basketball all-stars, well ... consider this like getting a jump on New Year's Eve. It's so much fun, why not whoop it up early.

The rules for this celebration are simple: Nobody before 1940. If comparisons between Dike Eddleman and Kenny Battle are a stretch, comparisons between 1922 All-American Chuck Carney and 1990s star Deon Thomas are impossible. So Andy Phillip and the Whiz Kids are in. Lou Boudreau and Pick Dehner are out.

And no current squadmen are considered, even if Cleotis Brown is one of the five best juco transfers ever at Illinois.

Here we go.

All-Time Illini Five (with apologies to Eddie Johnson and Kendall Gill):
    F-Don Freeman, explosive scorer
    F-Ken Norman, shot 60.9 for career
    C-John Kerr, MVP in Big Ten
    G-Andy Phillip, 1943 All-American
    G-Derek Harper, dominant on floor

Second Illini Five (apologies to Eddleman and top scorer Deon Thomas):
    F-Nick Weatherspoon, glass wiper
    F-Dave Downey, led '63 co-champs
    C-Skip Thoren, all-time rebounder
    G-Nick Anderson, Mr. Everything
    G-Kenny Battle, non-stop hero

Best in one year (apologies to Flying Illini Anderson (1989) and Gill (1990).
    Freeman, 27.8 ppg in '66
    Norman, all-league in '87
    Kerr, scored 25.3 ppg in '54
    Thoren, 14.5 boards in '65
    Harper, put points with D in '83

Most popular Illini (apologies to Paul Judson and Mannie Jackson):
    Kenny Battle, dunker deluxe
    Dike Eddleman, bigger than life
    Doug Altenberger, still a star
    Gene Vance, athlete's athlete
    Kendall Gill, caught fans' eye

All-time best on defense (apologies to Randy Crews and Steve Bardo):
    F-Mike Price, NBA first rounder
    F-Preston Pearson, tough as nails
    C-Derek Holcomb, 174 UI blocks
    G-Bruce Douglas, had 324 steals
    G-Derek Harper, octopus arms
    Sixth man-Jack Smiley, whiz on D

All-time best out-of-staters (apologies to Texan James Griffin):
    F-Nick Weatherspoon, slim Ohioan
    F-Mike Price, infrequent Hoosier
    C-Bill Burwell, no Brooklyn bum
    G-Tal Brody, Israeli-Jersey pickup
    G-Derek Harper, Florida flash

All-time best playmakers (apologies to Bill Erickson and Steve Bardo):
    Don Sunderlage, led two Final Fours
    Tal Brody, sparked 100-point fever
    Derek Harper, broke up the press
    Kiwane Garris, always in control
    Bruce Douglas, started 117, won 95

All-time most improved (apologies to Quinn Richardson and Don Ohl):
    Perry Range, talent harnessed speed
    Kendall Gill, overcame sophomore slump
    Derek Harper, learned to shoot
    Kevin Turner, caught fire in '98
    Chris Gandy, emerged as senior

All-time most overlooked (apologies to Rick Schmidt and Jim Dawson):
    Irv Bemoras, in two Final Fours
    Wally Oskerkorn, led scoring in '50
    Rod Fletcher, '52 All-American
    Dave Scholz, 20.5 career average
    Mark Smith, versatile four years

All-time Mr. Tenacity (apologies to spin-driver Andy Kaufmann):
    Fred Miller, Harv's whirlwind
    Kenny Battle, award is for him

Neil Bresnahan, backboard demon
Doug Altenberger, relentless
Nick Anderson, rugged in clutch

All-time best from area (no, Otho Tucker and Dick Foley, it's 60 miles to Paris):
Ted Beach, Champaign deadeye
Rod Fletcher, Maroon baseliner
Rick Schmidt, Royal piledriver
Deon Flessner, St. Joe-Ogden ace
Gene Vance, Clinton's Whiz Kid

Some played, even showing flashes of greatness, but crashed and burned. No apologies here:
Rich Jones, in "slush" scandal
George Bon Salle, grades cost title
Bill Morris, returned to St. Louis
Alvin O'Neal, Peorian didn't last
Rennie Clemons, failed in classroom

There they are, my purely arbitrary picks. If you want non-arbitrary, you can have five single-game scoring leaders: Downey 53, Kaufmann 46, Scholz 42, Phillip 40, and Thomas 39.

But, shucks, what's the fun in that?

You would see changes today in order to make room for Brian Cook, Frank Williams, Deron Williams and Dee Brown. It was difficult enough without them, so I don't think I'll try.

ILLINI FIND KANSAS HARD TO HANDLE
MARCH 19, 2002

Illinois ripped Kansas 80-64 in the NCAA regional a year earlier, but fell to a young Jayhawk team, 73-69, this time.

MADISON, Wis. — Illinois can make history Friday against Kansas. No Illini basketball team has defeated a No. 1 seed in the NCAA tournament. Fact is, no Illini team has beaten a team seeded ahead of it.

Here's a nutshell wrapup:

— With World War II interrupting the Whiz Kids, the UI made its first three NCAA appearances in an eight-team field in 1949 and 16-team fields in 1951 and 1952, bowing out in the semifinals all three years.

— In the 28 years from 1953 through 1980 — until 1975, only league champions advanced — Illinois appeared in the playoffs once, losing in the quarterfinals to Loyola's 1963 national champions.

— Numbered seeds were instituted with a 48-team field in 1979, and it was expanded to 64 teams in 1985. Illinois has made 17 appearances since 1981, posting a 20-16 record. Of the 16 losses, 11 came against lower seeds.

Of the Illini's 20 tournament wins, all came against lower seeds, in part because the selection committee has been generous in seeding the Illini through the years. Ten of 17 UI teams have been seeded fourth or higher, the 1989 and 2001 teams being No. 1 seeds.

As they face a No. 1 seed Friday night, the Illini are 0-5 against teams placed ahead of them, losing to No. 1 Kentucky in 1984, No. 2 Georgia Tech 1985, No. 3 Vanderbilt in 1993, No. 6 Tulsa in 1995 and No. 4 Maryland in 1998.

A further look reveals that if Dame Fortune has gazed down on Illini teams in the NCAA, mostly she has frowned.

Of the UI's first 13 tournament losses, 10 came by margins of three points or less. The 1951 and 1952 squads each came within two points of the title game. Kentucky escaped 54-51 in 1984 at Rupp Arena. Two years later, the Illini lost a last-shot thriller to Alabama 58-56. This was followed, in consecutive years, by a 68-67 loss to Austin Peay when Ken Norman missed a game-ending 15-footer, the rash of missed free throws that handed Villanova a 66-63 heartbreaker, the memorable 83-81 loss to Michigan in Seattle and an 88-86 crash-and-burn loss against Dayton in 1990.

The Kansas teams that Illinois defeated the last two years — 84-70 in Chicago and 80-64 in San Antonio, respectively — presented the same Collison-Gooden-Hinrich-Boschee nucleus as this one. These Jayhawks rededicated themselves to a weight-training regimen after Illinois outmuscled them a year ago, and they deserve the favorite's label. All the better. The pairing provides Illinois an opportunity to pull its first upset in NCAA history.

It was disheartening to see all those Kansas freshmen prevail when the Illini got such a strong game from Robert Archibald and had makeable shots by Brian Cook and Frank Williams with the score 71-69. I had long since become hardened to narrow NCAA losses. Bill Self left for Kansas one year later.

ILLINI LOST GROUND IN THE 1960s
MARCH 14, 1995

Indiana schools dominated as the UI basketball program had more than its share of problems beginning in 1953 and running through the mid-90s.

CHAMPAIGN — Purdue repeated as undisputed Big Ten Conference champion Sunday. In the last 30 years, the Boilermakers and Indiana's Hoosiers have won or shared 18 of those titles.

In three decades, Illinois has shared in one, that in 1984. Illinois came within one game on one other occasion, finishing 14-4 to Indiana's 15-3 in 1989. Face it, when Illinois fielded its best team of the modern era — the Flying Illini in 1989 — they still finished behind a typical Indiana champ.

No one who watched the Illini in the Final Four with chiefly underclassman lineups in 1951 and 1952 could have predicted such a turn of events.

In 1953, the two-time defending champs had veterans Red Kerr, Bob Peterson, Irv Bemoras, Clive Follmer, Jim Bredar and Max Hooper, and Harry Combes had a stranglehold on state talent with the Judson twins, Billy Ridley, George BonSalle and Harv Schmidt on the way.

What happened? How could such a talent-laden sector produce only two co-champions (1963 and 1984) in a span of 43 years?

It is a winding story marked by several devastating developments.

To begin with, Illinois was beaten fair and square by Bobby Leonard, Don Schlundt, Chuck Kraak and the Hoosiers' NCAA champions in 1953. Indiana's dominance was followed in the mid-50s by some of the finest Iowa teams ever (featuring Carl Cain, Bill Seaburg and other Illinois products).

During the transition period of the late '50s and '60s, the UI lagged in the acceptance and quest of black athletes who steadily and surely changed the game. The university had no bridge program to help marginal students. The recruitment of Mount Vernon's Walt Moore and several others backfired when they failed to meet academic requirements, and Chicago superstars of that era chose other universities. George Wilson joined the bandwagon at Cincinnati and

Cazzie Russell became a "founding father" at Michigan. The UI's falling out with Chicago prep coaches lasted deep into the 1970s.

Three debilitating run-ins over rule violations led to multiyear setbacks. The "slush fund" was revealed by assistant AD Mel Brewer in December 1966, and tall standouts Rich Jones, Ron Dunlap and Steve Kuberski were declared ineligible just when the Illini appeared ready to capture the 1967 title. Lou Henson inherited a team on probation and looked back on two 18-loss seasons when he took over in 1976. The latest haymaker came in the Deon Thomas case. Probation and reduced scholarships detoured a red-hot program.

While fans take pride in the UI using in-state players, no long-term elite teams ... not Kentucky or Duke, not Kansas or North Carolina, and certainly not Indiana or Michigan ... restrict themselves to state boundaries. And Purdue has struck gold with the innovative use of Eastern prep schools to prepare Boilermaker athletes like Cuonzo Martin and next year's projected standout, Luther Clay.

UI recruiting efforts are concentrated on a Chicago area where academics are notoriously weak and state loyalty questionable. Some of the best, Quinn Buckner and Isiah Thomas, led NCAA title teams at Indiana. The Big Ten's all-star centers last year and this, Juwan Howard and Rashard Griffith, are Chicagoans who played for Michigan and Wisconsin, respectively.

Even when Henson has rounded up an "Illinois all-star team," he smacks into elite teams featuring stars from all over the country. Furthermore, many northern Illinois stars are frequently overrated because of the strong prep coverage in Chicago.

This is an overview that does not attempt to detail the idiosyncrasies of a given year or two. But, once again, we see a current situation that is typical.

Chicago has its greatest player ever in Kevin Garnett, a 6-11 athlete who, like Chris Webber and Glenn Robinson, expects to play no more than two college seasons before turning pro.

For all the good that the summer bridge program offers, it's obvious Garnett would not be enamored by spending July in a hot classroom. If he qualifies, he can attend almost anywhere else without fulfilling that summer obligation. So, while the UI has profited from the school's proximity to Chicago, there always seems to be a problem in fitting the stars of that city into the school's academic format.

To make a point, I have often exaggerated by saying that Chicago is not politically, socially or educationally a part of the state of Illinois. The Illini have made breakthroughs but, face it, Chicago is from the state of Chicago. And that tells you all you need to know.

IT WAS A WEIRD DAY IN SAN DIEGO
MARCH 18, 2006

Bruce Weber's Illini defeated Air Force in as wacky a series of circumstances as you'll ever see.

SAN DIEGO — A surreal week evolved into a surreal basketball game.

A surprising seed sent Illinois 2,000 miles from home. Then came the delayed charter flight ... the broken bus near the San Diego airport ... the fouled practice schedule ... and the Thursday morning overreaction by two bomb-sniffing dogs to a standard hot dog cart.

All those were unexpected. They caught the Illini by surprise.

But the weirdest development was planned. Evidently pushed by numbskulls at CBS-TV — surely, NCAA execs knew better — a mere 25 minutes were allowed to empty 12,000-seat Cox Arena after UCLA's defeat of Belmont, and refill for the Illini-Air Force game.

How odd it was to compare an empty arena Thursday night to a year ago when Illinois drew thousands for practice, not to mention its playoff games. Two minutes prior to the lineups being announced, a thin line of carefully inspected fans began to trickle back in. At the first four-minute timeout, there were perhaps 2,000 fans in their seats, and the building was roughly half full with 9 1/2 minutes gone.

"It reminded me of our AAU days," UI senior James Augustine said, "when we played games in the morning with no one there. When you're playing, you don't look much at the crowd anyway. The (security enforced) delay in the starting time didn't bother us. We just thought it was spoiled mustard. That's what we thought."

Then there was the game itself. In no way did it progress in a fashion that anyone expected.

Two of the nation's top 10 defensive clubs, which allowed a combined 112 points a game, produced 147. The Illini enjoyed their highest field goal percentage, .580, as Bruce Weber's big men, including Brian Randle, sank 19 of 26 shots. The Big Ten's worst free throw shooters drained an efficient 12 of 14. And the UI outscored Air Force reserves 32-5, as Warren Carter sparked the first-half attack and Jamar Smith closed fast with six treys, more than the Peoria freshman had produced in the last seven games.

A furious offensive skirmish broke out where a slowdown defensive duel was expected.

Smith was so hot that on several occasions he waved for the ball in open-court situations, and Dee Brown had a cross-court eye out for him.

"On Smith's shot by the bench, he was right in front of me, and I was calling for patience," Weber said, "but he just shot it in and smiled back at me."

The 78-69 result left losing coach Jeff Bzdelik upset with "terrible defensive closeouts (out of a leaky zone) and too much missed communication." But he also opined that Illinois was the best team Air Force faced this season. Illinois led 78-62 going into the final minute.

Carter and Smith were critical to the victory because Randle and Augustine, while strikingly effective during their time on the court, joined Rich McBride on the bench with two fouls during the last five minutes of the first half, and neither played 30 minutes. Yet Randle and Augustine combined for 25 points and drew the attention of the Air Force interior defense, thereby creating openings for Smith on the perimeter.

The 6-foot Brown garnered eight rebounds himself, more than any Falcon, and came close to a triple-double with 10 assists and eight points. Unable to connect early, Brown didn't attempt a field goal after going 1 for 7 in the first half. He seldom has played a better floor game, a fact that both coaches recognized.

That's the kind of week it was, the Illini careening from one unexpected development to another to produce arguably their most efficient offensive performance of the 26-6 season.

There was Randle, sitting out 13 consecutive minutes, and then exploding for 15 second-half points. There was Carter, breaking out with 5-for-6 shooting in the first half and helping the subs hold the fort before the break. There was Smith, nailing a clutch trey after Air Force used three consecutive steals to cut the UI lead to 39-38 with 16 minutes left.

It was anybody's game to that point, and it was still a nervous 50-47 when Carter connected in the lane, Augustine popped an 8-footer, Smith drained a trey, Brown converted three free throws and Randle tallied a putback for the UI's second 12-0 run that ended all doubt.

What we learned is that (1) athletes are resilient and often unaffected by events swirling around them and (2) always expect the unexpected.

Some good teams bit the dust Thursday and more will today. "We're alive to play another day," Weber said.

And that's all that matters.

Nothing seemed to go right on this trip, and it was particularly odd to be held out of the arena while security officers tried to figure out why their dogs overreacted. Frankly, I wasn't concerned because I thought it was some kind of mistake. It was even more eerie to start the game while fans entered single file. The Illini got through it but then lost to Washington, 67-64.

BASS KICK ENDS THRILLER IN MADISON
OCTOBER 24, 1982

Few Illini football victories had a more dramatic ending than the 29-28 triumph at Wisconsin in 1982.

MADISON, Wis. — During three tight and incredibly fortuitous Big Ten victories, Wisconsin coach Dave McClain has offered the opinion that God had aligned himself on the side of Bucky Badger.

For 59 minutes and 57 seconds Saturday, Illinoisans had to shake their heads and agree.

The Badgers grabbed three pass deflections — one off the intended receivers' foot — and executed three trick plays for touchdowns after capitalizing on grievous Illinois mistakes that left the visitors trailing 7-6 at halftime.

When end Al Toon took an intentionally bounced lateral and wobbled a 40-yard TD pass to Jeff Nault with 52 seconds left, it certainly appeared that Wisconsin had received devine intervention for the fourth straight week.

But Californian Tony Eason, New Jersey's Tim Brewster and barefooted Floridian Mike Bass hauled it out of the fire for Illinois 29-28 on a sunny Wisconsin afternoon that will be remembered as the sweetest, most exciting Illini triumph since the Rose Bowl days of Pete Elliott.

That Mike White's athletes trailed in the final quarter was no surprise. They've trailed in the closing 15 minutes in each of their last four games. But this time they were behind 28-26 with :52 showing and hadn't reached their own 30-yard line when the clock showed :22.

That's when Eason read the Badger defensive strategy as (1) dropping deep to stop the bomb and (2) leaning to the sidelines to prevent clock-stoppers. He fired to Oliver Williams for 22 over the middle, and tried again only to have linebacker Jody O'Donnell nearly intercept. Nine seconds remained when he called Brewster's number in the same general direction and Tim bounced up from his eighth reception to call timeout with :03 left and the ball on the 29.

Those who recall Bass hitting the upright from 56 yards with the score 21-21 against Ohio State last week recognized the upcoming 46-yarder was well within his range. And, after a Badger timeout to increase the pressure, Bass boomed it unusually high and true to keep Illinois in the Rose Bowl chase.

White's melting-pot aggregation of Chicagoans, juco transfers and Sunshine Staters are 6-2 overall and will fly to Iowa next Saturday with a 5-1 conference record, a half-game behind Michigan, 5-0. It was the third triumph in four harrowing weeks, all those victories viewed by Big Ten commissioner Wayne Duke and a growing corps of bowl representatives. More than that, a regional television audience swelled to national proportions in the closing minutes as CBS beamed those last few minutes from coast to coast, capping the contest by taping an interview with White while more than 3,000 Illini followers mingled jubilantly on a foreign field.

For Eason, it was his most impressive showing in two seasons and perhaps the second-best ever by an Illini quarterback (surpassed only by Dave Wilson's 43-for-69, 621-yard spree against Ohio State). Eason completed and incredible 73 percent of his passes despite having three dropped, hitting 37 of 51 for 479 yards. Illinois was so dominant offensively that Chris Sigourney was called on to punt only once.

Bass, playing before father Tom (defensive coordinator for the San Diego Chargers), broke a hallowed UI single-season scoring record held jointly by Red Grange, Buddy Young and John Karras, who scored 13 TDs and 78 points each on 1924, 1944, and 1951. Bass has 80 on 26 straight extra points and 18 of 21 field goals, and his five field goals Saturday tied a Big Ten record held by former Illini Dan Beaver and two others. His 13 field goals in Big Ten games are just two short of the record in league games only.

An official turnout of 78,406 watched a promising Badger start turn into a wild Illini finish.

Bass contributed a 44-yarder for a 26-20 lead with 4:03 showing, and when Charles Armstead intercepted Randy Wright's long pass on the UI 11-yard line, the Illini were in a hole they couldn't dig out of. On fourth down, Sigourney ran back into the end zone and accepted a two-point safety in order to kick off safely from the UI 20. Only 1:47 remained when the Badgers put the ball in play from their 46, and Illinois appeared to be bracing when the clock passed 1:00. It was then that they pulled the cleverest trick of all, Wright intentionally bouncing a long lateral to Toon, who passed to Nault for the TD.

While the Badger fans were celebrating the Illini planned one last assault. And when Wendell Gladem's extra point bid struck the left upright everyone came to the realization that a 28-26 lead wasn't exactly safe, not when Eason, Brewster and Bass had 52 seconds to work their Illini magic.

The Illini locker room was crazy. Players were all over Brewster and Bass. And there was receiver Mike Martin seated atop the lockers in an apparent daze and watching the wild scene. I just wandered around asking stupid questions, in something of a daze myself.

FIRST OF FOUR COLUMNS ON UI-INDIANA BASKETBALL SERIES

MARCH 2, 1987

Illinois served Indiana's third-ranked Hoosiers their last loss before their national title run in 1987.

CHAMPAIGN — "We wanted to go out with a bang and I think we did," Tony Wysinger said.

He spoke for three Illini seniors and received — from Illini fans, at least — a thankful "Amen" following Sunday's 69-67 defeat of Indiana.

It was a long time coming but worth the wait.

No Top 20 team in recent memory has played so consistently hard and taken such courage-questioning abuse as these Illini. No reconstructed team, having lost three full-time starters and a part-timer, has come to have so much expected of it.

These Illini and their coach, who was demeaned again by faulty comparisons with Bob Knight in Sunday's ABC-TV broadcast, have paid a fearful price by daring to overachieve, by daring to play more talented opponents so close.

One network broadcast at midweek said the Illini have no backbone. The Associated Press began one of its stories on the game, in a reverse slap that will be read from Maine to New Mexico, "For once,

Illinois didn't blow a big lead at home."

So, apparently, a cattle-brand has been ironed that can't be erased, and a 13-2 home season will be remembered for the two losses, both in overtime and both after the Illini had built big leads on Purdue and Iowa.

That's life and, while others celebrated, Wysinger still seemed a bit grim after missing some makeable shots down the stretch and making some errant passes. Even in winning, some of the same old late-game tightness was apparent.

But they did win and those were REAL TEARS in the eyes of coach Lou Henson's wife, Mary, and it was a TRULY ENTHUSIASTIC gang of worshippers that stood behind Henson's postgame show even though no one could hear what was being said.

Henson has been telling anyone who will listen that these Illini are fighters, that they'll come back no matter how devastating the setbacks. And they hung on Sunday when the general attitude, with 8:00 left and the score 57-57, was: "Oh, my, here we go again."

Doug Altenberger, who combined with fellow senior Ken Norman for 44 points, stepped forward when the score was knotted.

"I told myself that I'm a senior and I took it upon myself to hit some of those three-point attempts. They were quick shots and maybe I shouldn't have shot them, but I just told myself that this is my last game here and I'm not going to let this happen again, and I got lucky enough to hit a couple of them. It sort of picked us up and got us going, gave us a little momentum."

After hitting two to put Illinois ahead 65-63, Altenberger was knocked flat on his next attempt by Rick Calloway without a whistle, a surprise for a game officiated closely and fairly by three Big East referees.

"That was ridiculous," Altenberger said. "That's not even worth talking about. If you have a semi coming right at you, you're not going to take your normal shot."

On another day, perhaps, the Illini would have limped off the court remembering that unexplained no-call. Not Sunday. Illinois was long overdue for a break and got it when Indiana ran off 30 seconds and Steve Alford ducked and dipped to launch a long, off-balance shot at :08 with the score 69-67. It wasn't close and a gambling strategy backfired on the Hoosiers.

Defending against Indiana's record-breaking Alford and permitting him just four points in the second half, Altenberger said:

"Steve made some great inside moves in the first half (13 points) and I just figured if he could make those, I'd just have to give them to him. I got some help from (Steve) Bardo on him, and Alford seemed to tire as the game went on. He wasn't running as much."

In fact, one of Alford's three-point shots missed everything, bringing an "air ball, air ball" chant from the crowd.

Altenberger saw Norman's take-charge attitude at midgame as giving Illinois the boost it needed when Indiana threatened to pull away. Nineteen of Norman's 24 points came during an 11-minute stretch before and after halfttime as Illinois went on a 31-14 run to build its biggest lead of 50-40.

Norman, scoring 19 or more for the 21st time this season, sank 10 of 17 shots, holding his 16-game Big Ten field goal percentage at 57.0 and his rebound average at 9.6 as he seeks both individual titles in the final two games in Michigan next week. Norman has 583 points overall, leaving him 84 shy of Don Freeman's UI single-season record with at least three and possibly more games remaining.

Squeezing in a few extra seats, it was the largest crowd in Assembly Hall history (16,793). And for a time they watched, perhaps without realizing it, a duel of junior college transfers. First it was Norman vs. Keith Smart, and then it was Norman vs. Dean Garrett, with Garrett maintaining his momentum down the stretch, just as he did in an earlier 69-66 Indiana victory. But the Illini seniors received a lift when it counted from 7-foot sophomore Jens Kujawa and freshman Bardo, and that put them over.

It seemed somewhat daring but Knight set his strategy to win it with a three rather than seek the tie with some kind of penetration. This is good strategy only if the arc shot is open, which it wasn't in this case because the Illini were concentrated on Alford.

MARCH 6, 1989

Nick Anderson launched one of the most memorable game-winners in Illinois history as the UI beat the Big Ten champs, 70-67.

BLOOMINGTON, Ind. — Illinois trumped Indiana's ace Sunday.

In what will henceforth and for years be known simply as "the Shot," Nick Anderson mustered all the strength in his muscular 6-foot-6 body to provide a memorable moment in Illini basketball history.

Arching a 30-footer high into the stratosphere in the game's last second, Anderson's picture-perfect bomb beat Indiana, 70-67, and forced the Hoosiers to postpone their Big Ten championship celebration.

Anderson's incredible basket nullified an even more phenomenal 17-foot baseline rainbow that seemingly curved over and around the backboard as Indiana clutch shooter Jay Edwards catapulted over the end line with :02 on the clock.

No two more remarkable shots ever ended a Big Ten basketball game.

And these battle-back Illini, who rallied from a 35-25 halftime deficit to beat Indiana 75-65 in Champaign on Jan. 28, charged from a 47-34 deficit with 11 1/2 minutes left of this occasion. They wound up wallowing in a pile in the corner of the court while seated, disbelieving Hoosier fans came to the bitter realization that there would be no overtime.

Many of the 17,311 fans thought the clock had run out in regulation, unaware that a quick-thinking Steve Bardo had signaled the UI's last timeout to referee Ed Hightower. Bardo acted instinctively, just as Edwards' looping shot cleared outstretched fingers.

Lou Henson came up with a strategy that Indiana did not anticipate.

Said Bardo: "He told me to run the baseline, look deep to Kenny (Battle) and Lowell (Hamilton) and, if they weren't open, throw to Nick on the right sideline."

Said Anderson: "Coach told me to come out from behind Kenny and Lowell, to use them as a screen and come out for the ball. He told me to take one bounce. That's what I did. I took one dribble and shot it. There was no time to do anything else."

Two years ago, in a similar situation at :02 against Austin Peay in the NCAA tournament, the Illini had an extra timeout and called it at :01 after Bardo caught a pass at midcourt. Then they set up Ken Norman for an open jumper from medium range that missed as Illinois lost, 68-67.

This time Henson, who called time twice as Illinois faltered early in the second half, had no more timeouts.

Indiana sent no one to challenge Bardo's long baseball peg, preferring to double-team Larry Smith in the backcourt. Anderson came along the sideline to meet the pass, dribbled once past midcourt and rose up while Edwards held his hands high and did not challenge the shot. The basketball struck dead center, flicking the net up over the rim.

It was Illinois' longest game-winning shot since Derek Harper drilled a three-point bomb to beat Minnesota by the same 70-67 score in double-overtime March 13, 1983.

If it lifted a national television audience (ABC) out of their seasts, it left the packed house stunned, unaccustomed as they are to seeing Indiana beaten. Six times during the Big Ten season the Hoosiers have won by four points or less, two of them on last-ditch jumpers by Edwards against Purdue and Michigan.

"Great shooters do things like that, and I've seen Edwards do it before," Anderson said.

"For me, it's never happened before and it'll probably never happen again. This is the shot I'll always remember. I arched it, and it felt good when I got it off, but I didn't know until it neared the basket that it was going in. When it was coming down, I could see it was falling. I could see it was good."

Jim Turpin and I, in doing the radio broadcast, had barely recovered from the tying baseline prayer by Indiana's Edwards when Anderson launched his bomb. Later, in hearing my rantings replayed, it was somewhat embarrassing. It seemed inconceivable that two shots of that nature would come back-to-back. This stunning win over No. 3 Indiana led to a string of 10 straight late-season wins, six against ranked teams.

FEBRUARY 25, 1998

Coach Lon Kruger tuned out the ugliness as Bob Knight challenged ref Ted Valentine, the Illini winning 82-72.

BLOOMINGTON, Ind. — What rabid Indiana fans regard as a travesty is sweet music to Illinoisans.

In the most foul-mouthed and ugly atmosphere any Illini quintet ever has been subjected to, they held the Hoosiers to eight field goals in the first 27 minutes and capped an amazing Big Ten season with an 82-72 triumph Tuesday night.

At 13-3, still alive for a share of the Big Ten basketball championship — if Purdue wins Sunday at Michigan State — Lon Kruger and his athletes kept their cool amid some of the most explosive and embarrassing activity ever witnessed at a conference game.

Three bench technicals (it easily could have been 10) were just part of it as irate Indiana fans tossed coins, hurled racial epithets at ref Ted Valentine and booed themselves hoarse.

Shocked by Sunday's 112-64 loss at Michigan, these fanatics were determined to lift their favorites on Senior Night. But the Hoosiers smacked into a three-point underdog that excels in that role and would not break.

"I don't know how I could be prouder or happier," Kruger said. "We started out a little jittery, but our guys hung together. They came over here expecting to win, and they took care of business. We were starting to get into foul trouble but not to the point where it damaged us.

"However it (the championship) turns out, we can be proud of what we have done. We can cherish it for a lifetime."

Consider what this Fighting Illini team has accomplished:

— Five seniors started every game except one in a 21-8 season, growing stronger while several of their rivals were set back by injuries, defections and underachievement.

— These Illini broke the Big Ten record for togetherness and complementary play, not to mention a remarkably deep relationship with a head coach who demonstrates that you don't have to browbeat athletes to get the most out of them.

— With the NCAA committee using the last 10 games as a critical portion of the selection process, the UI finished on a 9-1 roll before the first Big Ten tournament.

— The UI was outrebounded for the 16th time in the last 20 games, but it didn't matter.

— Illinois posted a 14-1 record at home, handed Penn State its only home loss so far, started Iowa on its tailspin out of the rankings and swept Indiana for the first time since 1990.

— In 16 Big Ten games, ever-ready Illinois led after 10 minutes 15 times and tied Purdue at 17-17 in the 16th.

— In the last 45 years, Illinois twice posted six Big Ten road victories, this season and in an 18-game schedule in 1984.

— Continuing a decade of solid overtime play, the Illini broke their losing spell at Wisconsin with their 13th triumph in the last 16 OT contests.

— Increasing their offensive production in late season, jump-shooters Kevin Turner and Jerry Hester combined to average nearly 40 points a game in the seven February contests.

— Four misses Tuesday cost Matt Heldman the Big Ten free throw percentage title, but he was a tower of strength at the line in a series of hard-fought triumphs. He finished 54 for 62 on free throws in the Big Ten.

It boiled down again to the whole being greater than the sum of its parts. And the Illini never played with more determination than in the second half, shooting 56.5 percent and holding the Hoosiers without a field goal in the first seven minutes after the break.

"We began to click in the second half," Kruger said. "Indiana tried to pressure us, and we were able to penetrate and kick out for good shots. We got in a good flow."

How did they deal with the raucous interruptions, and the lengthy two-technical episode with 9:37 left?

"We were huddling," Kruger said. "We didn't really see everything that was happening. And in each case, we came out of those situations to make nice runs."

The most important spurt came after halftime when the Illini quieted the crowd in building a 50-33 lead. It was 54-46 when Heldman went to the line on the double-technical, and the Illini shot out again, 66-51. Then Hester, cashing a trey and a dunk, applied the hammer as he silenced the crowd for the final time.

Several memories remain. If ever a crowd was ready to spill over with European soccer venom, that was it. Bob Knight's actions had those people irate beyond description. And for the umpteenth time, I left with the certain feeling that Knight had allowed himself to be outcoached by the rival bench.

FEBRUARY 21, 2000

Lon Kruger had Indiana's number, and never more so than in his final season at Illinois when the Illini ruled, 87-63, at home.

CHAMPAIGN — Oh, boy. An 8 o'clock start. Late for old-timers. Wonder how that'll affect Tuesday night's basketball crowd?

"Fret not," came the response, "It's a 'Who's your Daddy?' night!"

Indiana and Illinois would produce sold-out intensity at midnight. It's guaranteed to be electric when the Classic Bully comes to town. This is the Hatfields and McCoys ... a Wolverine-Buckeye football game. When both teams are good, it doesn't get much better.

Our good judge, Fred Green, set the stage for a half-century of torrid UI-Indiana conflict in 1949 when his soft hook pulled out a 44-42 road win, and kept the Illini rolling toward the Big Ten title. Green's game-winning goal came a year after he scored the last four points in a 52-51 Illini squeaker.

Even with a 53-37 series deficit since 1950, Illinois holds some of its most treasured triumphs vs. Indiana. Following are 10 of the more memorable.

— Feb. 19, 1951: Having suffered their only Big Ten loss at Indiana, the Illini and captain Don Sunderlage wowed a packed Huff Gym crowd with a riotous 71-65 defeat of All-American pivotman Bill Garrett & Co.

— Jan. 14, 1957: Unaware of what was to come, a high-flying Illini team topped 90 against Indiana for the fourth straight time, breezing 112-91 at Huff to reach 9-2 on the season and 173-46 under coach Harry Combes. Less than three weeks later, star center George BonSalle was declared ineligible after scoring 27 points in a 96-89 defeat of Ohio State, and the Illini went into a swoon that carried through the next five seasons.

— Feb. 16, 1963: At the peak of the high-scoring Jimmy Rayl era at Indiana, the Illini outlasted the Hoosiers at Huff, 104-101. Less than two weeks later, Indiana won at home 103-100 despite Dave Downey's record 53 points, but that loss did not prevent the Illini from capturing the Big Ten's lone NCAA tournament berth.

— Jan. 4, 1965: Seniors Tom and Dick VanArsdale were the most famous twins in college basketball history and they brought an 8-0 IU team to a rowdy Assembly Hall. The Illini met the challenge with an 86-81 triumph on the scoring of Tal Brody (23), Skip Thoren (21) and Bogie Redmon (20).

— Feb. 17, 1977: Kent Benson, a carryover from Indiana's 1976 national champions, scored 25 points but Lou Henson's second UI team ended the Hoosiers' nine-game dominance, 73-69, at home with balanced scoring from Rich Adams (16), Neil Bresnahan (13), Audie Matthews (12), Levi Cobb (11) and Ken Ferdinand (10).

— March 4, 1984: Illinois had a half-game edge on Indiana late in the Big Ten race when the Illini avenged a loss at Indiana with a 70-53 romp at home. Bruce Douglas drained 13 of 19 shots and the Illini went on to share their first league title since 1963.

— Jan. 27, 1985: As punishment for sloppy play, Indiana "name players" Steve Alford, Winston Morgan, Stew Robinson, Marty Simmons, Daryl Thomas and Dan Dakich rode the bench throughout the Assembly Hall contest as center Uwe Blab was the only non-freshman to play for the Hoosiers. Efrem Winters, George Montgomery and Anthony Welch dominated the boards as Illinois took a 24-12 halftime lead and won that unusual contest, 52-41.

— March 1, 1987: A national TV audience and record home crowd of 16,793 saw the final home game for Ken Norman (24 points), Doug Altenberger (20) and Tony Wysinger (10). Illinois won 69-67 as Alford missed a game-ending trey for an Indiana team that never lost again in taking the national title.

— March 5, 1989: Flying Illini star Nick Anderson launched a last-second bomb to stun Indian's Big Ten champs, 70-67, for the Final Four Illini.

— Feb. 24, 1998: Ref Ted Valentine caught the full force of an irate Hoosier crowd as his technical foul calls played a major role in the crucial 82-72 triumph for Illinois' Big Ten co-champs. Matt Heldman, Kevin Turner and Jarrod Gee hit 16 apiece to overcome A.J. Guyton's 25-point effort.

— And one extra last March: Beaten twice by Indiana earlier, and last in the Big Ten standings, Illinois ignited a three-game sweep of ranked foes by upsetting Indiana 82-66 in the Big Ten tournament in Chicago. Lucas Johnson outscored Luke Recker 17-7, and Damir Krupalija brought his three-game rebound total against Indiana to 38. The war continues tonight.

This night was easy, 87-63. But worries returned when Illinois met Indiana in the Big Ten tournament. In Chicago, Knight again violated coaching strategy by electing not to guard the passer on the UI's last out-of-bounds play on the sideline. Sergio McClain tossed it in, took a return pass, drew the defense to him with penetration, and kicked to Cory Bradford for the winning trey.

FIRST OF FIVE COLUMNS ON ILLINI-MICHIGAN FOOTBALL
NOVEMBER 6, 1966

In the final meeting of the brothers Elliott, Pete's Illini defeated Bump's Wolverines on a chilly day in Michigan.

ANN ARBOR, Mich. — They say the scales eventually balance.
Pete Elliott must wonder if he'll live long enough to catch up with Bump but at least he took the first step.

Mick Smith could have dug a hole after letting a punt hit him in the 6-3 loss to Stanford but Saturday he was named by WDWS as the "star of the game" in the 28-21 win against Michigan.

And Bruce Sullivan, well ... he's always where the action is. The tall Watseka senior fumbled a kickoff return Saturday and was being run ragged by star end Jack Clancy whose pass patterns and sharp cuts on a slippery field had him open for 11 receptions from Dick Vidmer.

But Sullivan's two late interceptions, and his record-tying 98-yard return on the first one, broke the Michigan spell as surely as the prince's kiss on Sleeping Beauty's lips.

Saturday's triumph proved several things: (1) Illinois can also return punts, (2) the Illini really do have a rushing attack; and (3) they can defeat a strong opponent when a few breaks come their way.

Pete Elliott said the team "needed this victory" after the tough defeat at Purdue. But it was really the other way around. The Illini wanted this victory for Pete, and they lifted a 20-ton weight off his shoulders when they did it.

Pete clutched the game ball awarded him by co-captain Kai Anderson and said:

"This is the first chance I've had to say it, but we (Pete and Bump) don't relish this brother vs. brother business. We are both very fortunate to be coaching at two such fine institutions, and we'd like to see the game viewed as Illinois vs. Michigan."

After his team had lifted him up in celebration of the long-sought triumph, Pete went to Bump and received his older brother's congratulations.

"We got the last touchdown this time," Pete said, "and this has not usually been the case."

And what a last touchdown it was!

As it turns out, an errant or lazy pass pattern by Michigan's running star, Carl Ward, may have made it possible. With Phil Knell guarding him man-to-man Ward drifted into the path of the sideline pattern being run by Clancy, and Knell was able to tip Vidmer's pass. Sullivan picked it off and the rest is history: 98 yards and the winning TD.

Seniors Sullivan and Knell now have 11 interceptions between them (12 if you count a sixth by Sullivan on an extra point), and this was supposed to be a weak point of the Illinois team! Actually, injuries to offensive halfbacks set them up in their present positions, Knell moving to safety to replace Rich Erickson when the latter switched to offense, and Sullivan moving up to the first unit at halfback.

"I've been lucky." said Sullivan to the swarming reporters from Ann Arbor, Detroit, Chicago and you-name-it. "Clancy was the toughest I've run up against since Jerry Levias of SMU!"

Levias made two TD catches in SMU's opening win against Illinois but Clancy was more prominent because Vidmer used him so frequently.

Elliott said the Illini adjusted their defense twice to stop Clancy but it was Sullivan who generally had primary responsibility. On both interceptions he was man-to-man with Clancy. Knell and Sullivan have now led an Illini team to eight interceptions the past two weeks against two of the country's most accurate quarterbacks. All-American Bob Griese of Purdue and Vidmer, who entered his 20th quarter of 1966 Big Ten play without an interception.

At the same time, while Bob Naponic has a mediocre completion percentage, he's had only two interceptions all year.

Mick Smith and I played cards on that trip. I'm don't remember for sure, but either he owes me a couple of thousand, or I owe him. In any case, he drew the right cards on his punt return because two Michigan tacklers hit him simultaneously and he emerged upright and running. The other memory is Sullivan diving into a snowbank after his 98-yard return of a pass that Michigan, with victory in hand, should never have thrown.

NOVEMBER 3, 1985

Chris White's deflected field goal bounced back off the crossbar as Illinois and Michigan tied, 3-3.

CHAMPAIGN — There he was again, the coach's son, holding center stage in a slow-motion sequel to Ohio State.

Another critical Big Ten game was balanced right out there on Chris White's big toe.

And in that split second after the center snap, your mind flashed back to your childhood, watching the pages of a flip-book, each leaf telling you a little more ... and in this painfully slow drama, bringing the football ever higher and closer to anticipated victory.

That lazy ball just hung up there with 76,397 mouths gasping for air, 76,397 pairs of knees bent to erupt. Illini security officers glanced anxiously toward the goal posts. It was stampede time. The celebration would last all night. Oh, how we hate Michigan.

But something was wrong. Even as a true swipe from White's hoof carried it dead center, the ball wobbled crazily and lost power like a rocket fizzling after liftoff. This wasn't the anticipated 37-yard shot into the cheap seats.

Still, look again, it might carry. IT IS, it's going to make it. Come on, flip those pages, get to the punch line.

Then, in an eye-blink that at first no one completely understood, the ball landed flush on the crossbar. Hearts soared in the distant north bleachers as it appeared to bounce up and over. But, no, that was only their imagination. The wounded duck, detained short of target by little more than an unseen inch of Dieter Heren's index finger, fell harmlessly back into the end zone.

And Illinois, victorious over Michigan just twice in 27 years, was repulsed again on this dreary afternoon, the stinginess of two proud defenses resulting in a 3-3 stalemate.

This is not to be confused with the 0-0 tie with Northwestern that signaled the hopelessness of Gary Moeller's Illini regime in the 1-8-2 season of 1978. This was a fierce, high-level shootout between the No. 4-ranked Wolverines, boasting the premier defense in the land, and Mike White's resurgent Illini.

Just minutes prior to the blocked field goal attempt, Bo Schembechler's infantry trapped and countered 68 hard-earned yards to the Illini 12, cocksure of winning before Illini linebacker Mark Tagart forced the lone Michigan turnover of the day, shaking the ball out of Gerald White's grasp and into the hands of Illini Bob Sebring on the 9.

That's when quarterback Jack Trudeau, cobwebs in his mind clearing during the Wolverines' time-consuming drive, entered to spearhead a gutty UI comeback. He picked away meticulously, tossing short completions of 8, 14, 9 and 8 yards, Stephen Pierce making a particularly courageous second-down catch as he was nearly dismembered in the air at the Illini 35. Past midfield rumbled the Illini, guard Scott Kehoe pouncing on a bungled snap between Trudeau and Mike Scully at the Michigan 33, and Trudeau himself rolling out for 4- and 6-yard gains to the Michigan 20.

Far enough. No sense taking further chances. A two-time All-Big Ten place-kicker can boot wind-aided 37-yarders in his sleep. It was only 17 yards longer than an extra point. This was precisely why Papa Mike arranged to have the wind in the fourth quarter. It was as though the result was preordained. The clock was stopped at :04. Michigan, beaten 12-10 at Iowa, would lose for the second time without giving up a touchdown.

But fate, which had allowed Chris White's earlier three-pointer to survive by scant inches a similar deflection by Heren, balanced the scales on this one.

It was a bitter pill to swallow. As the ball caromed off the crossbar, the disbelieving throng didn't seem to know what to do. They stood as though in a painting. Silence reigned except for the celebrating Michigan players, who jumped up and down in stark contrast to the crestfallen, paralyzed Illini.

"They were ecstatic and we were devastated," said a thoroughly wrung-out Mike White. "Maybe the differing reactions show how far we've come, but there's not much satisfaction in that now."

Chris White explained the differing emotions.

"What you're shooting for changes," White said, "when there's only four seconds left and one team has the ball in field goal range. It's a very empty feeling for us because we feel we should have won. In the end, all Michigan could hope for was the tie. But I would presume they were happier right then than they will be later."

Chris, whose perfect kick beat Ohio State 31-28, said he did nothing different on this one.

"I never alter anything whether it's a 50-yarder or an extra point," he said. "They're all the same. This one felt good coming off my foot. I heard the impact and then I heard the deflection immediately afterward. I knew it had been tipped. The ball was struck well, otherwise it wouldn't have carried as far as it did."

So it was another frustrating Illini afternoon against the rugged Men of Michigan. Chris White missed a wind-aided field goal from 43 yards in the second quarter — "I should have been shot for that one," he said — and Trudeau, 27 for 36 passing, made critical mistakes at the most inopportune times. Moeller's bend-but-don't-break defense, featuring son Andy Moeller with 19 tackles, worked to perfection.

Illinois is 2-1-1 in games winding down to the final seconds, beating Southern Illinois and Ohio State by three, fizzling at the Purdue 13-yard line in a 30-24 road loss and settling for a tie Saturday.

On days like that, you ask yourself: "What does it take to beat Michigan?" Fans and media alike were stunned by the closeness of this one. White's teams had victories over Michigan within their grasp on the last play twice, but came up short, winning only in the unbeaten Big Ten season of 1983.

OCTOBER 24, 1993

Johnny Johnson's clutch pass to Jim Klein resulted in a stirring 24-21 defeat of Michigan in the Big House.

ANN ARBOR, Mich. — This one came from the depths.

It was a comeback reminiscent of Jeff George against Indiana in

1988 and Southern Cal in 1989, and Jason Verduzco against Colorado and Michigan State in 1990, and Wisconsin and Purdue in 1992 ... and all those squeakers with Ohio State.

But this was Michigan, with one loss to Illinois in 26 annual meetings, and one loss in 25 previous homecoming games.

This was Michigan, too confident to imagine it could happen, too arrogant (or unaware?) to kneel on the football on second down with 1:18 showing and the Illini out of timeouts. If the Wolverines couldn't have run out the clock completely, they'd have been so close after two-25 second countoffs that it wouldn't matter.

But as the darkness began to settle on Michigan Stadium, the Wolverines lost the good luck charm that saved them on Joe Smalzer's disallowed end zone catch in 1975 (21-15), on the Illini march that ended on the 2-yard line in 1982 (16-10), on the Chris White field goal that caromed off the crossbar in the tie (3-3) in 1985, on the fourth-down pass to Chris Calloway that saved them in 1987 (17-14), on the late-game miscalculation between Verduzco and Shawn Wax in 1990 (22-17), and on the Peter Elezovic field goal that preserved the tie (22-22) one year ago.

A guy could spend a lifetime watching Michigan dominate this series. Some of us have.

But not Saturday. For six games and 59 minutes of persistent distress, this Illinois team had more bad luck than the last 10 UI teams combined. Suddenly through persistent effort, through a 25-16 dominance in first downs and a clear rule of the trenches, the tide turned.

Simeon Rice provided the opening with a strip and recovery, similar to the one the officials overlooked in the 13-7 loss to Oregon. And it was a third-stringer, 152-pound Jim Klein, who applied the knockout punch when he found a soft spot in the end zone while Johnny Johnson was escaping the furious, clutching Michigan rush. Only Johnson's dexterity allowed him to get the pass off with a Wolverine draped around him.

"This is the greatest moment of my life," Klein said. "I didn't catch it with my hands. I clutched it to my body in case I was hit."

Was he hit?

"I don't remember," said Klein.

On the field and inside, these Illini celebrated like never before. Accolades fell all around. Ty Douthard ran harder than ever before, gaining 176 yards in rushes and receptions. The offensive line rose to new heights, and tight ends David Olson, Ken Dilger and Kraig Koester blocked up a storm and combined for nine receptions. The swarming defense, fourth-ranked against the rush, held Michigan to

76 net yards.

But the hero Saturday was Greg Landry. The former Chicago Bear coordinator put together a masterpiece. He had the Wolverines off balance all day with cleverly-schemed runs and short passes. They couldn't solve his two-TE formation and the lead play featuring Douthard to the left. The play-action TD pass to Dilger was perfection.

It was a crime that Illinois got just three points from a 94-yard march before halftime. And in the second half, Illinois literally bowled over the Wolverines, only to fumble the ball away at the 6- and 16-yard lines.

And, finally, when Michigan called time to settle its defense with 41 seconds left, Landry was granted time to analyze the situation and change the call that Johnson had taken from his wrist band reminder.

Landry sent three receivers left, hoping to at least break Jason Dulick or Shane Fisher open underneath. But Klein, in the game because Gary Voelker was injured, broke wide open for Johnson's bullet.

"After Dilger fumbled (at the Michigan 16 with 4:06 left), I didn't know if we'd have one more shot," said Landry. "They had reached the point where all they had to do was run out the clock, but Simeon Rice gave us a big break and we took advantage of it."

Landry, who played so long in nearby Detroit, is suddenly 1-0 vs. Michigan. He can't imagine what it's been like all these years since Bump Elliott started the the trend with repeated victories over brother Pete.

But if it hadn't been for so many UI penalties (10) and fumbles, so much pent-up frustration, Landry might have made it look easy.

I was on the field near the end zone when Klein caught the winner, and I was swept up with the emotion of celebrating players to the point of tears. They wanted this so badly, and they had it coming. Looking back, Illinois was within a play or two in seven Michigan losses between 1982 and 1994.

OCTOBER 25, 1999

Illinois broke out of a slump and pulled a rousing upset at Michigan with diminutive Chicagoan Rocky Harvey making the key runs.

ANN ARBOR, Mich. — You can't plan these things.

Just when you least expect it, you reach out the bottle in a thunderstorm and capture a bolt of lightning so powerful that it lifts the nails right off your toes.

That's what Ron Turner's Illini did in the Big House on Saturday.

With 110,000-plus sitting in horror ... with thousands of ESPN viewers switching back on in disbelief ... with Michigan's proud athletes in full panic ... Illinois rallied from 20 points down to Conquer the Heroes.

This 35-29 stunner was, all things considered, the biggest Illini upset since the UI's upset master, Ray Eliot, retired in 1959.

"Little Old Illinois came in and took it away from them," said Illini defensive end Fred Wakefield. "Not many teams do that here."

Consider that Michigan was ranked No. 9, was 26-3 under Lloyd Carr at Michigan Stadium, and was 33-3-2 against Illinois since 1959.

Consider that Illinois was a 24-point underdog and had lost 23 of 25 Big Ten games after blowing a 28-7 lead at Indiana and losing a week ago to Minnesota, 37-7.

Talk shows had begun to field questions about team motivation, Turner's tenure, Kurt Kittner's mobility, and perceived recruiting losses. Then, in an unlikely final 18 minutes, with the unlikeliest of heroes stepping forward, the Illini rattled off four touchdowns — the first by QB-turned-end Walter Young, the second by QB-turned-end Brian Hodges, and the last two by little-used Rocky Harvey.

"Nobody, and I mean NOBODY thought this would happen except the guys in that locker room," said Turner.

Truth is, most UI fans didn't even dare to get their hopes up after seeing what Minnesota did to the UI homecoming.

But the Big Ten, which has emerged as the nation's premier conference — ask Notre Dame! — offers a full store of surprises every week. One day Michigan State is Pasadena-bound, and two weeks later the Spartans are not only losing, they're being dismembered. One day Wisconsin is counted out, and two weeks later the Badgers are kicking tails and taking names.

On Saturday, the Illini had a plan. It was, basically, a commitment to "fight to the death" regardless of the score.

Unlikely hero Jameel Cook followed his coach's plan to a T.

"I wasn't even looking at the scoreboard," said the stocky Floridian. "The coaches said it would be a 60-minute game and our job was to keep fighting regardless of anything."

The change in momentum was subtle. After scoring two TDs, the Wolverines' Anthony Thomas left with a finger injury. No one thought much about it with the score 27-7. Never in its history had Illinois rallied successfully from a 20-point deficit.

Using his tight ends, Kittner marched Illinois to the Michigan 31 where, on fourth down, the blitzing Wolverines blew a coverage and Young coasted down the middle for a 31-yard jail break.

That's when Robert Franklin, subbing for Eric Guenther, went wild at linebacker, personally getting the ball back for Kittner, who responded with a seven-minute, 77-yard march to make the score 27-21.

As we know, when the score is 27-21 with six minutes left, it's anybody's game. And, would you believe, the panicking Wolverines backfired on offense and blew another defensive coverage that allowed Kittner to switch off his primary receiver, the closely covered Michael Dean, and hit Harvey for 59 yards down the middle.

If no one could have imagined the outcome, it's also true that no one could have scripted the final three minutes. With Michigan penetrating into Illinois territory trailing only 28-27, center Steve Frazier snapped the ball high over Tom Brady's head to take the Wolverines out of field goal range. Then Illinois, needing only a first down to kneel out the clock, got a 54-yard TD run by Harvey that, in actuality, gave the Wolverines a chance to tie if they could get a TD and a two-point conversion.

And just when Illini Tony Francis saved the day with his goal line interception, he fumbled into what could have been a Michigan touchdown if teammate Muhammad Abdullah hadn't recovered for a safety.

But if it was messy at the end, if it was nerve-wracking until the final second, this only adds to the mystique of a stunner that was conceived on Mars and declined by Hollywood ... the biggest comeback and the least expected Illini football triumph of the modern era.

Colleague Bob Asmussen was the first to call for Harvey not to score when he broke that last Illini TD. And I quickly realized, "Yes, all Illinois needs is a first down. It's better if he doesn't score." Michigan could have climbed back into a tie, but the Illini hung on in a scary finish to ignite an 8-for-9 win streak over two seasons.

SEPTEMBER 24, 2000

Miscalled fumbles resulted in 10th-ranked Michigan snapping Illinois' seven-game win streak, 35-31.

CHAMPAIGN — The cry of the underdog has always droned on loud and unheard.

Go back to the 1940s, and old-timers will swear Ted Williams always got the call on outside-corner pitches. "If he took the pitch, it had to be a ball," goes the age-old complaint.

And it's louder today. When Greg Maddux strolls out with immaculate control, how many strikes are called on pitches 2 inches off the plate? Time after time, broadcasters suggest as though it is fact: "If you're around the plate, you get those calls."

So is it, or is it not, imbedded in the psyches of honest refs and umps to unconsciously lean to the favorites?

Wasn't it impossible to get a fairly officiated basketball game at Indiana in the 1980s? Wasn't there an Indiana-UI game so outlandish that Lou Henson was able to circle 28 legitimate officiating mistakes (favoring Indiana) on the tape?

We should not be surprised, then, that in the final four minutes of Saturday's UI-Michigan game, the zebras committed not one, but two mistakes on one play — a non-fumble by Rocky Harvey — and overlooked a game-turning fumble by Michigan's Anthony Thomas on the Illini 3-yard line.

I mean, Michigan was supposed to win, right? So it's perfectly natural, in the great scheme of things, that an Illini runner might fumble under pressure ... and equally illogical that a great back, Thomas, would cough it up.

But Harvey's head-over-heels bobble was caused by the ground, which means he was down when it happened. And then he scraped the ball back under his arm, which means the play had ended a second time before Michigan's diving players rooted it away from him on the ground. To give Michigan the ball under the circumstances was as ridiculous as it was sad.

Yet, within moments, Thomas fumbled it back, only to have the officials give his miscue a blind eye.

Get over it, you say. Put the 35-31 heartbreaker in the past.

What a terrific idea! Forget that an eight-game win streak would have been the longest in the Big Ten. Forget what it means in terms of revenue, bowl positioning and national ranking. Forget what it means to the mood of a community that is into its eighth season without seeing a win at Memorial Stadium over any Big Ten rival other than Indiana, Northwestern, Iowa and Minnesota. Eight seasons!

What you have to accept is that there is no recourse for unintentional mistakes. It's just like 1993 when Arizona scored two illegal touchdowns to beat Illinois 16-14. Afterward, in referring to Wildcat fumble returns of 76 and 46 yards, Big Ten supervisor of officials Dave Parry indicated both plays should have been ruled dead and neither score should have counted.

That's your satisfaction: the realization that you got scr ... ah, er, wronged.

Through all this, you've never heard me say Illinois is better than Michigan.

If they played 10 times, Michigan would probably win seven or eight. It would take a special performance by Kurt Kittner & Co. to defeat superior talent, the kind he produced with 352 aerial yards Saturday night.

Michigan is always a mountain. If you've watched over four decades, you realize how difficult it is to win from in front. Three of the UI's four triumphs over Michigan since 1959 were accomplished via surprising late rallies.

To forge ahead of Michigan is to unleash the full force of the monster, to cause cautious Michigan coaches to throw that caution to the wind. When that happens, the next word is unstoppable.

Consider last year, and note how the Illini game at Michigan differed from others. Illinois caught the Wolverines off guard. On other days, Michigan trailed in the fourth quarter vs. Notre Dame 22-19, Michigan State 34-17, Indiana 24-20, Penn State 27-17 and Ohio State 17-10, and rallied to defeat all except Michigan State, falling short 34-31. In addition, Michigan edged Alabama in overtime (35-34) and skimmed past Syracuse 18-13 and Wisconsin 21-16.

So, you see, the Wolverines are accustomed to late-game pressure. And it would not be surprising if the zebras, like close-following fans, get caught up in the momentum swings that routinely go their direction toward the end.

There's no script for these events. In the first upset, David had a sling and a rock. Illinois needed bazookas Saturday night ... to repel those tank-like blockers ... and awake the zebras.

These missed calls allowed Ron Turner to increase his cry for TV replays which, in this case, would have preserved the Illini victory. What we've learned in this replay era is that officials are frequently wrong because plays happen so fast and they are often blocked.

ILLINI CELLAR DWELLERS COME ALIVE
MARCH 7, 1999

Lon Kruger's rebuilt Illini, 3-13 in the Big Ten, defeated three ranked teams before bowing in the 1999 Big Ten basketball tournament.

CHICAGO — Wow! We're still here!

It'll be a Sunday of soiled undergarments and wrinkled pants. I mean, who based Wednesday's packing decisions on the likelihood of Illinois turning a last-place season into a United Center marathon of miracles?

Following a script Hollywood producers would turn down as unrealistic, Lon Kruger's inspired athletes have climbed over three ranked teams and a lineup of future pros ... Quincy Lewis, A.J. Guyton, Michael Redd, etc. ... to face Michigan State in Sunday's 2 p.m. Big Ten tournament finale.

Who's sweating? Bubble sitters Minnesota and Purdue, that's who.

Another upset today would assure the Illini of an NCAA berth, creating certain resistance within the selection committee to the idea of extending eight bids to the Big Ten.

"Four wins in four days against these teams would be a monumental accomplishment," Big Ten Coach of the Year Jim O'Brien said after Ohio State's 79-77 loss Saturday.

Sure, it's a pipe dream, but Kruger has his Illini challenging history with a coaching effort that tops last year, when a lineup of no-name seniors tied for first in the league race.

Piecing together a sick and injured club early in the week — "We never had the full team available for practice," Kruger said — he embarked on a system of two players sharing each position.

"For a while, we kind of passed that bug around," the coach said.

"But the coughing subsided Wednesday and Thursday. We started rotating players, and it became easier because the guys coming off the bench were playing so well. That gave us the best of all worlds because, while we're tired, we're not as fatigued as we would be if five guys were playing 36 minutes."

After shocking Minnesota 67-64, the Illini hit their highest production with 82 against Indiana and 79 against Ohio State. Saturday's effort marked the first time Illinois shot better than 50 percent all season.

This is a club that was drowning itself in turnovers and missed opportunities two months ago, with players who were being mentally discarded by their own fans. You heard it: Fess Hawkins lacks skills, Sergio McClain can't shoot, Lucas Johnson is overmatched, Cleotis Brown is a disappointment.

Then the persistent Kruger hauled out his wand, and the UI box scores are flooded with heroes.

Cory Bradford kicked it off with six huge treys to repulse cold-shooting Minnesota, Johnson coming to life just two weeks after he was limited to four minutes in a home loss to Iowa.

"Coach took me aside and told me what he expected from me," Johnson said. "He helped me with my jumper, and he instilled confidence in me. He wanted me to be strong with the ball and knock down open shots. Every time I hit one, it makes the next one feel like it's automatic."

Johnson set the tone for the defeat of Indiana, virtually mauling Luke Recker into submission while gathering 17 of his 41 tournament points ... stealing the Friday spotlight from Hawkins' unexpected 16-point effort.

On Saturday, the main source of inspiration came from Brown. The sore-ankled transfer defied Ohio State defenders in fierce basket drives and hauled down seven rebounds.

"We're riding on each other's shoulders," Bradford said. "It's a great feeling."

And before you think the Illini are out of gas ... a natural assumption ... remember that Brown and Robert Archibald saw no second-half minutes Thursday, that fouls limited Bradford and Victor Chukwudebe to 24 and 21 minutes Friday, that Damir Krupalija saw just 12 minutes Saturday.

Maybe a nine-man rotation, with Nate Mast also giving workhorse Bradford a few valuable minutes of rest, won't work against a No. 1 seed like Michigan State. But they wouldn't have come this far without Kruger's decisions.

When the Illini played ranked foes Iowa and Indiana close in late February, I thought they might pull a surprise in Chicago. But I never dreamed they would win three straight, and I am still amazed at Lon Kruger's clever manipulation of his squad. No Illini coach was ever better at matchups.

IT WAS A SPECTACULAR NIGHT IN CHAMPAIGN
JANUARY 12, 1979

In Lou Henson's biggest UI win up to that time, Illinois beat Magic Johnson and national champion Michigan State.

CHAMPAIGN — A young, starless University of Illinois basketball team is No. 1 in the nation today.

Oh, sure, the ratings don't come out until next week. And the Illini could be beaten by then. Rugged Ohio State is the 1 p.m. NBC-TV foe Saturday.

But just ask any of these orange-waving fans. The Illini are No. 1 because on Thursday night, playing before the largest crowd in UI history, they outfought, outrebounded (50 to 22) and outscored No. 1-ranked Michigan State, 57-55.

It took a last-ditch corner jumper by sophomore Eddie Johnson to do it, but this was a game that the Illini controlled after a nervous beginning. A jumper by the same Johnson — Eddie, not Earvin — sent the Illini ahead 47-46 with 9:25 remaining and they never trailed thereafter.

Taking a 53-49 lead with a taunting, four-corner offense ahead of the five-minute mark, the Illini saw the 1978 Big Ten champs battle back to tie it 55-55, on a dunk by leaping Greg Kelser and a 20-footer by sub Don Brkovich with 2:27 showing.

Both clubs missed opportunities in the holdout game that ensued, the giant crowd groaning as Eddie Johnson's jumper rolled off and tips by Neil Bresnahan and Derek Holcomb failed to go down. But, at 1:12, the Illini got it back when Earvin Johnson, shackled effectively much of the contest, attempted a driving shot and missed.

Earvin tried to save it when he tied up Illini Levi Cobb with 40 seconds to go, but Cobb got the tip to Eddie Johnson and the Illini held for the final attempt. As the clock dipped under 10 seconds, Steve Lanter found room down the middle and passed it off to an open Johnson in the corner.

"I knew it was going in when it left my hand," said the grinning Westinghouse forward. "That's my favorite. I didn't know how much time was left but I knew somebody had to shoot, and it happened to be me."

It was the shot heard 'round the nation. The victory extended the season's longest winning streak — 15 — and set the stage for another showdown of 3-0 conference teams, Ohio State and Illinois, here Saturday.

"We played a fine game," said Henson, "and I just can't believe those rebound figures (50 to 22). But we can't afford to celebrate. The job now is to get mentally ready for Ohio State. The Buckeyes knocked Duke out of the No. 1 spot and they have a super team."

As it turned out, Ohio State won that game in overtime, 69-66, with the help of a late block on a breakaway by Eddie Johnson. And as dominant as the Illini were in going 15-0, they lost 11 of the last 15 games. I laid this slump primarily on Steve Lanter's injury and erratic guard play.

FIRST OF TWO COLUMNS ON ILLINI-MIZZOU SERIES
DECEMBER 20, 1988

Lou Henson's Flying Illini rallied to down 10th-ranked Missouri for the sixth straight time in St. Louis.

ST. LOUIS — In an uproarious setting with 18,561 equally divided fans screaming their lungs out, Lou Henson's Illini learned a twofold lesson Monday night.

First, in the era of the three-point shot and the 45-second shot clock, big leads can and often do evaporate in a hurry. Illinois fell behind by 18 points in 16 minutes, made up the entire amount in seven minutes, and still had 17 minutes to play.

Second, the Illini's chief nemesis isn't whatever hulk the opponents put at center. It is themselves, their own judgment, their own tendency to use their quickness and free-lance skills to excess.

Criticism, perhaps, isn't appropriate after such a splendid 87-84 triumph against archrival Missouri. But it was gained by the shear force of their enormous athletic ability, with an exceptional streak of shooting (65.5 percent in the second half and a string of free throws). The Illini used only a portion of the finesse they're capable of.

Downstaters Steve Bardo and Larry Smith combined at the point for 11 UI turnovers. Lowell Hamilton scored 21 but, in Henson's words, "took some ill-advised shots early" that disrupted Illini teamwork, and fouled out with 25 minutes of playing time. Sophomore Marcus Liberty had a stretch of shaky ball handling when the Illini bungled second-half breakaway opportunities. Fouls and turnovers (24) made it a tough hill to climb.

Down 39-21 before Bardo hit his only basket with 4:01 left in the half, the Illini had deadlocked it 43-43 in less than three minutes of the second half. It was a withering seven minutes that demonstrated once again what these Illini are made of. With their quickness and firepower, they're capable of some extraordinary runs.

Kenny Battle was brilliant just before halftime, then ran wild for 19 points thereafter. He overtook Missouri's Arkansas transfer, 6-foot-6 Byron Irvin, as the dominant force in the game.

For all the talk about Missouri's 7-1 Gary Leonard, the senior center was the least effective starter in the game. With extraordinary quickness all around him, he played 14 minutes and had four points and no rebounds. The top rebounder was Illinois' Nick Anderson with 10.

"We just kept playing," said Anderson. "We're not the type to quit playing when we get behind. We got a few turnovers and the momentum changed."

In fact, Illinois outscored Missouri by 21 points in the last 24 minutes. Down the stretch, while blowing some opportunities with ill-advised passing, the Illini shot free throws and field goals with precision.

"You learn a lot in a game like this," said Anderson. "We needed a tough game and we fought to the end. We look to Kenny as our leader because he plays hard all the time. It rubs off."

Battle called the second half "one of my best," adding:

"I'm a senior and I'm supposed to pick the other guys up. I tried to stay aggressive.

"The last play (when Missouri led 84-83) was designed for me. I made my move in the lane when I saw they weren't in position to draw the charge, and I thought my basket counted. When it didn't, I concentrated on my free throws. I hit 12 of 12 in the morning and I thought about that. I kept my rotation and the shots went in."

For me, this remains as the best game in the Illini-dominated series with Missouri. There was nothing quite like watching Battle and Anderson when they got on a roll, and knowing Norm Stewart couldn't do anything about it.

DECEMBER 23, 1993

Missouri's biggest win in the Braggin' Rights series was a triple-overtime thriller in 1993.

ST. LOUIS — Three days before Christmas, Lou Henson's Illini were in the giving mood.

Three times they had a fierce Missouri Tiger on the ropes, first in regulation and twice in overtimes.

But no matter how much you practice free throws, you can't duplicate knee-stiffening, wrist-tightening, late-game atmosphere with 18,000 fans screaming in the background.

After making 17 of their first 20 free throws, the tense Illini missed 16 of 31 when the pressure was on, and fell to gritty Tiger reserves 108-107, in the third overtime in a sold-out St. Louis Arena. This epic contest deserves further review.

End of Regulation:

Confusing Missouri with a late zone defense, Illinois led 74-65 with 1:15 left. But the Illini, fouled repeatedly by a desperate foe, converted just five one-pointers while Mizzou guard Melvin Booker sandwiched a short jumper between two three-pointers each by Lamont Frazier and Mark Atkins. That made it 79-79.

"With the three-point shot, no lead is safe," said Henson. "We tried to get a hand up on them, but they made the shots when they had to, and we couldn't put them away at the line."

First Overtime:

Ahead 86-81 on Richard Keene's two free throws at :43, the tiring Illini let 6-1 freshman reserve Jason Sutherland slip in for a three-point play on a rebound, and Kiwane Garris and T.J. Wheeler both went 1 for 2 at the line while Mizzou's Kelly Thames scored twice inside to tie it again. Illini Shelly Clark missed a 10-foot bank shot at the buzzer.

"We had the sick and wounded playing, and the women and children were next," said Tiger coach Norm Stewart. "It's a great feeling to see this kind of unselfish teamwork. This just proves that as long as you're in it, you can win."

Second Overtime:

With hard-muscled Mizzou vets Jevon Crudup, Marlo Finner and

Atkins fouled out, Illinois jumped out again, 92-88. But Morton rookie Derek Grimm sank two free throws at :19 to tie it, whereupon Garris ran down the clock and drew a foul.

With an irate Stewart debating the refs in the middle of the court, Garris went to the line at :00 needing one free throw to win it. The rookie who hit 26 straight earlier this season failed on both, giving him 10 misses in a school-record 22 free throw tries Wednesday night.

"I usually make my free throws, but I wasn't getting my legs into it," said Garris. "I was a little tired and I think I rushed it. After I missed the first one, I tried to baby the second one in. I was trying to put the fans out of my mind."

Third Overtime:

Missouri's spunky subs outplayed Illinois' weary regulars, and when Deon Thomas fouled out with 1:34 left, the Tigers built their leads to 105-100 and 108-104 before Garris made a meaningless trey at the buzzer.

"After Garris missed those two free throws in the second overtime, I felt like someone was watching over us," said Booker, whose 13 assists (in 52 minutes) set a Missouri record.

"When we needed those threes, I just penetrated and kicked back, and they went for it. We kept reaching deeper within ourselves."

The officials wouldn't look back at Norm Stewart, who was on the floor and screaming near midcourt when Garris missed his first free throw. It should have been a technical foul. Stewart, realizing this, ran back quickly as Garris missed the second one. I think the refs figured Garris would make one of them, and they didn't want to deal with Stewart with the game over.

HENSON GANG PULLS OFF ROAD SURPRISE
DECEMBER 3, 1995

Kiwane Garris sparked a gritty victory that shattered Duke's 95-game home win streak against non-conference rivals.

DURHAM, N.C. — In a relentless display of guts and teamwork here Saturday, the Fighting Illini survived:

... the magical basketball tradition of Duke, which had won 95 straight home games against non-ACC opposition;

... their own horrendous 2-for-15 stretch of free throwing;

... a frustrating siege of Big Ten officiating so mind-boggling that Illini coaches, including Lou Henson, were seething even after the game ended;

... a splendid 27-point outburst by Jeff Capel, who averaged 12.5 last season and showed 11.5 in Duke's 4-0 start this season.

So, how did they beat the Blue Devils, 75-65?

First, the Illini displayed a more integrated offense and had five players score between nine and 18 points. Second, the Illini had 11 more possessions by spearing more rebounds, 42-34, and making fewer turnovers, 16-13. Third, the Illini dominated inside and posted a better shooting percentage, 48.4 to 42.9.

And in the final 20 minutes, when the game was looking for a taker, the Illini had Kiwane Garris. All he did in that final segment was (1) make three clean steals, (2) handle the ball against fierce pressure, (3) convert free throws when no one else could and (4) score 10 of the UI's last 16 points.

"We held him out early because we wanted to save him," said coach Lou Henson. "He's a key guy, and we knew we'd need him at the end."

This is the same Garris who saved the 83-80 win against Texas-San Antonio with the last four points of the game, and had otherwise participated with the team only sparingly while trying to recover from a chronic groin strain the last two weeks.

"Garris is an All-American," Duke coach Mike Krzyzewski said. "We knew he'd play and we knew what to expect. But overall, I think it was Illinois' physical play and outstanding defense that beat us. Their kids hung in and played tough, and we didn't."

Krzyzewski downplayed the 95-game streak, saying:

"I've never paid attention to the streak, nor have I talked to my players about it. The most important streak for us was our two national championships (1991 and 1992)."

The Illini win was particularly big for Richard Keene and Jerry Gee, both of whom chose Illinois over Duke after long recruiting sieges.

Gee made huge strides, not so much because he went 6 for 7 from the field but because he ruled inside with 12 rebounds and physical defense. Keene, who had seven assists and no turnovers, was again in control of the game when his foul troubles permitted.

"This was a big win because it was a test of where we stand, and very much a confidence builder," said Keene. "We had the big lead (38-22) but you always expect a team like Duke to rally at home. The main thing we had to do was not get caught up in the crowd excitement."

Keene was prepared for intimidation efforts by the student fans who completely surround the court in 10-deep bleachers. But the personal attacks never really developed.

"They got me a few times during the warm-ups," said Keene, "but it didn't carry over into the game. I didn't hear anything personal after the game started."

Krzyzewski is all business and hard to reach for the media. His time is so valuable that my pregame radio snippet with him was done while he rode a stationary bicycle. It is amazing what he has accomplished with a modest arena and stiff academic requirements.

ISSUES

FIRST OF FOUR COLUMNS ON DEON THOMAS CASE
1990

Allegations against Jimmy Collins, Deon Thomas and the UI fail to meet a reasonable standard of logic.

CHAMPAIGN — My lantern is lit and my cane is strong.

Lead me, now, to a man who cherishes logic over intellect, reason over cleverness.

I spend my mornings reading pages of ivy tower pontification, detailed recitations of a university's troubled history, and all manner of invective, innuendo and exaggeration.

But has anyone tested the NCAA's allegations of misconduct by the University of Illinois against simple logic?

The NCAA has elected to believe that Jimmy Collins offered Deon Thomas $80,000 and a Chevrolet Blazer in 1988. We know they believe that because they don't bring charges on an official inquiry unless they have reason to believe they'll stick.

Now, let's think about that. Imagine the uproar in coach Lou Henson's office if he found out a freshman without "visible means" was driving a new car around campus.

Henson threw a tantrum when a fifth-year senior, Ken Norman, used his likelihood of future earnings to obtain a loan for his auto. Henson wasn't even happy when the well-to-do parents of Kendall Gill and Stephen Bardo provided these multi-talented seniors with cars last year.

As for the thousands of dollars, it would have left a paper trail a mile wide. And how could you have Thomas residing in grandeur, and his mother and grandmother suddenly enjoying new furnishings, when the same wasn't being done for Kenny Battle and Lowell Hamilton and Nick Anderson and Marcus Liberty? Where do you stop with that sort of thing, and how large a secret organization would be required to quietly fund it?

Furthermore, how could you permit Anderson's mother to be

overwhelmed by hospital bills and be facing an eviction notice if you had a "slush fund" that could kick out $80,000 for a single player?

And if you could raise that kind of money, how could you allow Liberty to have his telephone cut off and face a court date for his inability to cover his apartment damage done by his dog?

Oh well, it must be a joyful journalistic journey to tweak the Big U., because everybody's doing it.

But where is the logic? And while we're at it, how pertinent are 25-year historical reminders to this case? Past UI run-ins with higher authority involved different people. That's what a university is, people. Not buildings. It doesn't make sense to carry on like there's an infectious disease, some brain-muddling "bad water" that carries over from one regime to the next.

Furthermore, to suggest a medium-sized city, with a population of nearly 48,000 students, faculty and staff, has "gone bad" because of the unproven and apparently trumped-up allegations against one assistant basketball coach is absurd.

The UI's real problem is that it is located in the state of Illinois, which is located adjacent to the state of Chicago. The two states are intertwined but have little in common culturally, politically or economically, much less spiritually.

The UI exists for the purpose of education. Based on records and surveys, the state of Chicago pays its bills by avoiding paying for education wherever possible.

Only a small percentage of the high school students from the state of Chicago are prepared to attend the UI — and yet an inordinate percentage of blue-chip basketball players come from there.

In the early years, some of the best Chicago athletes enrolled and promptly flunked out. Then, with Cazzie Russell as an example, they stopped coming, and Illini basketball languished. Ultimately, a truce was called in the 1970s as enlightened university leaders initiated a long-range plan to meet the needs of otherwise gifted but academically marginal Chicago students.

All through these years, the state of Chicago has been considered open recruiting ground for universities everywhere. Allegiances and loyalties seldom figured in.

Therefore, it should not be surprising that the vice-grip applied in the 1980s by Lou Henson and two assistants, first Tony Yates and then Jimmy Collins, would be met with stiff resistance from other universities.

"The attitudes around us are interesting," said Henson. "We can't go to Indianapolis and recruit a top basketball player. We can't go to Davenport and have any degree of success. We don't attempt to recruit ANYBODY from beyond our state boundaries unless that individual tells us from the start that he isn't interested in his state institution.

"And yet it's obvious that the University of Iowa became very upset when we signed Deon Thomas, even though he had every reason to come here.

"Look at it logically (logically?!?). We had two former Simeon players on a Final Four team, our games are televised on WGN Channel 9, we're within easy driving distance, and this university offers the best possible opportunity for him to get a job back in his Chicago home someday."

But Henson was asked at Michigan State on Saturday, can major universities really reach the Top 20 without cheating?

"Yes," he replied.

"Where?" persisted the questioner.

"We have five or six in the Big Ten right now," Henson replied, obviously including the Illini.

No coach has been more of a stickler for the rules than Henson. Stories abound about his efforts to run a tight ship.

Once, when Jens Kujawa had a summer job making deliveries, the boss let him make drops on the way home and keep the car home overnight. Henson found out and stopped it.

Once, when he heard Doug Altenberger was planning to play in a summer golf outing in West Frankfort, he called Doug back out of fear someone would pay his entry fee or give him a free meal.

Those stories go on and on. But so have the rumors. And it isn't anyone's fault. It is the fault of the fact that everybody, from Digger Phelps to Jud Heathcote to Tom Davis, believes down deep that the poor kids from the state of Chicago have their hands out, and that you can't recruit them without paying them.

It is a perception that will never change. As long as Chicago sits by the lake and the university is located in central Illinois, it will be the same.

So the NCAA enforcement department will always have rumors to chase here because those rumors never cease. Most recently, Thomas ignited those rumors with his own "trash talk" to Iowa assistant Bruce Pearl, seemingly admitting he accepted a "deal," then denying it.

But does that mean the university is a bad actor? And does it say that Jimmy Collins must pay for the past crimes of others and the setup tactics of a desperate Iowa assistant.

When it all comes out — and the NCAA's Iowa-raised investigator should know this — it will be revealed by members of the Thomas family that Pearl went to the NCAA and charged Collins with some of the very offers that he himself made in behalf of Iowa.

If this is true, it was a master stroke by Pearl, and it applied a twist unlike any case the NCAA has run across. It remains to be seen whether the NCAA can decipher the confusion.

The NCAA investigative team couldn't prove anything related to the major charges, but still penalized Illinois for minor infractions as a penalty for challenging the hierarchy. Pearl was never investigated despite obvious infractions on his part.

JANUARY 1990

With Illinois already under investigation, LaPhonso Ellis claims Illinois made illegal offers in his recruitment.

CHAMPAIGN — The mystery charge is still a mystery, but there is no longer any question where it comes from.

Deon Thomas is sitting out his freshman season (1989-90) at the University of Illinois not only because of his acknowledged misstatements with an Iowa assistant coach and NCAA investigators, but because the UI has been charged with strikingly similar allegations involving former East St. Louis Lincoln star LaPhonso Ellis.

"But for that, it's very likely that Thomas would have been cleared to play," said UI athletic director John Mackovic on Saturday.

Chancellor Morton Weir said the same thing in December. Far from pleased with Thomas' handling of critical conversations with Iowa's Bruce Pearl and the investigators, Weir stated firmly that he was nevertheless prepared in early November to initiate an appeal to the NCAA eligibility committee for Thomas' immediate eligibility, and then to carry the case before the NCAA Committee on Infractions if need be.

Weir was ready, that is, until the mud hit the fan in the form of the Ellis allegations. That's when the administration began to reconsider the case and rethink the Thomas matter.

How does Ellis, a sophomore at Notre Dame, affect Thomas?

Because aspects of the supposed payoffs are frighteningly similar. These weren't, you see, lump sum deals. They were incremental, one source citing an initial outlay of $15,000 with annual follow-ups.

Thomas, claiming coercion and trickery by Pearl, "sort of went along" when Pearl mentioned that the UI had offered him $80,000 and a Chevrolet Blazer. When asked why he didn't emphatically deny it, Thomas said he was "talking trash ... not paying a lot of attention."

Said Weir:

"When I first heard the $80,000, I thought it was preposterous." Preposterous, that is, until he was informed of the proposed system of incremental payments apparently described by Pearl ... and then discovered, to his shock in early November, that the NCAA (and not Mike Slive) had in its possession an allegation of incremental payments intended to encourage Ellis to attend Illinois.

Said an administrativel source:

"One of two things happened. Either someone made an offer (to Ellis) that was similar to the offer Pearl said Illinois made to Thomas, or it is a fabrication along similar lines. And it is hard to understand why he (Ellis) would put himself at risk in this if it didn't happen."

Could it be a copy-cat case, Ellis learning of the Thomas story andcopying it?

"We're checking into that. Anything is possible," he said.

So, looking back, you can build an understandable scenario in the Thomas aspect of the case. Insiders report that Thomas' high school friend, Renaldo Kyles, worked with Pearl to watch after Thomas and encourage him to attend Iowa. Kyles may have been influenced by Pearl in any number ofways, Thomas telling intimates that Kyles was paid.

When Thomas chose Illinois, Pearl asked Kyles what happened. That's where the $80,000 was supposedly born, Kyles explaining away his failure, and Pearl calling Thomas on several occasions to find, undoubtedly to his surprise, that Thomas was willing to go along with it. Perhaps, some say, Thomas was protecting his friend, Kyles, by admitting that Iowa had been outbid for him.

The latter is conjecture but the next is not. Pearl called Minnesota, which had also recruited Thomas, and told Gopher basketball coches of his material, asking if they'd join him in going after Illinois. Clem Haskins and assistant Silas McKinnie, a 1968 Iowa grad, listened and declined.

So Pearl, presumably with the support of Iowa head coach Tom Davis, moved ahead, eliminating part of the information on the tape and turning over the portion he wanted the NCAA to hear ... and adding a list of charges against UI assistant coach Jimmy Collins.

By itself, Pearl's information would not have been enough to convince Weir to keep Thomas on the sidelines. Weir didn't believe

Pearl's allegations and was ready to release Deon until Slive carried the NCAA-uncovered information on Ellis to him.

As the UI awaits the letter of official inquiry, there are assorted other nuisances — technical and minor, they're called — but the university's real problem is getting to the heart of the Ellis charges.

If someone made him an offer, who was it? When was it made? Did the same person approach Thomas and Ellis? Even if it happened, why would Ellis report it now? If it didn't happen, why would he make it up?

What is Irish coach Digger Phelps' involvement in this? What do Weir and Mackovic mean when they refer to "conflicting statements?"

And how would the NCAA Committee on Infractions treat an unsubstantiated allegation of this nature, or do they consider Thomas' recanted statement on tape substantiation for the Ellis allegation?

Weir and Mackovic, with the aid of Slive, are searching for answers to these questions. And that's why Deon Thomas, whose only mistakes may have been his own self-incriminating words, isn't playing.

UI administrators are generally private, but Mort Weir called me into his office to explain his quandary. How could he let Thomas play, and how could he release Jimmy Collins to recruit, after the Ellis allegations hit? He faced charges from two directions. Was there a connection? It would be a long time before it became clear that all the major allegations against Collins were fabricated.

THE EARLY '90s

Back-tracking finds that exaggerated stories may have originated with Renaldo Kyles in Chicago and Arlander Hampton in East St. Louis.

CHAMPAIGN — Why LaPhonso Ellis?

Why did Ellis, early in a promising basketball career at Notre Dame, alter testimony he had given to Richard Johanningmeier in Operation Intercept, and tell NCAA enforcement staffer Bob Minnix that Illini assistant coach Jimmy Collins had committed a series of recruiting infractions?

Many people, including former NCAA investigator Randy Rueckert, make an unanswerable point when they demanded: "Why would Ellis lie?"

With new information as to how the process evolved, a fresh theory has materialized.

Bruce Pearl, Iowa assistant coach, made a series of nonconsensual telephone tape recordings with Deon Thomas in April 1989, and obtained rough admissions of an $80,000 offer by Collins to Thomas on April 9. Telephone records indicate Pearl was in close contact with the NCAA throughout the process, and the NCAA sent Minnix and Rueckert to interrogate Thomas on the UI campus that spring.

After two showdowns with Thomas, the enforcement officers must have realized that Thomas would strongly deny the information on the covert tape, and that UI Chancellor Morton Weir would never believe the contrived and far-fetched story. The staffers needed corroboration of UI indiscretions from another source.

As Minnix explained to the Committee on Infractions, he contacted Digger Phelps, Notre Dame coach, who in turn told him to call John Shumate, Southern Methodist head coach who had recruited Ellis for Notre Dame.

Shumate asked to speak to Phelps before replying to Minnix, and then told Minnix that a good source would be Arlander Hampton in East St. Louis.

Hampton was a teacher's assistant at an East St. Louis junior high and a friend of the Ellis family. By his presence (and antagonistic attitude) in the Ellis home, he had spoiled UI coach Lou Henson's home visit, forcing Henson to leave early, and he had influenced Ellis to attend Notre Dame.

Furthermore, in a time of great stress that spring, Ellis later acknowledged that Hampton encouraged him to remain at Notre Dame when he was thinking of transferring.

Since Notre Dame would not release its telephone records, and Hampton refused to cooperate with UI attorneys, one can only imagine the calls from Minnix, Phelps and/or Ellis to Hampton in this period.

Minnix said he interviewed Hampton and then went to see Ellis in Phelps' basketball office. It seems likely that Ellis became a dupe and, rather than originating the story, merely confirmed the wild and inaccurate charges that Hampton had given Minnix.

"This would explain everything," said Henson on Friday. "I thought LaPhonso was tricked into it. That's why he told a different story every time."

So Ellis may have done nothing more than confirm exaggerated "street talk." It's likely that Ellis may have been convinced, at the time, that his information was basically correct. But those charges broke down one by one under scrutiny ... though this didn't happen until the UI got rid of its blinders-wearing investigator, Mike Slive.

The key development in clearing Collins was the Ellis interview by former Judge Frank McGarr representing Illinois, in which Ellis was found to be inaccurate. Later documentation and additional testimony proved this beyond any reasonable doubt.

Thus the Illinois case, for all its complexities, boils down to NCAA investigators and committeemen actually believing the outrageous "street talk" that originated with an Iowa-linked, story-changing junior at Chicago Simeon (Renaldo Kyles) and an athletic hanger-on who became associated with the youthful Ellis (Hampton).

"The NCAA investigators knew their case was weak," said Steve Beckett, attorney for Thomas.

"If you had what you believed was good information from Ellis, why wouldn't you be on the plane to see all the other players Collins had sought to recruit — Sean Tunstall, Shaquille O'Neal and Litterial Green? The answer is that they didn't want to talk to these other people and receive information that wouldn't support their allegations.

"If you find there are no offers to anyone else, it attacks Ellis' credibility. They were trying to make a case, not find the truth."

Mark Goldenberg, attorney for Collins, added:

"How do you explain that the two people closest to Ellis didn't know about any offers? I'm talking about his mother, who made a taped statement to me, and Mark Chambers, his school friend. Chambers refuted the allegations, and yet the NCAA never did a memo. Byron Higgins (UI counsel) and I interviewed Chambers last July, and we came back stunned that he had been interviewed by Rueckert, and there was no written memo on it.

"I knew we were in trouble on the second day (Aug. 13) in Colorado Springs when David Berst (director of enforcement) said, 'Just because we withdrew all those allegations by Ellis, we don't think that says anything about Ellis' credibility.' "

When the university decided for itself that the allegations weren't true, and took an offensive position with the NCAA, this set in motion the Rueckert-committee philosophy of non-cooperation.

The committee took the step from non-cooperation to "lack of institutional control," clearing the path for severe sanctions despite the elimination of all major charges in the Official Inquiry.

You may have read stories about Rudy Giuliani's ruthless vindictiveness when he was mayor of New York. Power often corrupts and it was never more true than in the UI's dealings with the NCAA's investigative arm. When Mike

Slive represented Illinois, he was prepared to accept all charges and throw the UI on the mercy of the "court." The UI fired Slive and uncovered the truth, but Berst & Co. got the wanted pound of flesh anyway. As Giuliani demonstrated, you can't beat city hall.

1990

UI counsel Byron Higgins disagrees the NCAA's institutional control sanctions.

CHAMPAIGN — Institutional control.

It's a simple term with a vague, complex, almost mysterious definition.

The NCAA Committee on Infractions invoked it but didn't explain it. Nor did the committee give University of Illinois Chancellor Morton Weir an opportunity to debate the subject.

Some will argue the committee had to unearth something to justify serious basketball sanctions — scholarship limitations, three years of probation and no NCAA postseason tourney in 1991 — when, in fact, the committee really believed the UI was guilty of terrible crimes that couldn't be verified.

"We can find no guidance, no definition in this situation that shows us where we crossed the line on institutional control," said Byron Higgins, UI legal counsel. "We disagree with the committee's decision."

Institutional control was never fully discussed in two meetings between UI officials and the committee. But, in what wound down to discussions on mostly self-reported minor items, UI officials made a point of presenting evidence showing institutional control in each case.

Studying each finding from an institutional control viewpoint, Higgins went back over them in search of how the committee reached its conclusions. He found no answers.

— Illegal contacts:

"In the chance encounters between (assistant basketball coach) Jimmy Collins and Simeon athletes at Aunt Sonya's Restaurant and at Simeon High School, institutional control can't prevent such meetings, and Collins acted appropriately in each case," said Higgins.

Recently, Henson has accidentally bumped into teen-agers at

various functions here and elsewhere, and has felt the need to make a formal report of each one. He was told to stop because it's so ridiculous.

— Auto purchases:

"In the case of the automobiles purchases by Illinois players in Decatur, you find strong institutional control," said Higgins.

"Within a matter of days (after Steve Bardo and his parents purchased a car), the car dealer, Miles Schnaer, was contacted, and he sent us copies of all material he had in his possession.

"Rick Allen made inquiries, obtained additional information from the loaning agency (bank) and was satisfied that the price was appropriate and everything was handled properly. Two weeks later, Bob Todd went to Allen for further clarification.

"So, before we even received our notice of preliminary inquiry, the material had been checked by Todd and Allen as well as (hired investigators) Mike Slive and Mike Glazier.

"This had been on Slive's back burner for months when a woman in Decatur, who had a friend in the business of repossessing cars, called Bruce Pearl to tell him that Illinois players were getting cars without making down payments. Pearl told the enforcement staff, and the charge was repeated in October (1989) to Slive, and he arranged for Rich Campbell to run another exhaustive investigation to make sure Bardo and (Kendall) Gill were eligible."

It was then that the UI discovered the loan applications weren't fully completed — as is frequently the case — and the UI declared Gill and Bardo briefly ineligible, and appealed on their behalf. Gill and Bardo were quickly cleared by the NCAA eligibility committee Jan. 4.

"I don't see how anyone could conclude that the university lacked institutional control in this matter," said Higgins, noting that a request has been made for the committee to reconsider its "show cause" ruling that forces the UI to separate itself from Schnaer for three years.

— The double visit:

Lou Henson and Jimmy Collins were charged with visiting Simeon on separate days in the same week. Henson's records and testimony from Bloom High School administrators and teachers verified that Henson was at Bloom when Simeon student Renaldo Kyles — called by Henson "the broker" for Iowa — said he was at Simeon, but the committee found otherwise. The ruling questioning Henson's veracity came as a total shock to the UI coach.

"We disagree with the committee's findings," said Higgins, though acknowledging "sloppiness and looseness in coordinating travel." In other words, Collins didn't keep perfect records and, according to a UI athletic board member, actually failed to turn in vouchers that would have repaid him for a trip involving LaPhonso Ellis.

But sloppiness in record keeping isn't the same as cheating. And, as Higgins said, "the degree of sloppiness doesn't carry over into institutional control."

— Complimentary tickets:

"Slive audited our comp ticket operation in both 1986-87 and 1987-88, and gave us a clean bill of health," said Higgins.

"We were already taking precautions that few schools do. We called people listed as relatives to make sure they really were relatives of the players. We felt we were doing more than 95 percent of other schools in terms of institutional control."

Still, two problems were uncovered in an exhaustive investigation. A few players put down the names of relatives and allowed friends to pick them up. And the UI kept a ticket list of high school coaches in the basketball office, and not in the ticket office, as is required. The latter policy is OK for regular-season road games, but not for NCAA games, and that policy wasn't caught by Slive in his audits. It was a simply mistake of having the calls taken by the wrong office.

For all his legal and collegiate background, Higgins can't understand the institutional control ruling.

"There is an array of speculative answers as to their motivation," he said, shaking his head. "It was our third appearance before them in six years, and they hold an institution with our history to a higher level of control.

"Cynical people would argue that they had to seize on institutional control to give the sanctions they wanted to give, that they conjured up this ill-defined concept, said we're on the precipice, and handed out the penalties they wanted to give.

"Another theory is that this was a compromise."

Perhaps the compromise was deemed necessary because (1) the committee felt obliged to appease the enforcement staff after testimony and common sense forced the committee to reject the staff's major allegations and (2) the committee felt Collins was guilty even though they couldn't prove it.

Illinois was developing a history during the Neale Stoner era of challenging the enforcement staff, and the institutional control gimmick was simply a way for the NCAA committee to get back at the UI for daring to do so. In the final analysis, never was a school penalized so much for doing so little.

REPLACING LOU HENSON
APRIL 1996

The Illini fandom's reaction was inappropriate when Lon Kruger was hired.

CHAMPAIGN — Jimmy Collins and Dick Nagy have landed safely, and Mark Coomes will soon rejoin them. It's one big happy Henson-bred family again just a couple of expressway hours north.

But the community attitude about this coaching issue lingers like a fish in three days of sun.

As one who prides himself in maintaining a reasonable feel for community attitudes, the disapproval rating of Lon Kruger as Illini basketball coach still confuses and bewilders me.

It raises questions that won't stop.

— Why did Collins' backers pretend the decision was unexpected when athletic director Ron Guenther had made it clear he had embarked on a national search? And wouldn't Kruger, the hotshot of the 1994 Final Four, remain on the short list of a director who attended that event while beginning to make contingency plans for Henson's ultimate retirement?

— If Kruger was a far-out reach, why did our Bob Asmussen circle his picture when he was shown what we believed to be the "final three" candidates, and how could Decatur sports editor Mark Tupper have Kruger among the last five he had standing?

— Did Collins' old run-in with the NCAA, and the UI's decision to pull him off the road during the long investigation, have an unmentioned impact as Guenther sought to make a decision that would be welcomed on campus and not draw negative attention in NCAA headquarters?

— Why would people be taken in by the wild Mike Krzyzewski rumors when (1) Krzyzewski made his position clear, (2) they received no such encouragement from this newspaper and (3) anyone who follows the Chicago rumor mill knows how much misinformation it churns out?

— How can you say "where there is smoke, there must be fire" when you're the one who walked along dropping lighted matches?

— Did the personable Collins build a network of hopeful friends who felt they'd be close to the program if he was hired, and are reacting because they now feel out of the loop?

— Aren't we all aware Lou Henson really didn't select Collins as his successor, but rather told Collins and Nagy his loyalties would be with either, and they should decide among themselves who would have the best chance rather than compete against each other?

— Is the local focus so narrow that a top coach from another sector ... one who meets all the appropriate criteria for this job ... is a virtual unknown?

— Was DePaul smarter in retaining Joey Meyer, and Ohio State in retaining Randy Ayers? Did Northwestern, Michigan State, Penn State and Wisconsin make better, wiser hires when they had recent opportunities?

— Couldn't you anticipate that Guenther, knowing the nature of this university and having lived through the Mike White period, would not seek a coach who built his career on junior college transfers?

— Why do folks question Guenther's motives when he has been Illini-dedicated first, last and always, and his hires in other sports have been so appropriate ... or don't you like Mark Johnson, Theresa Grentz and the others arriving in his brief regime?

— Has the talk radio phenomenon created an underground world of people who sit home and form opinions without background, and feed on themselves in controversies? Is this the Cub syndrome that former manager Lee Elia went berserk about when he complained, "Ninety percent of the people have jobs. The rest come to Wrigley Field and boo my players"?

Lon Kruger was razor-sharp and an excellent basketball coach who fielded well-prepared teams. He struck gold with his Peoria-Lincoln recruiting but he was unable to crack the Chicago area during the loaded Maggette-Richardson era, and left for the NBA money in Atlanta after four seasons.

A SAD STORY ABOUT A WAYWARD ATHLETE
APRIL 10, 1988

From the locker room to the lockup, former Illini football player Harry Gosier committed double murder of his wife's mother and sister.

CHAMPAIGN — In Minneapolis, millionaire receiver Anthony Carter set an NFL playoff record for receptions in upsetting San Francisco. A Northlands hero, he came within an eyelash of carrying the Vikings into the 1988 Super Bowl.

In Dallas, the NBA's Mavericks rewarded Derek Harper with a 10-year contract worth more than $8 million.

In Champaign, their one-time ball-playing buddy, Harry Gosier, sits in the county jail. On Feb. 22, police say, Gosier terrorized, shot and killed his wife's mother and sister.

Gosier spends his days in solitary confinement, seemingly oblivious to the potential death penalty hanging over his head, still caught up in his earlier athletic triumphs. It is as though his once-powerful 195-pound body is unscarred by the ravages of his life, as though his violent nature has never spilled beyond the white lines of the playing field.

Gosier, a native of West Palm Beach, Fla., was a three-sport star in high school — a four-year starter in football, a starter with Harper on a state championship basketball team and a near winner of the state track decathlon.

"I could have gone to any school in the country," he said.

While eligible for only two collegiate football seasons, he became the first athlete since 1918 to play in two Rose Bowls for different schools, Michigan and Illinois.

But not everything was roses.

Abandoned by his mother, he bounced from foster home to foster home as a teen-ager. Entwined with his high school athletic successes were discipline problems. Later there were problems with college, problems with drugs, problems with two marriages and problems stemming from his own violent temper.

But a football career — and the success of old Florida friends Carter and Harper — is still an obsession.

"Derek and I were on the state (basketball) championship team at North Shore, and I had my pick of any school for football," he said in a telephone interview from the Champaign County jail.

"Anthony (Carter) had gone to Michigan the year before. I admired Anthony and I used to work on my defensive skills by covering him down there. He only lived a few blocks away. Bo (Schembechler) said there was a place open for me, so Derek and I planned to join Anthony at Michigan. Derek and I grew up together and we intended to go to school together, Derek playing basketball and me football."

Gosier signed with Michigan in 1980. Wolverine recruiter Bill McCartney recalls having reservations about his temperament:

"Harry had a lot of warp to him. He was undisciplined."

Carter voiced similar recollections:

"Harry had all the ability in the world, but he always just seemed to be in the wrong place at the wrong time. He wanted to play right away (at Michigan). When he didn't, he became frustrated."

Harper was a signature away from joining Gosier at Michigan when basketball coach John Orr decided to leave Michigan for Iowa State. Illini assistant coach Tony Yates was hot on Harper's trail and signed the 6-foot-4 guard, later acclaimed by some as the premier basketball player in UI history.

"Harry was a great athlete, always one of the best from childhood on up," Harper said. "He grew up real rough — his mother gave him away early — and he was in foster homes the majority of his life. He always had problems here and there.

"I don't know what happened in the later years. He had to be on something. He couldn't get things squared away with Linda. This wasn't the Harry I knew."

Friends and relatives say Gosier's problems originated with his upbringing. He moved from one foster home to another after his mother handed him over to his ailing grandfather when Harry was 7 or 8. He ran away from several homes seeking his mother.

"But he was always with good families. I was trying to give him a chance in life," reflected Gosier's mother, Mrs. Irene Brown.

Mrs. Brown, who was married last year, had six children. Two of the three still living are now in jail. Before Harry was incarcerated in Champaign County, she hadn't heard from him since November 1985.

Gosier began dating Linda Tillman, a neighbor in Riviera Beach, when they were teen-agers. They were married Aug. 6, 1983, just as Gosier was earning the necessary credits from Parkland Junior College to make him eligible for the UI's championship football season.

Their daughter, Terrenie Nikia Gosier, was born Aug. 18, 1985, and Linda filed for divorce Nov. 22, 1985. The final judgment for divorce came through Dec. 3, 1986. But Gosier had already married his second wife, Lesia Halcrombe of Champaign, two weeks before on Nov. 22, 1986. Their child, India Ashley, had been born two years earlier on Oct. 5, 1984, nearly a year before the birth of Terrenie Nikia in Florida.

However confusing his personal life, those who knew him say Gosier always believed he could make it work out through football.

"Football was the driving force of his life," said Lesia's father, Porter Halcrombe. "He said he didn't want to do anything else."

But Gosier never played as a starter anywhere after high school. He performed sparingly at Michigan in 1980 and took out his frustrations as a "hitter" on special teams. He joined the Wolverines in the Rose Bowl as they defeated Washington 23-6.

He was arrested later that school year for disorderly conduct and resisting officers outside a bar.

"Bo told my folks I needed discipline," Gosier recalled. "The officers accused me of being intoxicated in public, making too much noise and stuff. It was a bad scene, but I was doing all right up there."

Michigan had its entire defensive backfield returning in 1981, and Gosier's bid was further hampered by a knee injury that spring. He attended summer school but problems in and out of the classroom caused him to leave that second year.

Hoping to regain eligibility, Gosier went to California and enrolled at the College of the Redwoods, where he led the junior college region in punt returns in 1982. Intent on being reunited with Florida friends Harper, Mike Heaven, Craig Swoope and Richard Ryles at Illinois — "I had lots of friends there," he said — Gosier transferred to Parkland in the spring of 1983 and received his associate's degree late that summer.

But by then Harper had decided to turn pro, and an unhappy Ryles had elected to transfer to San Jose State. Gosier, enrolling at the UI without an athletic scholarship, lined up behind Dave Edwards at safety. Gosier had an early confrontation with coach Mike White for talking back to coaches over his lack of playing time and, again, found his niche on the kick coverage teams.

Gosier was in sufficient good graces to be allowed to address the UI squad before the Michigan game in 1983 on the subject of "how Michigan feels about Illinois."

According to a News-Gazette story late that year, Linda Tillman Gosier was one of four players' wives joining their husbands at the Rose Bowl. This was Harry's last game. When the January grades came in, he had flunked out.

"Our main problem with Harry was that we couldn't get him to go to class and we couldn't get anyone to help him," said Ed Swartz, Illini assistant director.

"He was a tragedy as a person. We contacted (scout) Ray Newman at Edmonton in the Canadian Football League and got him a tryout — I told Harry it was his last chance — and the next thing I heard was that he took the guy's credit card and ran up a four-figure telephone bill.

"He was bad news for everyone he associated with, and even his friends on the team wanted to stay clear of him. I have reason to believe he was involved with drugs."

I met with Gosier in person later in the jail. He still had a jock image of himself. I later learned he had threatened his first wife in Florida but didn't carry out the threats as happened in Champaign. The state's moratorium on the death penalty has left him on death row for two decades.

JESSE JACKSON FUDGED ON HIS SCHOOLWORK
LATE 1987

Jesse Jackson was engaged in the 1988 presidential run when it was discovered that he left the UI for plagiarism.

CHAMPAIGN — Acquaintances at the University of Illinois say Democratic presidential candidate Jesse Jackson left the UI in the spring of 1960 after a plagiarism incident in a freshman English class.

Jackson has repeatedly maintained he departed after two semesters for North Carolina A&T because racial prejudice prevented him from playing quarterback on the UI football team.

Former Illini teammate Mel Meyers and Champaign's Arnie Yarber, a former UI assistant trainer, offer a different story.

Meyers, who is black, was the UI's quarterback then. Now employed by Southwestern Bell Telephone in Dallas, he pledged the same fraternity as Jackson. He recalls him as an athlete "without great talent."

"Jesse was smart and I don't think he had any real problems in the classroom, but I was told at the time that he plagiarized a paper in a class taught by Phil Coleman."

Meyers remembers Coleman because the former UI teaching assistant was the top U.S. steeplechase runner in the 1956 and 1960 Olympics.

"I was told Jesse took the material from Time Magazine and used it as his own. As for the authenticity of my word, all I can say now is that I got it through the athletic department," Meyers said.

Yarber, a close friend of many black athletes who have attended the university, tells basically the same story, recalling both Coleman and Time Magazine.

"Jesse left school for plagiarizing," Yarber said. "I remember him real well. I was a trainer with the freshmen that year and we talked a lot. He was supposed to turn in an essay and he took the article from

Time. Coleman had already read it. That's what happened. But it was pretty much hush-hush at the time."

The charges, if accurate, are similar to those in a college incident that contributed to Delaware Democrat Joseph Biden's decision to withdraw from the presidential race earlier this year.

Questioned by Mike Augspurger, a reporter for the Ottumwa (Iowa) Courier, Jackson denied the charges.

"I knew Dan Coleman but I don't recall Phil Coleman," Jackson said. "I don't know a thing about it."

Jackson declined to comment further as he completed his Iowa campaign tour, returning to Chicago on Tuesday for "down time" that will carry through the Christmas period.

According to the UI Office of Admissions and Records, Jackson was enrolled in the college of physical education in the fall semester of 1959 and the spring semester of 1960.

His grade point average, related in a letter from former coach Ray Eliot to a member of the UI Board of Trustees and released in a column by The News-Gazette's Chuck Flynn 3-1/2 years ago, shows Jackson earned a 3.25 grade-point average the first semester and a 2.75 GPA in the second. The latter sub-C average placed him on probation, according to Eliot.

Grades in individual classes have not been made public.

Now a professor at California State College in California, Pa., Coleman recalls the plagiarism incident but not the name or the face of the student involved.

"I do remember a young black man who wrote an article, and it had come from somewhere, Time Magazine I believe," Coleman said. "Are you telling me it was Jesse Jackson? That's unbelievable. I have never made that connection. I wouldn't remember if you hadn't brought it up. But I don't know the name of that student."

Nor does Coleman remember the resolution to the incident.

"I've searched my memory and my records," said Coleman several days later, "and I can't confirm that I had Jesse Jackson in my class. I've moved around since I left Illinois and I've had a lot of students since then."

Former UI assistant coaches Tom Haller, Bill Tate and Brody Westen have only vague recollections of Jackson. And Coach Pete Elliott, who took over in the spring of 1960, recalls the name but can't recall whether Jackson played halfback or fullback that spring.

But Lou Baker, a Monticello man who served under both Ray Eliot and Pete Elliott, recalls him well.

"I sure do remember Jesse. He was a loud talker and, even as a freshman (when freshman were ineligible), he kept saying he belonged on the varsity," Baker said. "I recall his claims that Illinois was against blacks, but we had an outstanding black quarterback at the time, Mel Meyers."

"Based on his ability, I thought Jesse was a walk-on, and I thought he quit after he was caught turning in a paper that he had copied. Of course, you hear a lot of things and I never knew the absolute truth of it. I felt that Jesse was more of a talker than a player, a politician just like he is now. He had a big ego. He thought he was better than anyone."

Ray Eliot's secretary, Margaret Selin, also had some recollections.

"I can't recall the exact circumstances but I know he was dropped. I thought he flunked out," Selin said. "He made some speeches later that upset Ray, and Ray said if he ever came here for a speech, he would go on stage with him. Jackson had a chip on his shoulder."

But Jackson, in a number of speeches and publications, has repeatedly maintained that prejudice was the chief reason he transferred to North Carolina A&T.

Despite evidence to the contrary, that account has been widely reported in the media.

U.S. News & World Report offered a comment: "Jackson suffered discrimination — on buses, at restaurants, at the University of Illinois, where he was told blacks didn't play quarterback."

Similarly, Vanity Fair reported: "What he was not prepared for was the rejection. In the dormitory, the classroom, and on the football team, where Negroes were allowed only to be linebackers, he was humiliated. 'It was traumatic for me,' he admits, 'black players being reduced to entertainers.' And so he turned his back on the fine white northern school and entered A&T, then a mediocre black land-grant college."

But the record clearly shows that Ray Eliot didn't restrict blacks to linebacker. The late coach fielded a particularly impressive list of running backs, a group headed by All-Americans Buddy Young and J.C. Caroline and including such memorable performers as the late Paul Patterson, NFL stars Bobby Mitchell and Abe Woodson, as well as Mickey Bates, Johnny Counts, Harry Jefferson, DeJustice Coleman and Marshall Starks.

The captain, most valuable player and defensive signal caller in 1959 was black: Bill Burrell, an All-American linebacker. The quarterback and leader in total offense and passing was Meyers. And the first sophomore to start for the varsity a year later, end Thurman Walker, now a policeman in Joliet, did not consider the athletic department discriminatory.

Jackson's denials to the contrary, I found undisputable evidence that he plagiarized, including a statement by former secretary Glenna Cilento that she typed Jackson's paper from a magazine article (with minor changes). Jackson would have been on probation if he had returned to the UI. He became a backup quarterback at North Carolina A&T.

FIRST OF SIX COLUMNS ON CHIEF ILLINIWEK
APRIL 8, 2001

Anti-Chiefers attempt to influence prospects that Illini campus is racist.

CHAMPAIGN — Aggressive adversaries of Chief Illiniwek, in their creative, ever-more-brazen and increasingly damaging efforts, have struck the rawest of nerves.

Cleared by a federal court injunction, they now threaten to "hold hostage" prospective basketball recruits by calling them to paint their version of racism on the UI campus.

These prospects are mostly young blacks for whom racism is a sensitive issue. The plan might work. One of Bill Self's blue chippers, in weighing a career decision about universities he knows little about, could be turned away.

But it is a dastardly scheme. In any business where tenure is not involved, those working at cross purposes internally would be summarily dismissed.

At the UI, there is no acceptable solution. The chancellor's memo referring to NCAA limitations hit a free speech snag, and was overruled by U.S. District Judge Michael Mihm who concluded that NCAA rules penalize those who seek a "competitive advantage" but aren't concerned with those who want to create a disadvantage.

OK, we're long past the day of tar and feathers. You won't see e-mail addresses or telephone numbers in this column. We don't want to see anyone flooded with calls, classes disrupted or, as happened at Indiana University, a professor (Murray Sperber) who felt obliged to spend a semester in Canada.

Nor is capitulation an acceptable alternative. Civil war has become the obligation of energized rivals.

Anti-Chiefers must do their worst, stiffening resistance in the process. No matter how many celebrated battles they win, no matter how many athletes are turned away, regardless of time and expense, the Chief will be left standing.

What was once a sports-related fuss has now burrowed deep into the heart of the institution ... even deeper in the community. And we have a front-row view of strife on three major fronts:

(1) With interviews set for chancellor candidates, anti-Chiefers are seeking to crack through the secrecy and present their case before Michael Aiken's successor is named.

Effects: They have succeeded in impacting the interviews and might "chase off" a candidate who doesn't want to spend major time on a never-ending distraction. But, long-range, the UI Board of Trustees has been forced into a virtually unanimous pro-Chief position. And despite all the denials you'll hear on this subject, they won't hire a chancellor who isn't at least neutral on the issue.

(2) A visiting accreditation team left campus with a one-track mind, infuriating UI officials and forcing the recent "dialogue" that revealed overwhelming public support for Chief Illiniwek.

Effect: UI officials are prepared to fight back on this one, and will be prepared to meet the opposition head-on when the accreditation team comes to town. Furthermore, the Trustees "did their duty" in meeting dialogue requirements and are "as one" in support of the Chief.

(3) Attacking Ron Guenther's athletic department at its heart — recruiting — anti-Chiefers have obtained federal injunction which allows them to bypass NCAA rules and contact prospective athletes with their views of a so-called racist campus.

Effect: Again, whether or not they actually make the calls, this nasty tactic has accomplished its purpose. The headlines and stories are right there for rival recruiters. But, ultimately, this move may bring the might of the NCAA's legal team in alongside the UI.

It has been mentioned here that the alternative to capitulation is to don helmets and live with the collateral damage. That's where the UI finds itself, on the defensive, digging trenches and waiting for the next bomb to drop.

Very innovative people, with a cause they fervently believe in, are using every device at their disposal to force the Chief's retirement. They are striking from all sides ... legal, institutional, racial, emotional, etc.

A great, multi-faceted university is being hurt in terms of its image elsewhere and in time-expense required to deal with each new diversion.

Pro-Chiefers won't give in, and the anti-Chiefers have come too far to give up.

In actual practice, the scheme didn't impact Illini recruiting. But it left a sour taste among those who want to see the Illini succeed in sports, regardless of the Chief outcome. Oh, by the way, they DID HIRE an anti-Chief chancellor, Nancy Cantor.

MID-JULY 1995

The battle over Chief Illiniwek was just warming up when the governor changed a legislative bill from "shall" to "may."

CHAMPAIGN — This Chief Illiniwek fuss seems to be never-ending, but consider:

— From the political side, Gov. Jim Edgar and the state Legislature, as well as U.S. Rep. Tom Ewing, R-Pontiac, strongly support the continuation of the Chief as the honored symbol of the University of Illinois.

— From the UI administrative side, outgoing UI President Stan Ikenberry and incoming Jim Stukel are outspoken backers, and the UI Board of Trustees is solidly behind the Chief.

— From the legal side, UI chief counsel Byron Higgins says the UI is prepared to appeal if the Department of Education rules against Chief Illiniwek, and would take it all the way to the U.S. Supreme Court.

— From the public side, the numbers are overwhelming in favor of the Chief, to the extent that any politician who would "shoot down" the Chief could expect a difficult job getting reelected in these parts.

If that's how the cards are stacked, what was the latest furor about?

What we had was a freshman representative, Rick Winkel, who used the Chief issue to help get elected, and then took a track into the teeth of two high-powered and politically savvy locomotives, Edgar and Ikenberry.

By carrying a popular issue through the General Assembly against their wishes, Winkel set those heady veterans to scratching their heads about how they could have their cake and eat it too ... and they found a way via the governor's amendatory veto.

By simply changing "shall" to "may," the governor arranged a permissive (nonmandatory) bill that accomplishes four objectives.

One, Edgar upholds the right of the UI to maintain the Chief as its honored symbol. Two, he has allowed the Legislature, by a simple majority vote in the fall, to make the Chief a part of state law for the first time. Three, he avoided a micromanaging situation, leaving the Chief question on campus where it belongs. Four, he reaffirmed a positive, working-together relationship with UI leadership.

Of course, Edgar's "veto" could be overridden by a three-fifths vote by both chambers, but it won't be. The General Assembly isn't looking for a fight on this ... there are bigger fish to fry ... and will happily give him the majority vote he seeks. State Sen. Stan Weaver, R-Urbana, understands the political realities, and is quietly stationed in the governor's corner in exchange for help in renovating UI athletic facilities.

And an outmaneuvered Winkel can return to his constituents as a hero who fought the good fight and came away with a few bruises and new respect for his elders.

For those who say nothing has been accomplished, consider that the Chief will soon be on the books as a state law ... in a process whereby state leaders demonstrated more support for him than any of us believed possible.

For Ikenberry, it means he can leave office satisfied that the Chief is sitting on high ground without impacting the UI's autonomy. He said:

"I appreciate the governor's reaffirmation of the university's ability to run its affairs. The trustees consider the Chief a positive tradition, and I don't see trustees returning to the Chief as an issue in the near future."

Said Edgar: "Interference from the governor and state Legislature into affairs of the university could take darker forms such as direct intervention through state law into the content of academic programs. Chief Illiniwek is an appropriate, respected and respectful symbol of the university. The Chief has enhanced, not diminished, respect for native Americans."

The battleground now switches to the UI's legal department, which has been responding to complaints for 30 months, and is still providing the Department of Education with voluminous reports denying that the UI has created a "hostile environment" for native Americans and minorities.

The legislative action seemed like a strong Chief-supporting development at the time. But even if Chief Illiniwek had been decreed the UI symbol by state law, that would have ultimately have changed due to NCAA pressure.

MARCH 15, 2002

The UI Board of Trustees came out in strong support of a challenged symbol, Chief Illiniwek.

CHAMPAIGN — The afternoon of March 7 was a momentous occasion for Illini Nation.

After years of ever-heightening controversy, after Chief Illiniwek critics gained strength from past administrative concessions, after colleagues on other campuses expressed their disapproval, the UI Board of Trustees came out more strongly in favor of the Chief than ever before.

Of 10 voters, only the student trustee from the Illinois-Chicago campus, Arun Reddy, called for the Chief's removal. And Reddy's term soon ends.

If it had been a vote — for many of us it was — the count was 8-1 with one abstention ... and it was 8-0 by the permanent non-student members.

More than that, trustee statements were well researched and non-repetitive, showing thought and consideration honed through the dialogue period. Each speech offered a high degree of individuality. If a public relations firm shaped some of the comments, the basic ideas were original.

Now, for all the good intent of forming a panel to seek a compromise, it boils down to this: either Chief Illiniwek is on the field at halftime, or he is not. That is the flaming point, and there can be no compromise on that.

If the Chief is not permitted to dance, that will be a celebrated victory for anti-Chiefers and will be proclaimed as a forerunner to eliminating the UI nickname, Fighting Illini.

Now, about this nickname business:

Illini is derived from the state name. Pro-Chiefers incorporate into their arguments a contention that his ouster would weaken support for the nickname. Don't believe it. No assault on a state-derived nickname would gain steam. Oh, sure, extremists with an exaggerated sense of victimization would target it and fan flames of discontent giving the administration more unwanted moments. But such a quest would never gain groundswell support.

The nickname fuss is simply a red herring. This is a conflict over a halftime dance, inciting those who can't understand the popular feeling that an arm-raised Chief, regardless of dance authenticity or regalia, is the heart-swelling personification of the indomitable spirit of men. Believers are touched, non-believers offended.

Peace has one avenue. Pro-Chiefers must give it up and acknowledge that the tradition they're clinging to is an "illusion of permanence" ... misguided sentimentalism ... racist. Chief worshippers, being the more moderate group, would eventually get over it. The next generation won't care.

The only other course is to don helmets and live with the bombshells.

There is too much fever on campus for it to go away. The administration will be forever assailed by aggrieved activists. Big-city columnists will have a field day. One way or another, rumors of a racial climate that doesn't exist will reach UI recruits. And heady anti-Chiefers will dig for remedies via legal and accreditation lanes.

Once again, here are the choices:

The UI can drop an honored symbol that was born of good will and maintained with uncommon respect, and weather the majority's unhappiness in hopes of reaching a less contentious day. Maybe, eventually, UI leaders would be allowed to concentrate on more important matters of education.

Or, refusing to let go, the UI can continue to resist in a conflict that admittedly distracts from the primary mission, and is seemingly without end.

For now, gritty trustees have bowed their backs and taken the latter course. There is no hint that they're succumbing to combat fatigue.

What we saw March 7 were trustees universally in agreement and downright proud of their solidarity.

If there was slippage during the dialogue period, they were firmly reunited by Stephen Kaufman's self-defeating threat to contact prospective recruits. Pride in their unity was obvious, and was driven home when Pres. James Stukel lauded them for their eloquence and thoughtfulness.

They support the Chief because they, like thousands of others, believe in what he represents. What happens as a result will just have to happen.

The UI Board of Trustees remained steadfast in support of the Chief until the NCAA barred the school from hosting NCAA events and, behind closed doors, began to discuss the idea of preventing the UI from participating in bowl games. The outcome soon became inevitable.

NOVEMBER 12, 2003

With a dramatic change in the UI Board of Trustees, the push is growing stronger to push out Chief Illiniwek.

CHAMPAIGN — Alarm bells clanged again this week.

Catching pro-Chiefers by surprise, new board of trustees member Frances Carroll beat Tuesday's 8:30 a.m. agenda deadline with a resolution calling for the retirement of Chief Illiniwek.

If it seems hasty, don't be misled. It's been in the works. Carroll is in league with another recent Gov. Rod Blagojevich appointee, Robert Sperling, who is probably Chancellor Nancy Cantor's closest board ally.

So the Chief once again is walking on hot coals and, even as backers celebrate Chief Week, their favorite could be wired for history tomorrow.

Here's my problem with it.

If thoughtful former board member Roger Plummer, after analyzing the lengthy dialogue and devoting a year of study on the subject, concluded it was appropriate to pull the plug, his view would deserve consideration.

If the great John Cribbet, former chancellor and a Goliath among his law peers, opined that the Chief had become too much of a burden, his argument would be respected.

If the worldly Stan Ikenberry, who spoke eloquently on the subject during his grand tour as UI president, made a strong declaration, the staunchest Chief supporters would have to stop and ponder. But for a Johnny-come-lately to march into this hurricane with slim background and a large agenda, someone who didn't attend the UI, someone who hasn't experienced and doesn't appreciate downstate traditions, someone who by her presence brings race into the debate, someone named to Tom Lamont's unexpired term to ease pressure on a governor who had named three straight males, well ... that's unacceptable. She clearly doesn't understand the Chief is "of the people," with meaning that goes far beyond the university.

The Chief at least deserves an executioner with time in the struggle.

Make no mistake, Carroll's resume is long and impressive. She started her college education in Sarasota, Fla., and finished in Chicago. She is on the Chicago Area Alliance of Black School Educators, among others.

She is part of a board with four members who didn't even attend the UI. And a student, Nate Allen, holds one of the precious 11 votes. OK, perhaps the Chief's time has come. The NCAA is applying not-so-subtle pressure. The issue distracts from the university's primary mission. It hampers coaches' recruiting efforts. Years of administrative concessions have permitted anti-Chief gains that only make opponents more determined. It won't go away.

But, how did we reach the jumping-off point where a global university is being run by a student, two members who did not graduate from college (Champaign's Marjorie Sodemann and LaSalle's Robert Vickery), and seven political appointees with Chicagoland backgrounds and lifestyles?

It's all part of a warped trustee setup, and here's one example. In what appears to be a tap dance around the rule that permits no more than five members of one party, we see "independents" who can miraculously swing from one governor to another (of a different party).

OK, that's the way the game is played, as politically devious as redistricting. But when a new governor, already falling into such disorder that his own party is overriding his legislative vetoes, uses an important board for political favors, it's agonizing reappraisal time. Already in the works are three recommendations for changing the trustee system (none will pass; they need the governor's signature).

But back to the Chief. The governor, remember, has a vote (if present) and can be the tiebreaker in a 5-5 standoff. Who knows where he stands? Would Blagojevich allow Carroll to be chopped off this limb when he desperately needs Chicago's black vote to be re-elected? How rocky is Blagojevich's relationship with Emil Jones, the Senate president and close friend of Carroll? How much control does Blagojevich have over the votes of his four trustee appointments?

Stay tuned. The last time this came to a boiling point, President James Stukel lauded board members for their eloquence and thoughtfulness. If a vote had been taken, it would have been 8-1. But only Dr. Jeffrey Gindorf remains from that board. It's a different world today. A distant city with arguably the shoddiest political reputation in America is running the UI campus.

Few things bother me as much as Chicagoans, with their vastly different social, political and educational backgrounds, running the downstate university. This system of political appointments needs change, but there is no acceptable solution.

MARCH 5, 2007

Chief Illini was laid to rest despite the outcries of George Will, Robert Novak and a long list of mourners.

CHAMPAIGN — If you never experienced the Chief Illiniwek as a youth or longtime resident you may not understand.

If your background happens to be Chicago, Detroit or Indianapolis, or the far reaches of this country, the feelings built from one generation to another in downstate Illinoisans may be a mystery. Recent arrivals on a diverse, multicultural campus don't come easily to the tradition.

Nor are national editorial writers and pundits generally favorable. And yet two of the nation's most respected political wordsmiths, two who grew up with the tradition — George Will and Robert Novak — view the Chief in strikingly positive terms.

"One of America's booming businesses is the indignation industry that manufactures the synthetic outrage needed to fuel identity politics," chastised Will, an Urbana native.

He pointed out that in 1995, the Office of Civil Rights, "a nest of sensitivity-mongers, rejected the claim that the Chief created for anyone a 'hostile enviroment' on campus."

In words that only Will can muster, he spoke for many when he asked:

"When, in the multiplication of entitlements, did we produce an entitlement for everyone to go through life without being annoyed by anything? Civilization depends on, and civility often requires, the willingness to say, 'What you are doing is none of my business' and 'What I am doing is none of your business.' But this is an age when being an offended busy body is considered evidence of advanced thinking and an exquisite sensibility."

Novak called Oct. 10, 1942 "up to then the best day of my life" when at age 11 he attended an Illini homecoming and "was privileged to watch Chief Illiniwek proudly dance down the field to Indian war music."

Added Novak: "The accusation that Illinois and other schools degrade Native Americans is absurd. These schools picked Indian symbols in admiration of their valor, ferociousness and indomitable spirit in the face of overwhelming odds. Native Americans were honored in naming states. Illinois is Algonquin for 'tribe of superior men.'"

For Illinoisans who grew up cherishing the four-minute performance of music and dance, it became a brief, imaginary return to the state's heritage. It can be heart-thumping and spellbinding ... a semi-religious halftime experience that matched the sincerity of the pre-game national anthem at University of Illinois athletic events.

Who can explain his deepest feelings to another? An experience that draws one person's devotion may have an opposite effect on his brother. Can we accept our differences?

In this case, as it pertains to UI fans and supporters, the minority ruled. The year 2007 brought an end to eight decades of exhilerating Chief performances. It was for many "a death in the family." Tears flowed. An uncommon number of Illini fans made their unhappiness known through the media.

Many saw the Chief as a link to the past and, with the associated singing of the UI's "Alma Mater," a linked connection to the state university. Described one true believer, "He is a tangible symbol of an intangible spirit filled with qualities a person of any background can aspire to: goodness, strength, bravery, truthfulness, courage and dignity."

The comments poured in:

"He is all men; he is every man."

"I have watched the Chief, first as a child, then as a student and now as a longtime fan and ticketholder. The Chief is in my heart, like a part of my family, and definitely an integral part of the Illini family."

"As I watched Chief Illiniwek, I saw nobility, courage, respect and honor."

Support far outweighed the negative responses. They continued:

"The Chief brings people together. I never put my arm around my dad, but I did when the Chief came out."

"I cried during his last dance. That tells you how I feel."

"He brought treasured memories to so many disappointing football seasons."

"I didn't attend the University of Illinois, but I feel a connection through the Chief."

The feelings cut across age, gender and race. No single issue, not even a hotly contested election, has drawn such feverish debate in around Champaign-Urbana.

The late Ray Eliot, who retired as Illini football coach in 1959, was perhaps the Chief's most profound spokesman when he delivered a resounding and oft-used speech emphasizing that "the Chief is not a nut (buckeye) or a burrowing animal (badger), but the symbol and spirit of the Fighting Illini."

Put in the simplist language, Chief Illiniwek should at the very least be deemed harmless by those who don't comprehend. Why would it be different from recognizing without rancor another's religion that you don't agree with? The Chief was never a mascot nor a cheerleader. He was obliquely connected to the athletic event, and he danced for joy and in bringing togetherness. He represented nobility and spirit. The feelings expressed in this performance may have less to do with specific Indian ancestry than with the heritage of the land.

The ironies of the NCAA ruling, that go far beyond Florida State's ability to retain a spear-throwing Seminole horseman, were pointed out by Andrew Cline of the New Hampshire Union Leader:

"The Sooners (Oklahoma) were people who illegally occupied land confiscated from the Indians. Oklahoma is Choctaw for 'red people.'

"If North Dakota (which is suing the NCAA) removes Sioux from its jerseys and replaces it with North Dakota, it will still have a tribal name on its jerseys. Obviously, NCAA executives have not thought their plan through.

"The paternalism that comes from intellectual superiority has overruled common sense."

I was often too busy at halftime to watch the dance. My concern in losing the Chief was the disappointment that spread through Illini Nation. I knew what they felt because I felt it as a UI student. George Will's comments on the issue say it all for me.

JULY 30, 2006

Before Chief Illiniwek was officially retired, UI professors piled on by threatening Chicago's bid for the Olympic Games.

CHAMPAIGN — These 22 professors are, after all, intelligent people. They have advanced degrees. They are scholars and researchers at a world-class university.

But why, when they've obviously won, would they pile on with such a presumptive and bizarrely misplaced act?

Chief Illiniwek is clearly on the way out. It's just a matter of time. There's no need to sabotage Chicago's Olympic Games quest and sucker-punch the university. What's behind this activist overreaction? Can't they wait? Or do they want a midfield ritual in which the Chief's blood is spilled drop by drop? A stake in the heart?

What they overlooked at this juncture was an opportunity to be good sports.

It's clear that plans are being finalized to retire the Chief in an honorable way. There's been no official announcement but, barring an unlikely miracle from Congress or North Dakota, the timeline is set. It won't come fast enough for the Shameless 22, but it'll take place prior to the 2007-08 school year.

Again, it's not official. But the UI president and chancellor are in tune with the board of trustees' master plan. Ron Guenther and the coaches know they can't host NCAA events for one more year. Most pro-Chiefers don't want to face it, but they understand. And above all, anti-Chief provocateur Stephen Kaufman, the outspoken architect of this activism, knows it.

A levelheaded winner would step aside and let the inevitable play out. Further backstabbing of Guenther's athletic program isn't called for. Nor does it make sense to embarrass the institution that pays the salaries.

But the Shameless 22 found it appropriate to send a highly presumptive letter encouraging the U.S. Olympic Committee to skip Chicago (the UI might host some Olympic events) if the Chief isn't retired.

By the way, that's the same city that supports the Blackhawks. If the Olympic Committee had a concern about Native American imagery, the Blackhawks in Chicago would far outweigh the Chief in distant Champaign-Urbana.

And remember, we're talking about 2016 here. The 2016 Olympics. That's a long 10 years from now.

Hey, you are professors! Think! This is off the wall. Or if you can't think, at least be quiet.

We are left to wonder what's behind conduct so imprudent and obviously impotent in terms of actually impacting the U.S. Olympic decision (the committee must think we're crazy here).

Some say the professors are driven by self-identification with an overcooked issue that soon will be clarified and are demonstrating for the sake of "hey, look at me!"

Maybe the Shameless 22 can't stand the idea of the Chief getting a rousing sendoff through his final football, volleyball and basketball seasons. They must want the firing squad mustered at dawn.

Or perhaps they're unhappy with not being asked to the table for the complicated wrapup (the devil's in the details).

Former Chiefs and caring administrators are mulling over some sort of lasting memorial. And UI higher-ups have apparently acquiesced to Marching Illini desires to retain the halftime music, a fact that will surely rile anti-Chiefers as fan memories are jogged in a raucous stadium every time the UI band plays the part where he formerly danced. Those four minutes of the 3-in-1 still will have a solemn and inspirational connotation for many, a fact that ultimately will unleash the fun-killing PC police for another fuss over the Marching Illini halftime production.

The Shameless 22 should, for the time being, be willing to quietly celebrate their part in the destruction of a symbol that is cherished by throngs of UI graduates and fans. In terms of his impact on the local fandom, Chief Illiniwek might be the most revered symbol in the land. By contrast, do you think Michigan people cherish a furry carnivore? Do you believe many Ohioans care about a nutlike seed? Certainly Oklahomans aren't proud of Western settlers who cheated to get free land.

The irony is the Shameless 22 can't understand that they're making more difficult the task of careful UI leaders who are actually on their side.

In the world of activism, there is a time for a take-no-prisoners assault. That is no longer necessary. Even before the NCAA brought intense pressure on the Chief debate, operation of campus affairs had become a time-consuming headache for every UI president, chancellor and board of trustees.

President Joe White and this board understand what must be done. They are in lockstep. From an institutional standpoint, the Chief has become too divisive. With the NCAA available as blame taker, UI leaders have begun the delicate work of solidifying relationships with financial contributors who hold pro-Chief leanings. The massive Memorial Stadium and Assembly Hall renovations are just around the corner.

There is also the matter of the university's upcoming $1.4 billion fund drive for refurbished buildings and faculty pay increases. Public relations efforts are already underway to ease the inevitable dip in contributions when the Chief is retired.

The Olympic letter signed by these piling-on activists is way out of line. It stiffens the resolve of pro-Chiefers and inserts more bitterness into the march toward resolution.

Hey, profs, your side has won. Don't disgrace yourself further. Go away.

It was presumptive of Kaufman and his friends to write an Olympic committee obviously unconcerned by the Chicago presence of the hockey Blackhawks, and absolutely disgraceful that they couldn't wait for the inevitable announcement that everyone knew was coming. As a UI graduate, I was ashamed.

FIRST OF TWO COLUMNS ON UI SLUSH FUND
MARCH 21, 1999

"Slush fund" revelations were an earthquake among the ground-shaking scandals in the Illini history.

CHAMPAIGN — In a century of competition, no game, no season impacted Illini athletics like the infamous "slush fund."

Nothing in the sports realm has been so traumatic here, an entire community groaning in shock as the UI's most popular coaches and athletes were banned after assistant athletic director Mel Brewer, irate that "Michigan man" Pete Elliott had been chosen to succeed longtime AD Doug Mills, marched into the president's office to make public his multi-year record of improper payments to athletes.

This event, which culminated in the ouster of head football coach Elliott and basketball coaches Harry Combes and Howie Braun in March 1967, is this month's most significant UI sports happening ever. Other cases also traumatic

— The Deon Thomas case: Before Linda Tripp, there was Bruce Pearl. The Iowa aide led Thomas into incriminating comments on tape. That, coupled with accusations from Notre Dame and Indiana, halted a basketball program that had just reached the Final Four in 1989 and held national stature.

The long investigation and disruption of Jimmy Collins' recruiting efforts (particularly with Juwan Howard) were damaging, and the penalty limit of two scholarships for each of two years handicapped the late years of the Lou Henson regime, ultimately leading to his retirement.

— The Neale Stoner ouster: A flamboyant "idea man" who hired Mike White and helped fill Memorial Stadium for a string of sellouts, Stoner and assistant AD Vance Redfern were forced to resign in July 1988 because of their own extravagant misconduct. The incident began with Stoner's firing of strength coach Bill Kroll, who turned over a rock squirming with improprieties and led ultimately to the UI dissolving and taking over the incorporated Athletic Association.

Controversial and bitter as the Stoner case was, the on-field impact wasn't seen immediately as the basketball team reached the Final Four a year later, John Mackovic fielded four straight bowl teams (10-2 in 1989), and Augie Garrido kept baseball going strong.

— The Dave Wilson case: When White arrived, he landed with a bang. A monumental Big Ten controversy arose in 1980 about the use of a junior college quarterback, Wilson, whose eligibility was in question. Stoner was accused of pointing Wilson to an attorney, Bob Auler, after Wilson was declared ineligible for the 1980 season, and sparks flew as Wilson played under a court order.

It became so heated that Stoner talked of leaving the Big Ten, and league leaders threatened to oust the UI from membership. The UI absorbed sanctions, the first of three run-ins with authority during the White era ... infractions in the 1984 Elton-Delton case leading to White's removal for lesser mistakes (1987) and creating an NCAA attitude that later influenced an "institutional control" ruling in basketball.

But nothing changed the course of events quite like the "slush fund."

At that juncture (1966), the UI held a clear edge over every other Big Ten member in basketball, had reached the Final Four three times under Combes, shared the Big Ten title in 1963 and was the 1967 favorite after winning that December at Kentucky. The roots of Combes and Elliott burrowed deep in the community, Combes having led three straight Champaign High teams to the state title game and winning in 1946.

Since the initiation of the Big Ten-Rose Bowl pact in 1946, the UI had as many wins in Pasadena as Ohio State and Michigan (three), had beaten Michigan seven of 10 in the 1950s and had defeated Ohio State and Michigan in 1966.

Both coaches were highly popular.

It was like an earthquake striking the center of the Twin Cities when juniors Rich Jones and Ron Dunlap and sophomore Steve Kuberski were ruled ineligible before a game in Chicago.

The team was shattered, ongoing play by Big Ten MVP Jim

Dawson and high-scoring Dave Scholz offering evidence of what might have been.

Then came March when the three coaches and four football players were added to the list.

Illinois went the next 14 years with only one football team winning more games than it lost. The basketball team grinded through 17 years without another Big Ten title. And it's been a bitter, up-and-down struggle in both major sports ever since.

MARCH 20, 1967

Three Illini coaches had just one honorable alternative, and they took it by stepping down in the wake of the "slush fund."

CHAMPAIGN — We are gathered here today ... not to mourn the dead ... but rather to praise the living ... and to make the best of an impossible situation.

In everything they have done, University of Illinois coaches Pete Elliott, Harry Combes and Howard Braun have taken the honorable route.

And as the final Big Ten ultimatum sank in Sunday morning, they realized that it would be unfair to pit their leading defender — President David D. Henry — against two ruling boards which were willing to support the coaches only up to a point.

We refer to the Senate Committee on Athletics and the Athletic Association Board of Directors, neither of which would offer a statement a week ago because they did not want it known they would back the coaches only if Illinois could remain a bonafide Big Ten member.

The coaches could foresee a possible split over the issue, one which could ruin Illinois athletics — if it hasn't already — and they agreed to solve what could have become an embarrassing situation for President Henry. In resigning, they knew, just as both UI faculty boards did, that the NCAA could come along and concur with any and all rulings of the Big Ten ... and could hardly let Illinois slip the noose since Michigan's Marcus Plant, who issued Saturday's statement in Chicago, is president of the national ruling body.

In some ways the coaches were relieved Sunday. They are not

destitute and the character they have demonstrated through this long ordeal will tide them over in whatever field they choose. Pete Elliott has already received some excellent job offers and you won't have to run any tag days for Combes and Braun.

Combes' attitude was surprisingly calm as he appeared before national TV cameras at Elliott's home Sunday evening.

"I've had 20 wonderful years at Illinois, and I don't want this to sound corny, but it has been a real privilege just being associated with the university. I consider myself very lucky."

One of the official statements said the decision of Sunday can be a rallying point for Illinoisans.

I see the exact opposite happening. Not that Illinois will be hostile to new coaches. But it may take awhile for the old enthusiasm to be generated again.

Illinois is virtually dead from a recruiting standpoint and some of the strongest financial supporters of the program are not going to soon forget that the AA Board of Directors and the Senate Committee on Athletics were not willing to go the limit for the coaches.

I have tried to understand the ruling of the conference and can come to only one conclusion: Commissioner Bill Reed felt he had to make an example of Illinois in order to keep everyone else in line.
He would undoubtedly have dictated the same policy for anyone else who "got caught" at this time, since previous penalties had failed to halt what he calls "periodic outbreaks of infractions." He has never conceded that irregularities are widespread.

Through the entire episode, I held out the hope that some compromise would be worked out which would be satisfactory to both sides. I have presently lost faith in human nature, though I had prepared for the worst almost three months ago when I wrote:

"You are greeted ... this cold Christmas morning ... with terrible and very real possibility ... that if the Big Ten ruling body does not consider mitigating circumstances in the Illinois case ... ALL the football and basketball coaches involved and the designated players may be at the end of the line at Illinois."

It has been a great victory for the Big Ten.

As I sat in Elliott's home that night, already aware of the three coaches' resignations, I had an ill feeling about the future. Sure enough, the decade of the 1970s was not very productive on the football and basketball fronts.

FIRST OF THREE COLUMNS ON DAVE WILSON CASE
JUNE 14, 1981

Dave Wilson prepares to turn pro as Big Ten faculty reps limit him to a single season at Illinois.

CHAMPAIGN — While football officials in Calgary and New Orleans — not to mention Illinois — watch with mounting interest, the Dave Wilson case is meandering through the summer months.

With a self-imposed early-July deadline, Wilson has created stiff odds as to whether he'll ever again play quarterback for the Illini. Still, in a case already bubbling over with strange twists and turns, prejudgment would be ill-advised.

Here is the mid-June status report:

— Federal judge Robert Morgan has set June 24 (in Peoria) for a hearing on the Big Ten's motion for summary judgment. Conference attorney Byron Gregory is seeking an immediate dismissal of the case, encouraged undoubtedly by the judge's clear inference that conference matters should be resolved within the conference framework ... and such cases have no place on his busy calendar.

— Wilson determined through a personal meeting with Wayne Duke that eligibility issues are basically out of the commissioner's realm, and are the function of the faculty representatives ... and further than the faculty reps don't consider the progress-toward-graduation rule pertinent to his 1981 eligibility.

"I told them I'd take 15 hours this summer and get up to 105," said Wilson, "but they said that wouldn't make any difference. I have decided not to enroll in summer school (which begins Monday)."

— The trial, if it goes forward, is expected to revolve around whether the Big Ten is acting in a discriminatory manner by refusing to give Wilson a medical waiver for the 1977 season (when Wilson broke his arm in the first outing at Fullerton Junior College).

Robert Auler, Wilson's attorney, is taking the approach that the Big Ten is being arbitrary and capricious if it does not provide Wilson a fourth full season under the medical redshirt provision. Auler is also preparing a suit for damages to accompany his question for Wilson's 1981 eligibility.

The Big Ten counters that it does not provide the extra year for medical incidents that occur at institutions outside the Big Ten. Confusion stems from the NCAA, which does not allow a medical redshirt for JC athletes transferring into Division I, but then made a contradictory move by withdrawing from the Wilson case with the statement that (1) the medical redshirt rule is superseded by a different NCAA rule and (2) it will abide by whatever resolution the Big Ten or the courts come to.

— A compromising decision on Big Ten sanctions imposed on Illinois, stemming from the UI's handing of the Wilson case, is expected by early August. It is widely believed that a resolution to the Wilson court case would ease the pressure surrounding the negotiations, although Duke and the Big Ten faculty representatives have repeatedly stated there is no longer any connection.

That's where this complex matter stands. Meanwhile, football coach Mike White has sent Tony Eason back to California with the stipulation that he prepare himself to become Illinois' No. 1 quarterback. White and his staff have been cooperative with NFL teams seeking film and other information on Wilson ahead of the supplementary draft in early July.

The Big Ten informed Dave Wilson that he could not play in 1980 but could gain eligibility a year later. On advice from athletic director Neale Stoner, Wilson retained Robert Auler and went to court, and was allowed to play in 1980 under a court injunction. Since his 1977 one-game appearance counted against him, 1980 was his only season at Illinois.

JUNE 26, 1981

The complicated aspects of the Dave Wilson case taught us a great deal about the operation of the courts, the press, the Big Ten and human nature.

"I'm glad its over. I'm sick and tired of seeing all that Dave Wilson stuff in the newspaper. Maybe now the Big Ten will leave us alone."
— Anonymous Illini fan

CHAMPAIGN — That's one way to look at it. With Wilson heading into a professional football career, the sports pages will now have more space to report on the hardheads in the baseball strike and John McEnroe's tantrums.

But like it or not, the Wilson case has been something very special. Most important, it has forced its followers to think, to bear down. With all its complexities, it has demanded double reading. And that's the beauty of it.

The last year of the Wilson case has been the single most educational local event in modern times, growing into something far greater than a sports story. Look back at what you've learned:

— The courts: The workings of the circuit, appellate and supreme courts are now clearer, as well as their relationship to the federal judiciary. We saw how quickly the appeals system can operate when it wants to, and how slowly the wheels turn when matters are allowed to drift. We were also reminded that judges are human, that all of them don't agree, and that it is not perfect.

— The Big Ten: The case has provided a clearer view of the Big Ten's handling of eligibility matters, and has demonstrated that neither a Ph.D. nor vast experience — as with Iowa's Robert Ray and Wisconsin's Frank Remington — guarantee consideration and fairness.

The faculty representatives made a poor but understandable decision when they reversed the eligibility committee's ruling to allow Wilson to play in 1980, then disgraced themselves by turning their unexpected court losses into an irrational attack against the University of Illinois, a mistake they are belatedly attempting to rectify.

Yes, the UI made clerical mistakes, but not intentionally. Yes, UI attorneys took adversary positions (to the Big Ten) in circuit court, but Charles Palmer's chief "misconduct" was simply reading the Big Ten handbook and asking the judge to rule on it, and George Miller's famous "self-righteous hypocrites" statement was in response to insults directed toward the UI by Big Ten attorney Byron Gregory.

Whatever the Big Ten may feel about the Illinois court system, that does not excuse their stacked attitude toward UI appeals, their nasty treatment of UI Chancellor John Cribbet in Chicago, the severe and accusatory wording of the charges, and the refusal to allow UI President Stan Ikenberry a requested 48 hours so he could meet with the Council of Ten (presidents) before the outlandish sanctions were announced.

— Duke failure: The weakness of the commissioner became apparent as Wayne Duke shrank from the firing line and permitted Gregory free rein not only in the courtroom but — as all Illinois officials believe — in the writing of the damning charges against Illinois.

Illinois has discovered support within the conference in working toward the ouster of Duke, and that will become a major discussion point when the Illinois case is concluded. Duke is a stunning disappointment.

— Illini Fans: The Illini fan psychology, much of it steeped in the distant (1966) "slush fund," is an interesting phenomenon. Though some of the responses were irrational, Ikenberry found his position in the Bloomington meetings strengthened by an overwhelming public and faculty willingness to leave the Big Ten.

Fortunately for the UI, Ikenberry and Cribbet were not swept away by the raging sentiment and maintained their desire to retain league membership in tricky diplomatic discussions. Many fans still want to leave the conference regardless of the repercussions.

— The Press: There has been a flood of editorials — newspaper, TV and radio — on the Wilson-Illini subject, with minimal understanding of the basic facts. It took months before some "experts" figured out that the UI did not sue the Big Ten but was, in fact, a defendant.

The rantings got out of hand at times and the UI, claiming it was restricted by Big Ten edict, seemingly could not extricate itself from the public relations nightmare. Overall, the press did an erratic job and was only sporadically thorough in dealing with the complexities. These comments do not apply to the Chicago Tribune's Linda Kay or Sports Illustrated's Doug Looney.

— Wilson and White: Through the nerve-wracking year, Wilson and his coach, Mike White, acted with restraint and honor. They have had reason to lash out, but they have refrained.

And White has gone about his business of bringing quality California football talent into this fishbowl atmosphere, in the face of criticism from some of the state's high school coaches and amid grim warnings from UI academia about marginal students. In this past year, White has shown himself to be a determined fighter as well as a tactician.

So, looking back, there is no end to what has been learned from the Wilson case ... about human nature, about the Big Ten, about the judicial system, about the quality of university people like Ikenberry, Cribbet and Emily Watts, about Illini fans, and about a young man who took a chance and challenged the system.

This is a community built on education, and we have all learned a great deal more than if Dave Wilson hadn't made this whirlwind visit. Whatever excitement he provided in the 3-8 season of 1980, he has been far more valuable in force-feeding Illinoisans to gain a better understanding of our tiny corner of the world.

I, for one, am not glad it's over. What other teacher has taught us so much in one year?

Unless we attended law school, none of us in the media could imagine all the workings of this complicated case. I don't know where to start in explaining it. Dave Wilson was a qualifier and never did anything wrong. Neither did the UI, other than to stand up for his rights, which the Big Ten faculty reps perceived as an inappropriate stance. Wilson played one year and signed with the New Orleans Saints in the supplementary draft, receiving a five-year contract for $1.5 million.

AUGUST 7, 1981

While some Illini backers wanted the UI to withdraw from the Big Ten, the university accepted penalties over the Dave Wilson case.

CHAMPAIGN — Illinoisans who believe in justice and fair play have a right to be fighting mad today.

Even if Gov. James Thompson approves a legislative (lottery) plan to defray Fighting Illini penalties of $500,000 ... even if it turns out that Mike White's second UI football team isn't good enough to receive a bowl bid ... the Illini have received a monumental goring from a forever confused and misguided band of Big Ten faculty representatives.

This is not to detract from a skilled negotiating job by UI President Stan Ikenberry and Chancellor John Cribbet — the faculty reps, remember, had never before agreed to renegotiate sanctions — but those who call it an "Illini victory" are cautioned by Cribbet:

"If it was a victory, why am I not elated?"

The problem was, the faculty reps were more concerned with their reputations than correcting an awful wrong. So they swung from a concept of concern over the structure and attitude of UI athletic governance, and they attacked the key sport, football.

They voted to split up among themselves the UI's customary share of football TV revenue ($500,000) and they punished Mike White even though there hasn't been a hint that he did anything more wrong than (1) obeying a court order and (2) attracting transfer students from California's rich junior college system.

The reps, you see, have been suspicious of White and Neale Stoner from the start, a fact that has crept out of inside conversations along the way.

And the official charges against Illinois indicate their feeling that Stoner did not act in good faith in the initiation of Dave Wilson's court case, that he failed to provide notice to the conference of the impending suit and that he did not take the appropriate posture at the initial hearing.

Like most of their charges, these are part hearsay and part assumption.

The simple fact is that no judge in America could hand down severe penalties on such weakly supported circumstantial evidence and hope to retain a position of public trust. Only in a protected academic environment can such obvious vindictiveness surface as an unappealable final ruling.

The question remains: How could learned educations arrive at conclusions so outlandish as to bring the threatened intrusion of the Council of Ten (presidents)? How could they be so far off as to necessitate Wednesday's turnabout?

After all, no action better demonstrates their instability than Wednesday's reconstitution of sanctions and philosophy. It was the clearest possible admission of conference mistakes that far outstripped anything the university did.

How could this have come about?

One popular interpretation of the Big Ten mess, oft repeated, begins with the revelation of Wayne Duke as a shallow, insecure commissioner who allowed the conference power base to evolve toward counsel Byron Gregory and two long-time facultymen, Robert Ray of Iowa and Frank Remington of Wisconsin.

No other current faculty rep dates back farther than 1977. Minnesota's Robert Stein is brand new, and two others began their terms Thursday. Gone since 1979 are such long-time stalwarts as Marcus Plant of Michigan and Jack Fuzak of Michigan State. Whether a more experienced board would have knifed through the fog is speculative, but there is no question that this particular group is young and made tragic miscalculations. However impressive they may in their specialties, as a group they misread the Illinois case from the beginning.

Thus Illinois was left with two unappealing choices: (1) withdrawal from the conference, regarded by Ikenberry as a sure road to disaster or (2) accepting unfair and undeserved football sanctions.
A joint statement, neatly drafted to appease both sides, tried to paint a picture of healthy cooperation.

But the long-running Illini-Big Ten war did not end Wednesday. What the scorecard actually shows is that the faculty reps got so far out of bounds in their spring rashness that they couldn't come all the way back.

Illinois was severely shafted for vague misdeeds, and had no choice but to accept.

Let the record show that the Big Ten leaders disgraced themselves is this episode as surely as they did last spring.

An angry state legislature approved a lottery that paid back the UI for more than its $500,000 fine, and Mike White's team went on to successful seasons in the early 1980s. The 1981 team finished 7-4 and would have qualified for a bowl game if it had been eligible.

FIRST OF TWO COLUMNS ON NEALE STONER'S OUSTER
1988

A popular athletic director, Neale Stoner, and assistant Vance Redfern were forced out for "overspending their welcome."

CHAMPAIGN — Lee Iacocca, Chrysler CEO:

"The real problem is not the existence of perks; it's the abuse of them.

"I'm talking about freebies like trips to hunting lodges, or the use of a yacht — frivolities that involve charging the company for lifestyle you could easily afford on your own.

"When you see guys traveling to golf matches in company planes, you really have to wonder if the company is keeping records and billing everybody, as it ought to.

"If a worker is asked to mow an executive's lawn and trim the hedges, that's an abuse that's in a league with embezzlement. For those types, justice is swift — you get canned."

Iacocca's words hit home in the current investigation of alleged improprieties by Illini athletic leaders. But it's another question whether they could actually afford the life style.

For example:

When the Illini basketball team played in Hawaii last November, Doddson Travel Agency issued airline tickets for six Nov. 22 flights — five days prior to the UI's first-round game — for Mr. and Mrs. Ron Guenther, Mr. and Mrs. Wayne Williams, Vance Redfern, and athletic director Neale Stoner at a cost of $4,805.72. Stoner's wife, Lynda, arrived the same day on a flight billed at $967.62.

It was reported later that the Guenther's did not actually go. Records for that period, obtained by The News-Gazette via a Freedom of Information request, show "Guenther" was crossed out and replaced by "Beard" in the Kaanapali Alii condominium where the group stayed. Guenther is in charge of fund-raising in the UI's Chicago office. Ed Beard is the UI golf coach.

One two-bedroom condo was split between Beard and Williams, men's golf paying for Beard's half and St. Louis grants-in-aid handling Williams' half, at a cost of $265 per night for eight nights. Tax fees brought the total cost to $2,319.71. Three people were registered in a connecting condo signed for by associate director Redfern under "administrative travel."

Golf at Kapalua the next two days, Nov. 23-24, for Williams, Beard, Stoner, Redfern and his son, Kirk Redfern, was charged to the Athletic Association at $75 per round, coming to $750. A hospitality room costing $101.32 was set up for the 23rd, the snacks and refreshments also including Bayer aspirin, saline solution and lotion. That same day Stoner charged the AA with $217 bill at El Crab Catcher. The next day Stoner charged the department $107 for a "public relations" affair that included his close friends, Billy Rasmussen and Dick Martin, and Kapalua golf pro Gary Planos.

The incomplete material available to The News-Gazette did not explain how additional golf outings, meals and entertainment at Kapalua later in the week were handled. Planos, who attended the UI in the 1970s, informed by telephone that Stoner and the Illini group, who had come to Maui on previous occasions, loved their golf and played virtually everyday.

"I may have given them a few free rounds," said Planos.

Planos joined Vance Redfern, Kirk Redfern, Mr. and Mrs. Dick Martin and Tom Kelly for a $53 entertainment bill on Nov. 26. Later that same day a $653 meal was billed to the AA by Vance Redfern for a meal that included Vance and Kirk Redfern, Mr. and Mrs. Stoner, Mr. and Mrs. Martin, Mr. and Mrs. Williams, Tom Kelly and Ed Beard. Stoner also approved and accepted per diem of $4 for breakfast, $4 for lunch and $14 for dinner for himself that day, plus the automatic $10 for tips and taxis.

Are such expenses legitimate? Under what circumstances is it appropriate for the associate director to charge his son's golf to the department? Would the chancellor approve of $75 rounds for Stoner's top staff men? Was Planos being entertained at AA expense for free rounds he provided the department heads? Is a $653 meal excessive?

Questioned in this regard, UI vice president Craig Bazzani said:

"You're asking some of the same questions that we're seeking answers for. And whatever you're sitting on, multiply it by 1,000 for our auditors. There's a great deal of pick and shovel work here. You have to track the rabbit all the way through before you know absolutely what happened. Our auditors may be working for another month to six weeks."

Among other things, the auditors must be alert for slips of reimbursement made at a later date. In this case, according to Pam Hahn of the UI Public Information Office, there was no reimbursement. As for the dinners and entertainment, Bazzani said:

"We can't have rules for everything. The university has a broad policy statement and a procedural manual pertaining to gifts and that sort of thing. But in many of these cases it comes down to the 'prudent man' rule. If it's not defined, was it reasonable? What would prudent man do under the circumstances? That's a judgment we have to make."

Bazzani reminded that there are "fuzzy areas" in development (fund raising), that you have to spend money to raise money. Furthermore, it might be acceptable for a department head to bring his forces together for a planning session and then take everyone out to eat at department expense.

But only a few months before, the UI athletic department headed into severe cash flow problems requiring cutbacks and the elimination of graduate assistant coaches. There seems to be no justification for the department funding family vacation golf trips — fees, carts, entertainment, meals and even the aspirin.

A thorough investigation revealed that the popular Stoner and his right arm, Redfern, had gone too far in a number of areas, and they were obliged to step down. For me, this was a difficult time with many of Stoner's friends expressing their disapproval. It's 20 years later and some still won't speak to me.

JULY 17, 1988

Illini athletic director Neale Stoner and chief lieutenant Vance Redfern are removed after revelations of improper behavior in the department.

"The first day the maintenance department allegations ran in The News-Gazette (June 6), I realized that if they were true, we'd probably have to separate ourselves from Neale Stoner."

— UI Chancellor Morton Weir.

CHAMPAIGN — "What did you know and when did you know it?"

The question once asked by Howard Baker during the Watergate revelations was met squarely by the University of Illinois decision-maker, Morton Weir, in a meeting at The News-Gazette after Stoner resigned as athletic director last week.

"In my view, the charges were serious and could not be explained reasonably," said Weir in retrospect.

"I tried to keep an open mind, but I knew that if we verified the basic claims alleged by the maintenance workers, it would be very difficult to keep Neale.

"I felt a great part of the problem was that other staff people were engaging in the same improper behavior, that it was a widespread in the department. That was part of the context I described.

"I told Neale that he was responsible for the program, that the problems ran deep in the organization, and that this aspect was even more troublesome to me than his personal involvement with the maintenance department."

According to Weir, Stoner was brought down not only by his individual mistakes, but by the grand view of things. Also resigning was his senior associate director, Vance Redfern.

"We had a program that had lost its good reputation, that was widely believed to skirt around the ethical fringes," said Weir.

"In the 1980s, we've been placed on probation twice by the NCAA (and once by the Big Ten). We've been before the NCAA infractions committee three times and received sanctions twice. If we overlooked the current problems, the university would give the appearance of not being on the up-and-up.

"I did not see this as a media vendetta. I saw it as a case where disgruntled employees blew the whistle. The first story came out and started to snowball."

Weir wasn't prepared to discuss specific travel violations. But he acknowledged:

"I haven't studied the receipts, but if the November trip to Hawaii was as The News-Gazette described it, if that was basically a vacation trip for some staff members and their wives, then no, that's not permitted. If there was fund raising involved, as may have been the case for Neale, then his part of it can be justified. But vacation golf, lodging and meals for a group at department expense is not permissible."

So, when a visibly upset Weir conducted his first press conference June 15, he knew. And all those close to Weir also knew. The Stoner regime was over. It was just a matter of time.

Why, then, did Weir seemingly join Stoner in dumping the responsibility for Stoner's demise on the media doorstep at the press conference a month later?

"I was not aware that my comments would be interpreted in that manner," said the chancellor.

"I had several thoughts in mind as I wrote my statement. Stoner was out and, for humane reasons, I wanted to leave him with as much dignity as possible. At the same time, I wanted to present a positive face from the university perspective."

Weir doubtless was also aware that monied UI boosters, who have supported Stoner's flourishing grants-in-aid program and his $35 million capital campaign, needed to be retained.

"I had talked to some of the major contributors," Weir said, "and almost uniformly they reminded me of the great things Stoner has done. Many felt that he could survive this, but they also expressed an awareness of the difficult decision I had to make."

Weir said that his recitation of rumor denials in Tuesday's statement was done at Stoner's request. The former director was concerned about circulating gossip.

"Neale asked me to include that material," said Weir, "It did not occur to me that, by issuing those denials (of kickbacks, improper gifts-in-kind, etc.), it would appear that they originated in the media."

Actually, internal sources and former staff people turned out to be a main source of rumors and allegations that were handed over to the investigating team. Once it became clear that something might be done about the situation, the complaints grew.

Except for the allegations that were verified as improper, these were not published. Nevertheless, Stoner and his attorney, Dan Webb, cited a media vendetta as the reason for Stoner's ouster. And Stoner never acknowledged personal wrongdoing or the obvious internal problems that led to the outcry.

Said the chancellor:

"For me, it was a gut-wrenching, no-win situation from the beginning. Neale accomplished a great deal in the areas of fund raising and individual sports. He has a strong ring of supporters who will always feel I made the wrong decision, that I caved in.

"But the fact is, the university is better off to be starting over and moving forward with credibility. I know there are people out there that will help us do that."

As soon as the decision was made, Weir's main concern was avoiding legal bloodshed, and Stoner was allowed to return to California with kind words and a "golden umbrella" annuity. Stoner was brilliant and dynamic but should have been in private business, not collegiate athletics.

BACKGROUND FOILS CUNNINGHAM QUEST
1992

Gary Cunningham's past rose up to prevent him from interviewing for the Illini athletic directorship.

CHAMPAIGN — Gary Cunningham's quest for the Fighting Illini athletic directorship raises a juicy blend of pluses and minuses.

With the Fresno State director joining Ron Guenther for final interviews — behind Illinois State's Ron Wellman and UI interim director Bob Todd — let us weigh the factors:

First, The Bad News:

A university administrator says, correctly, that "long-term athletic success stems from stability at the top, cleanliness over time, and winning over time."

He says we "put too much stock in the personality of the AD. A good director isn't necessarily one who is out front, but one who rather puts the right coaches in charge and lets them to the work."

There are concerns that Cunningham's idea of a long-term commitment may be comparable to John Mackovic's. Most middle-aged Californians who come to the Midwest ultimately have one destination in mind — California. It's called "going home." Whatever promises he provides in discussions here can't be any more sincere than those he gave to Fresno State when he declined Iowa overtures 10 months ago.

Furthermore, with local candidates Todd and Guenther attracting powerful blocs of loyal support, and with the UI's most recent California dealings (Neale Stoner) ending up in disappointment, there is a strain of resistance to any outsider, and particularly one from the West Coast.

By going outside, it can be presumed that a lagging UI gift

That must be a youthful Sonny Tate in a day long gone.

As a Monticello sophmore, I'm wearing No. 33 and standing next to coach Wally Gregory on the Sages' 1946-47 Okaw Valley champions. Team leaders were seniors Dave Lord (25) and Ken Clouser (23) in the front row.

An early responsibility was handing out Hall of Fame certificates to Joe Fred Green (left), Tony Clements and others at Champaign Central in the late '60s.

Tony Yates, former Illini assistant basketball coach, speaks while Bob Brown, Tate and Bob Auler listen.

Look at the letters we received in naming the column in the fall of 1966. Ray Compton is credited with naming it Tatelines.

Jim Turpin calls an Illini game and I chipped in.

TATELINES 139

They let me sidle up next to the big guys,
UI football coach Mike White and announcer Jim Turpin.

Two of my heroes from Monticello were Illini basketball coach
Harry Combes (left) and assistant football coach Lou Baker.

Here I am trying to figure out that confusing computer.

That's Travis as a baby with
the proud papa and Lex.

That's Travis a lot of years later with his grinning parents.

Lou Henson gets in the picture with Lex, Travis and some guy in a hat.

Elizabeth Burden wins the State Amateur golf title in Peoria with her grandfather caddying.

It was a proud day when the family showed up for my induction into the Monticello High School Hall of Fame. To my left are son Travis, wife Lex, daughters Melinda Burden, Lori Simon and Kathy Meyer, and granddaughter Casey Burden.

That's me swinging in our 55-and-over old-timers softball league. Player shortages found me still hanging on at age 76 this past summer.

Friends sit down for dinner. The handsome ones are
Ralph "Shorty" Shafer, Lou Henson and Joe Thompson.

It must have been a serious moment at the golf course.

I broke out my New York Police Department hat for the Fourth of July parade with Tom Kacich driving and Stevie Jay in the back with former News-Gazette owner Marajen Chinigo.

There we are, the Tate and Turpin twins, doing our Saturday Morning Sportsline.

Veteran announcer Brent Musburger (center) takes time out to pose with Brian Barnhart and me.

Our sports staff ofetn practices what it preaches. From left, back row: Brett Dawson, Loren Tate, Bob Asmussen, Jim Rossow; front row: Tony Bleill and Jeff Mezydlo

Gerry DiNardo, former Indiana football coach, discusses the Big Ten TV Network in Chicago in 2007.

Jerry Hester, UI basketball analyst, must be wondering what the guy next to him is trying to point out.

Mayor Jerry Schweighart and News-Gazette personnel turned out for the naming of Fremont Street in my honor.

John Foreman, publisher of The News-Gazette, presented the Publisher's Award to me in 2003 with Lex standing by.

This computer age is getting the best of me but I'm hanging on.

Former UI President Jim Stukel gets some very good advice.

It is always fun being interviewed but
they don't always know what to expect.

Tiger Woods would be terrified to see this on the golf course. From left, that's me, Lou Henson, Bruce Weber, Brian Barnhart and Jason Elliott.

Our N-G sports staff, once a three-man operation, is almost as big as the news department. From left, front row: Tony Bleill, Fred Kroner, Mike Goebel and Marcus Jackson; middle row, me, Jason Randall, Mike Colgan, Bob Asmussen and Paul Klee; back row, Jim Rossow, Rich Barak and Jeff Huth.

program, which could account for a considerable portion of the $20 million athletic operation, would continue to lag. And the community motivation, waiting to be unleashed, would probably remain stagnant.

Next, The Good News:

Cunningham, already deeply involved as an NCAA committeeman, would offer wide-ranging political advantages in the highly political NCAA.

Under Cunningham, the UI might even approach the "favored" status of Duke, Indiana and — put your money on this one — Virginia. Under the NCAA's form of justice, incidents that draw a debilitating two-year investigation for one university wind up as a hand slap for another.

Consider, for example, that long-time basketball coach John Wooden, ably assisted through many of those years by Cunningham, has retained virtual sainthood despite revelations of 15 years of blatant cheating by Papa Sam Gilbert, the late Godfather of UCLA basketball.

In this case, perception rules over fact. A stubborn nation won't accept Wooden as a co-conspirator with the deceptive Gilbert when, the truth is, they were as closely united in seeking their common goal as Laurel and Hardy.

The Ugly Past:

In a flaming expose 10 years ago, Los Angeles staff investigators Mike Littwin and Alan Greenberg laid bare the truth about UCLA after interviewing more than 45 former Bruin players, coaches and others. The series of articles displayed Gilbert, a multimillionaire Encino contractor, as a "surrogate father and adviser" for UCLA players, and a man who helped them get cars, stereos, clothes, airline tickets, scalpers' prices for their basketball season tickets, and even abortions for their girlfriends.

Gilbert routinely negotiated pro contracts for the players before their eligibility expired.

Two NCAA investigations impacting the Lou Henson program at Illinois — the first at the end of the Harv Schmidt era — are wisps of wind compared to the Gilbert tornado at UCLA. But, for all of Gilbert's excesses, UCLA maintained an aura of respectability that the UI clearly lost along the way.

Brought in initially by UCLA to prevent Kareem Abdul-Jabbar (then Lew Alcindor) and Lucius Allen from transferring to Michigan, Gilbert handled Bruin players as though they were members of his own family. For many of those All-Americans, his Pacific Palasades home was a second home where they routinely gathered for meals on weekends.

"I buy 100 hamburgers at a time. These kids can really eat. Everyone drops by," Gilbert said.

The Times quoted one former head coach, presumably Larry Farmer:

"I knew he (Wooden) didn't have full control. If you've got a guy on the side where players can get cash, cars and clothes from, who's the player going to go to?"

Littwin and Greenberg wrote that "Wooden knew the players were close to Gilbert. He knew they looked to Gilbert for advice. Maybe he knew more. He should have known much more. If he didn't, it was only because apparently chose not to look."

According to the Times, "Cunningham was much closer to Gilbert," and Gilbert became directly involved in recruiting only during Cunningham's two-season tenure (1977-1979) as UCLA head coach. Darryl Mitchell, a Floridian who attended Minnesota, was one of the players who told the NCAA that Gilbert offered them cars as high school seniors in 1978.

Farmer said Gilbert became involved that year "because we were struggling so much. They (Gilbert and Cunningham) cared about each other a great deal. They had a warm relationship."

Why, then, with Gilbert common knowledge across the land, didn't the NCAA act?

The answer goes back to the NCAA's penchant for selective enforcement. Brent Clark, an NCAA field investigator in 1977, told the Times he looked into the Gilbert-UCLA relationship that year and was told to drop the case.

"They (the NCAA) just sat on it," said Clark. "If I had spent a month in Los Angeles, I could have put them on indefinite suspension. But as long as Wooden was there, the NCAA would never have taken any action."

Later, in 1978 testimony before the House Committee on Interstate and Foreign Commerce's subcommittee on oversight and investigations, Clark said: "The conclusions I draw is that it is an example of a school that is too big, too powerful, and too well respected by the public, that the timing was not right to proceed against them."

Eventually in 1981, the NCAA moved and gave UCLA two years probation for nine minor infractions. The most serious allegation was that Gilbert signed a promissory note so a player could buy a car. David Berst, head of the NCAA's enforcement division, cited a four-year statue of limitations in refusing to turn over the rocks in UCLA's past.

We learn from this what we already knew already, that Berst has favorites and Berst has victims. UCLA has been the former, Illinois the latter. It makes a fellow wonder what might happen if they are united.

The UI board apparently didn't know Cunningham's past and, when it was published, he didn't fly in for the interview. I felt badly for John Easterbrook, the former Illini quarterback from Champaign, who would probably have accompanied Cunningham as assistant AD. But I felt strongly that Guenther was the man for the job.

THIS MIGHT CHANGE YOUR MIND
1984

California junior college prospects bolster Mike White's Illini teams.

CHAMPAIGN — Excuse the repetition but I'm trying to alter your thinking on an old issue.

If you're a Midwesterner, you've undoubtedly raised an eyebrow over the Illini football team's dependence on junior college transfers.

You had long since formed your opinion on junior colleges. Students went there because they didn't have academic qualifications for college, right? Second-class citizens all the way, huh?

You justified the Illini approach temporarily as a needed "stopgap measure." You enjoyed the victories but you avoided philosophical discussions with your cousin from Michigan. You were a teeny bit embarrassed. You applauded Mike White's statements that he would soon return to the high schools for talent.

BUT IS THAT REALLY such a good idea?

Let's agree first that the Californians who form the nucleus of the JC contingent — Dave Williams, Todd Avery, Curtis Clarke, Jackie Johnson, James Gordon, Mike Piel, Shane Lamb, Guy Teafatiller, Alec Gibson, etc. — aren't exactly dead-end kids picked up on some ghetto corner.

"Everybody wanted those players," said White this week. "It's just that we have more contacts out there. We can make quicker, better evaluations and we've been able to demonstrate to these athletes that they can be successful here."

Of course, every barrel has its good and bad apples. But information provided by academic adviser Terry Cole last year revealed that nearly 90 percent of the JC transfers on the UI's two-deep 1984 roster were academic qualifiers out of high school. This is repeated to eliminate the theory that all these athletes took the juco route because they had to.

Some had to. The overwhelming majority didn't. Most went to junior college because they weren't highly recruited out of high school and needed time to develop their physical skills.

Point is, the JC transfers are at no particular disadvantage, when compared to the high school recruits, in terms of their ability to do classroom work. In fact, the record shows the JC products are more mature and generally better prepared for the effort ... and certainly far advanced over products of the giant Chicago Public School system.

And if Proposition 48 goes through in January, placing stiffer prerequisites on high school seniors, student-athletes with a junior college diploma will become even more vital to major college football programs. With that possibility so real, this hardly seems to be the time to reduce efforts in the JC area.

This JC vs. high school issue came to mind again this week as Illini rookies went through their paces. As expected, two individuals stand out. They are 297-pound offensive tackle Arael Doolittle and 275-pound defensive tackle Jim Blondell, both JC transfers. Seven other JC transfers enrolled in time to participate in spring drills, and all are rated good prospects who will eventually attain first or second-team status. Four already have.

Prize freshmen such as Steve Williams and Greg Boysaw look promising also but, generally speaking, the freshmen appear to have a long way to go.

You see, the real problem for White and his recruiters is making an accurate judgment on high school seniors. High school films are difficult to evaluate. There is an enormous discrepancy in the competition. There are huge inconsistencies in the play. Not enough is known about the personal characteristics of the individual prospects or their ability to develop.

It may develop, after the first of the year, that the Illini will recruit a large number of highly-touted preps from the surrounding area. This will please the fans, the professors, the in-state coaches and all those who don't believe the facts when they're placed on a plate directly in front of them.

The truth is, the best approach for the Illini, the one that has paid and continues to pay dividends, is to keep hauling in those marvelous athletes from out West. This could be Illinois' best team in modern times, and 22 of the top 44 squadmen are JC transfers, 14 of them on the defensive two-deep.

If Mike White could find a way to bring in 20 prime JC transfers in the next class, the entire community should be thrilled, not mortified. They're the ones who put the Illini on this winning roll and they're the ones the Illini will need to keep them there.

The recruitment of 17-year-old preps is high risk at best. To begin with, they're tougher to corral. You have to go head-to-head with Notre Dame and Southern Cal for the can't-miss blue-chippers like St. Rita linebacker John Foley. The Illini have been burned going to the wire for Alvin Miller, Eric Kumerow and Hart Lee Dykes. And once you get past the best five or six in the state, it's anybody's guess who'll make it and who won't.

If you could take 30 leading preps and wait two years to chose the top 15 from that group, you'd know. And that's exactly what the Illini are getting from the JC ranks.

It was hard to sell the notion on the UI campus that recruiting junior college prospects was a good idea. In truth, some of them were rowdy and got in trouble, and Mike White twice had run-ins with NCAA investigators. So White tried to change and concentrate on high school players, and that's when the level of talent dropped.

EDUCATIONAL COMPLEXITIES BOGGLE THE MIND
MID-1980S

In the 1980s, the wide use of ACT and SAT scores was one of the more controversial subjects in education.

CHAMPAIGN — Does a highly-competitive, state-supported university have an obligation to a segment of society that has not prepared its sons and daughters for the demands of advanced education?

This is not a sports question.

It is basic, whether you're pinpointing rural youths following Pa's footsteps from high school to the farm, young women reared with blinders by a sub-par school system or gang-oriented products of the Chicago ghetto.

Why should the University of Illinois, one of the nation's Top 10 public universities, feel the necessity of dealing with a cross-section of the unprepared? Isn't the university's reputation sustained by the young geniuses, those ACT scores at 30 and above, who clog the law, engineering and computer classrooms?

Wasn't the state's junior college system constructed, at considerable expense, to fill the gap for marginal students? Doesn't it make sense for the state's other universities, with less demanding enrollment requirements, to pick up the slack?

That's enough questions. Let's see what conclusions our educators are coming to.

The UI, through its Educational Opportunities Program, has long since demonstrated a compassionate interest in the culturally disadvantaged. In fact, the university is out there searching for those special talents that can be developed.

"I'd be saddened if a university in a major industrial state did not provide help for students from inner cities," said law professor John Nowak, the UI's faculty representative to the Big Ten Conference. Nowak expresses a widely-held viewpoint of academia when he adds: "We have a moral responsibility to help a variety of our population, to receive and prepare students whose test scores aren't quite up to what we would prefer. We serve the entire state.

"By using traditional criteria, the high school rank and test scores, we get a fair cross-section from small communities and the suburbs, and from private and public schools. But not the city. If we're going to be of service to all segments, we have to use more flexible admissions criteria in some situations. We've found that some high schools produce students with very low test scores, and yet students who finish high in those classes traditionally do well in a university setting if they're given the chance."

This supports Jesse Jackson's pronouncement that opportunity, coupled with effort ("to the third power"), will overcome sub-par preparation.

Many black leaders have described the national tests (ACT and SAT) as racially biased. If Nowak doesn't go that far, he at least conceded that ACT scores don't always predict the future.

But regardless of this, the fact remains that if there are 200 positions available in the prestigious UI College of Law, the state produces considerably more than 200 high school graduates who would make good lawyers. And even here, the college goes beyond the computer in deciding who gets in.

"We choose two-thirds to three-fourths of our incoming students from the formula," explained Nowak, "and the faculty studies a large amount of criteria to choose the rest, some of whom had been dropped by the computer. This is done all across the campus. All our decisions are not based on high school grades and ACT scores."

OK, if we agree (and everyone does not) that the university should have a broad-based policy, that flexible admissions policies are appropriate to serve as segments, that all decisions should not be strictly on academic prerequisites, that the ghetto should have its representatives in this institution of higher learning, it becomes only a tiny step into the world of varsity athletics.

If the university believes in developing the gifted musician or in making room for the computer genius with marginal writing skills, why not the blue-chip athlete?

For Nowak, the answer is clear. Yes, with such a high percentage of gifted athletes, particularly basketball players, emerging in the shoddy Chicago Public Schools system, it is perfectly reasonable to drop the standards for entrance in special cases.

"We don't want totally unqualified people, and we don't want to give degrees that aren't legitimate," said Nowak, "but the philosophy in this regard is the same as that at Cal-Berkley, Michigan and other top universities."

It is, of course, the philosophy of a nation. Universities from coast to coast, making up the NCAA, have for decades operated on minimum academic standards far below the average of the other students seeking enrollment.

Even with a bottom line drawn low, many athletes have fallen underneath it. In the Midwest, a common practice is for these athletes to spend two years at the junior college level. Greater numbers are expected to take this route in the future as the NCAA moves swiftly toward more stringent academic requirements in 1986.

But no matter where the line is drawn, many athletes will gain admission lacking academic background comparable to all those against whom he must compete in the classroom. So the question becomes: Why let them enroll if they're almost surely bound to fail?

Here again, the answer if obvious. If you're going to let them in, you're morally bound to provide support in the form of tutors and transitional programs. You're also morally bound, in words popularized by sports sociologist Harry Edwards, not to "exploit" them.

In other words, and this has become accepted in educational circles, it has become the obligation of the university to arrange a trade-off, a diploma in exchange for the athletes's crowd-drawing, dollar-attracting performances on the field. Just to "offer education" is not enough.

Nowak agrees, "I can't prove this, but my view of the world is that one's opportunity in life, particularly employment opportunities, improve with graduation," he said, "For most people, a college diploma enhances his career.

"Frankly, the university has a different relationship with the athlete than with the nonathlete. The university is not using the nonathlete for gain. We're here, he's on his own and we hope he makes it, but if he doesn't well …

"The athlete is here at our request, and the university is getting both direct and indirect benefits, and that gain diminishes the time and energy he can devote to studying. The football and basketball player is here to help our teams, to help produce thousands of dollars, and we have an obligation to be concerned about him.

"We know it's going to be difficult for him to succeed if we don't support him. If he leaves without graduating, we feel we've let him down. It's fine for the athlete who turns pro and makes it, Derek Harper, for example, but he's one of the few. There's nothing wrong with quitting college for a lot of money, but we worry about the graduation rates of the great numbers who don't make it in the pros. We want to prepare them for a better life."

The University of Illinois has come to a crossroads in this regard. The crisis is brought on by a myriad of social ills developing the last 20 years, the shocking educational slide dating to 1964 (when first effects of TV-watching began to appear), the gang culture in the cities and the drug culture everywhere, the flagging efficiency of high school teachers in the cities, the breakdown of the family structure and the explosion of out-of-wedlock births, and the marked increase of racial separation and unemployment in major cities.

These factors and others have contributed to an increasingly sharper division between the intellectual haves and have-nots.

So, on one hand, the UI is participating in a nationwide move to (1) toughen entrance requirements for student-athletes and (2) place greater demands on the high schools to emphasize "core curriculum" courses.

At the same time, in concluding that it is morally objectionable to recruit marginal people without a plan to help them succeed, both summer and in-semester courses are being coupled with more sophisticated counseling and tutoring to make the steps easier.

Former Chancellor John Cribbet provided the impetus. To his credit, the first "bridge" program was initiated this past summer and will be expanded upon next summer. And Gary Engelgau, director of admissions and records (also chairman of the committee that rules whether athletes will be admitted), is an architect of a transitional program which is scheduled to begin 1986-87.

The record seems to indicate that, when opportunity is offered, even at a university where academic competition is so strong, even where athletic demands are so great, the results can be positive for the marginally prepared student-athlete. The UI has made its decision and has embarked on a long-range program to make it work.

Because Illinois' summer transition program was not developed earlier, the Illini lost a number of key Chicago athletes for academic reasons, thus creating a long-standing split between the Windy City and the state university.

COACHES & ADMINISTRATORS

FIRST OF THREE COLUMNS ON RON GUENTHER
NOVEMBER 23, 2004

Ron Guenther fires Ron Turner and goes in search of a new Illini football coach.

CHAMPAIGN — Ron Guenther has accomplished just about everything as Illini athletic director ... except what he wants most.

He has changed the face of the south campus with new buildings. He has maintained the financial and operational integrity of a program disgraced by past indiscretions. He kept basketball purring in coaching changeovers from Lon Kruger to Bill Self to Bruce Weber. His men's teams are even now national contenders in tennis, wrestling and gymnastics. He has overseen the development of a women's program that this week sends a soccer team into the Elite Eight.

But, in his words, "after dissecting and dissecting for three years," he hasn't been able to solve the UI's football puzzle.

At this juncture, he is Phil Mickelson before he won his first major ... he is Gene Keady, who received six national Coach of the Year awards but never reached the Final Four ... he is Jim Ryun, who ran a 3:51.1 mile but never won the Olympics.

Basically, Guenther has a long list of accomplishments, but he can't win the big one. A 4-19 football record during the last two years have sent fans tumbling off the bandwagon, stymied recruiting and slowed further construction plans. A 4-19 record has cast a pall over the UI's autumn weekends.

So, even in the face of a budget-busting $2.2 million payout for the final two years of Ron Turner's contract, Guenther agreed with the majority of Illini Nation that a change was needed.

The decision to start over was easy compared to the difficulty of attracting the perfect successor. Mounting years of failure have made Illinois a treacherous coaching job. The last 10 football coaches were not all bad, but each one left with a full realization of how demanding and difficult it is. Some never again held a Division I head job.

One strength of Guenther, as he embarks on the hiring process, is that he is oblivious to that kind of thinking. He won't be dissuaded from his firm belief that the Illini job is an exceptional one. While others see the glass as half empty, while some winning coaches will shy away, Guenther maintains the opposite view.

Even as he reiterated the sadness attached to Turner's departure, he said: "We have some great young players. The sad part (as it pertains to Turner) is that someone else will come in here and have success."

Guenther calls it a "fragile business," implying that Lady Luck plays a major role. To be successful, he said, "You need to be a good recruiter and you need to get some breaks."

It's as though the world turned on a dropped pass here and a missed tackle there. He cited how Purdue was "talking Heisman (for Kyle Orton) and a Big Ten championship, and it turned on two or three plays this season." Similarly, he claimed that Turner didn't get the breaks.

Truth is, Illinois went sour in a string of inexcusable early losses to Missouri, Southern Mississippi and San Jose State in 2002, lost 15 of 16 Big Ten games the last two years and has built a string of 10 consecutive road losses. The Illini could have won some of those games with a key play here or there, but the overall performance was unacceptable. The defensive effort slipped from unsatisfactory to ridiculous.

To suggest that Illinois is on the verge of acceptable success is to believe Santa Claus can play quarterback, the Easter Bunny can catch passes and Paul Bunyan will come down to play defensive tackle. Decent talent in two young classes could make Illinois more competitive but is probably too thin to compete with the big boys.

The only good news is that Illinois has the right guy undertaking this enormous task. It shouldn't be attempted by someone who doubts the ending.

This is Guenther's last chance to get it right. He doesn't intend to be around for any more major hirings. He will have monumental decisions related to the Assembly Hall and Memorial Stadium, but this is the one that will make or break his legacy with the fans.

He will have moderate restrictions in the selection. He will begin by adhering to a two-week affirmative action requirement, noting that it'll probably take "three or four weeks" in any case. He is obliged to interview a minority candidate or face recriminations from the Black Coaches Association. He won't consider anyone with a shaky background (forget Rick Neuheisel). His timing might be thrown off by bowl game availability.

"A seated head coach is the first place you look," Guenther said, "although I can cite the examples of numerous coordinators who have done great jobs. I want someone who legitimately wants to be at Illinois. I'll go all the way to Mars to get the right guy.

"In our business, you can get coaches who can win but don't do it the right way. You might get someone you won't want to take to dinner. You might get a guy who doesn't support academics."

As for a cheerleader coach like Mike White, he responded: "What the masses want to see is winning and winning. We got close, but we didn't get it done. You can run it or throw it or push it, as long as you win. There is no magic to it."

So Guenther once again will go underground. He has a short list, and he will confer closely with interim chancellor Richard Herman as he whittles it down.

Don't ask about the perfect Christmas gift for the guy who has almost everything. It is obvious. Let Guenther locate a winning coach, and he will have everything.

Guenther is a "football man" and success on the field means everything to him. He found his man in Ron Zook, and they worked closely together as Zook brought in successful recruiting classes and reached the Rose Bowl as the Big Ten's runner-up team in 2007.

MARCH 18, 2007

CBS columnist Gregg Doyel severely criticizes UI athletic director Ron Guenther for his strong reactions during Illinois' 54-52 loss to Virginia Tech in the 2007 NCAA basketball tournament.

"If I offended someone, I apologize." — Ron Guenther

COLUMBUS, Ohio — The same bulldog tenacity that propelled Ron Guenther on the football field — a 200-pound guard, he succeeded Jim Grabowski and Dick Butkus as Illini MVP in 1966 — spilled over in an awkward place Friday night.

While the bulk of Illini Nation slammed their fists and cursed their TV sets, or at least considered the temptation, a frustrated Guenther was doing the same.

Ever the fan, he was waging his own personal battle ... just a few seats away from CBS SportsLine.com columnist Gregg Doyel in the Nationwide Arena press box.

"I didn't know who he was," Guenther said Saturday. "He never identified himself. He never even looked at me. It wasn't an interview, and I didn't intend for anyone to overhear what I said. But like everyone else, I was pretty excited. If I offended someone, I apologize. But my comments weren't directed at anyone in particular."

The game brought a devastating end to a bumpy UI basketball season. Seven turnovers in the last seven minutes and erratic Illini shooting allowed Virginia Tech to rally from a 52-42 deficit and bump Bruce Weber's gang from the NCAA tournament 54-52.

As Doyel departed, he said to Illini sports information director Kent Brown (seated between Doyel and Guenther): "You're not going to like my column tomorrow."

Doyel was right about that. In the latest of several blows to the UI athletic image, Doyel leveled a salvo at Guenther. His words follow:

"The Illinois AD is smart enough to ascend to the job he holds, but dumb enough to behave so ridiculously courtside, surrounded by media in general and sitting 30 inches from me in particular.

"Guenther is a table-pounder, in good times and bad. Since there were very few good times Friday — even when the Illini had a 10-point lead with less than 4 1/2 minutes to play, they looked awful — Guenther did most of his pounding in anguish.

"If only he left it at pounding. Alas, he did not. Guenther would on occasion rise and stare down an official, or rise and give Weber advice, generally something along the lines of 'Get (Brian) Randle out of there!' And after one miserable play by Warren Carter — which isn't nearly specific enough considering his vast array of miserable plays — Guenther pounded the table, rose from his chair and screamed, 'Warren, you idiot!' Screamed it, people."

Guenther, the fan, wasn't the only one screaming in those final minutes. Feelings intensified throughout the building in the heat of the moment. It was the most excruciating loss in an Illini season marked by late-game fadeouts.

But he is a public figure and must accept criticism like a president who drops a verbal bomb when he thinks he's not live and discovers to his chagrin that everybody heard it.

The fact is, Guenther cares about his athletic teams and, in some cases, cares too much. It is an ongoing joke that his friends, particularly buddy Bob Lynch, watch him closely at Memorial Stadium to make sure he doesn't jump off the back of the press box. He usually chooses his football viewing location carefully to avoid embarrassment. Putting it mildly, he is not a happy loser.

"The last six weeks have been pretty tough beginning with the (Ron) Zook situation," Guenther said, "and the basketball season has been particularly frustrating. What should have been a great football recruiting story turned the other way. I think the question in the New York Times was legitimate — 'How did Zook do it?' — and it should have been about contacts and perseverance and personality. It should have been a great story. Instead we had to defend ourselves from charges that had no merit, no substance and no accountability."

Internet and newspaper inferences of cheating were repulsed by Guenther's proactive investigation, but that story was followed by one major controversy after another, from Jamar Smith's DUI accident to the ouster of Chief Illiniwek to the arrest of two football players for residential burglary.

"Everyone knows how much I care," Guenther said. "We put in a lot of time and effort to do things right, and it hurts when we get bad publicity.

"Did I slap the table? Yes. But I didn't direct my comments to anyone in particular, and I certainly didn't intend for my words to be picked up. That did not represent the way I feel about our players, and they know it. I feel badly that (Doyel) felt he had to print it.

"I think my frustrations were built up by everything that happened this season. I care. I had a dog in this fight. We played so well for so long against Virginia Tech, and it was heartbreaking to see it get away.

"The Internet has changed everything. Comments can be posted with no responsibility. It's hard to know who you can trust. I guess it's the world we live in," he said.

Doyel didn't stop with criticizing Guenther. Piling on, he patted himself on the back when he wrote: "Weber can't recruit at the elite level, which I first pointed out during Illinois' magical 2005 season." He referred to Weber as "dorky" and the players as "mentally weak."

If the latter is true, how do you explain the fact that Illinois, short-handed with transfers Trent Meacham and Marcus Arnold in the injury-depleted eight-man rotation, clearly outmanned at every position by superior Hokie athletes, and statistically the worst shooters in the Big Ten, led into the final minute Friday?

And if Guenther and Weber and Randle are targets today, how would that have changed if Randle hadn't rimmed out that last trey from the corner? Ask Ohio State if one three-pointer can make a difference.

Unlike 1988, Friday's loss wasn't truly tragic because the Illini weren't good enough to advance far in the tournament. But they worked hard against the odds and were in position for a 12-5 seeding upset. Guenther desperately wanted it for them ... and reacted like the fan he is. He'll be more careful next time, but he won't care any less.

Guenther tends to get worked up for Illini games. It is as though he is still playing as an undersized offensive guard on every play. Seating arrangements usually keep him out of earshot, or within earshot of those who accept his emotional outbursts.

JULY 18, 2006

UI trustees break the bank to keep Ron Guenther seated as Illini athletic director.

CHAMPAIGN — How much is too much for the indispensable man?

How do you replace an athletic director who in 14 years has ... well, count the ways.

(1) Ron Guenther set the tone for an Illini fundraising operation that attracted more than $100 million in donations toward facilities — administrative, academic and various sports — that for decades in the pre- and post-World War II era were either unimagined or untouched. At the same time, DIA endowments have grown from zero to $23 million.

(2) Guenther has avoided coaches with shady backgrounds, and created a four-man compliance staff to back his personal insistence on a level of honesty that was not always apparent during the 1960-70-80s period when Illinois had too-frequent run-ins with NCAA investigators.

(3) In the face of football disappointments and the ongoing Chief Illiniwek controversy, Guenther has served as point man and facilitator for the upcoming $116 million Memorial Stadium renovation supported by gifts and the rentals of suites and boxes.

(4) Within a year Guenther will be the driving force in developing a plan to pay for another monstrous undertaking, the renovation of the Assembly Hall.

(5) Illini basketball has reached new heights under three Guenther-hired coaches, each coach contributing to 19 Big Ten champion-

ships (and an NCAA tennis title) during the Guenther term.

(6) The period is marked by a dramatic improvement in classroom accomplishment, as shown by nearly 100 Academic All-Big Ten award winners annually.

So, Guenther received a raise from $410,000 to $500,000.

Trustee Robert Sperling said last week Guenther now ranks No. 4 among Big Ten directors.

Well, that's not exactly correct. Or maybe it is. When it comes to salaries, almost nothing is perfectly accurate.

You see, if Guenther is to receive a bonus of $250,000 for staying through Dec. 31, 2008, that computes to more than $600,000 annually. When you add in such extras as a courtesy vehicle, country club membership and complimentary tickets, it flies well past that figure.

But that's the case with all athletic directors.

Here's what we think we know. All Big Ten AD's salaries are more than $300,000. At least six are more than $400,000. Ohio State was paying the nationally renowned Andy Geiger a base of $290,000 (plus up to $50,000 in attainable incentives) when he retired, and then had to give $465,000 (plus $60,000 in incentives) to pry Gene Smith away from Arizona State last year. The numbers at Penn State and Michigan are way up there.

And Barry Alvarez, whose AD salary reflects not only his fundraising qualities but three Rose Bowl triumphs, dropped football for a five-year contract as AD Feb. 1, drawing $600,000 (plus extras) the first year.

Alvarez, incidentally, succeeded Pat Richter who, in January of 1993, was the league's highest-paid AD at $147,000.

Why, knowing the criticism that follows an athletic administrator receiving more than the president and chancellor, would Larry Eppley and the gang feel it necessary to jump Guenther so sharply?

Part of it was the shock of imagining how they would go forward with the hot-button Memorial Stadium, Assembly Hall and Chief Illiniwek challenges if Guenther wasn't on the firing line.

Sperling said Guenther "had opportunities with TV and the new Big Ten channel" which he had worked to develop. Then too, Guenther had off-handedly mentioned retirement. As the senior AD in the conference and now in his 60s, it is something he thinks about.

Understand this: Guenther's contract would have been for four or six years if he preferred. The fact that it is less than 2 1/2 years is telling. He may stay longer and will be much in demand during the stadium and Assembly Hall facelifts. But, at this juncture, you might assume he intends to change his status on Jan. 1, 2009.

Meanwhile, he'll ride the whirlwind.

"Ron Guenther is critical to us," said Chancellor Richard Herman. "He runs a smoothly-oiled operation, and he has delivered on championships."

"Athletics is important to the life of the institution and in reaching out to the alumni. Ron is a citizen of the university and his status goes far beyond athletics. He is not a caretaker. He has set a standard in activism and ambition for the campus."

"We are hopeful he'll stay through the completion of the stadium and in launching the Assembly Hall work, and even longer. I think of him not as an athletic director but as a counselor. He understands the institution in many ways. He brings both stability and a sense of adventure."

At the same time, while Guenther supports the Chief and sympathizes with Chief backers, he has no say in the debate and can't prevent the Chief's projected retirement at the end of this school year. He is obliged to keep Olympic coaches in line while soothing emotional contributors who admire the Chief. It is a high-wire act not recommended for the uninitiated.

"It was critical for us to get Ron to agree," Eppley said. "He appreciates loyalty, and it goes both ways."

Loyalty, some say, is Guenther's one weakness. He has been chastised for keeping coaches past their date of effectiveness. But even his critics must agree that if you're going to be criticized for something, there are many things worse.

"If I was running a company, I'd be looking for a guy like this," Eppley said. "He's more than a fundraiser. He mixes high expectations with high achievement and high integrity.

"I don't begrudge anyone their salary. There are market issues. We don't make the market demands but we have to react to them."

Check the team hotel around 6 a.m. on a football Saturday and you'll find Ron Guenther winding through a stiff workout. His joints, now past 60, often complain but he keeps in training. And that good health has allowed him to stay in a high-pressure job longer than he ever intended.

MIKE WHITE FACED PSYCHOLOGICAL DISADVANTAGES
DECEMBER 29, 1983

Illinois' role as favorite gives UCLA a psychological edge that the Bruins used to defeat Mike White's team in the 1984 Rose Bowl.

"From a psychological standpoint, we're getting killed out here this week. Veteran members of the Los Angeles media are rehashing that 1947 game, quoting former Illinois players how they left the Bruins bloodied and beaten. And Terry Donahue is being quoted on how great this Illinois team appears on film. It's brutal."
— Neale Stoner, Illini AD

PASADENA, Calif. — From the end of glorious October, when Illinois completed its sweep of the Big Ten's five toughest opponents, the Illini have been a marked team.

The league's tailenders — Minnesota, Indiana and Northwestern — were too weak to capitalize although Illini slippage was apparent in the eroding emotion of the proud defensive unit. Those three rivals scored 68 points, three more than the previous six.

With his ear close to the ground in his home state this week, Neale Stoner said: "I'm really concerned about the psychology of it here. It's all going one direction."

What is being obscured, claims the Illini athletic director, is UCLA's talent and experience. This is a team, playing at home, that defeated Michigan soundly in the Rose Bowl last year. This is a team that faced a brutal early schedule, with two road games that almost no team could survive — at Georgia and Nebraska — while sustaining devastating injuries at linebacker.

Now healthy for the most part, the Bruins are on a 6-for-7 streak and Donahue is playing the Bruins' unrated status to the hilt. He's enjoying the role of the scorned lover.

"You can imagine my reaction when the Disneyland animal characters ran up to greet Mike White and left me standing there," said Donahue with tongue in cheek.

Then a day later, at Wednesday's Tournament of Roses breakfast, the media directed question after question at White while Donahue sat next to him in what was supposed to be a joint news conference.

"If the Mike White interview is over, I'll be happy to answer questions," interjected Donahue, adding, "Just kidding, Mike. Just kidding."

White had anticipated all this. Donahue is old news in Los Angeles. It's his home. White is the hero riding back into town on a white horse, or the villain on a black one, depending on your point of view. In either case, White is the center of attraction.

And he works the press like a sculptor manipulates clay. Because he sees it as important, from the psychological standpoint, he has demonstrated both endurance and patience in responding to the same questions over and over again, for the individual radio stations, then for TV, and collectively for the print media.

His public charm is overpowering, camouflaging the short fuse that connects to an electric mile-a-minute temperament.

No, you never see it on the sideline. There, he's cool and introspective. That's his laboratory, his courtroom. But sometimes, during the tense and tiring days of preparation, even his own assistants find it prudent to steer clear. And other times he feels the tension building and takes time away to avoid the "burnout" that rocked his closest coaching comrades.

Historically, in structuring his daring master plan for success, whether gambling on marginal students or seeking improvements in facilities, he has sometimes outrun his supply line. He has pushed harder and faster than those around him can react.

For those looking for a chink in his armor, perhaps that is it. Stoner balanced this aspect of the man against his X & O's genius, and felt careful handling and maturity would resolve it. Now, as White nears his 48th birthday next week, Stoner does not see it as the problem it was regarded at Cal.

But Stoner views it as an unfortunate distraction this week in that White's 1977 firing at Cal is being relived here. It's only natural. In contrast to Donahue, people are either captivated by his charisma or see him as a slick salesman trying to pawn off a used car without a motor.

He's one of their own out here, maybe the most dynamic and bright offensive coach who ever came along, and they let him get away without ever really replacing him.

Observers who know his personality don't have to look far to uncover why he was fired. A high-voltage, demanding leader, bent on pushing to the limit, White didn't mesh with careful, young athletic director Dave Maggard.

The problem developed when White began to dominate in a power struggle with his own boss. Some say Maggard set up rules which

White felt restricted his style. White, popular with the masses, basically did as he pleased. Maggard was concerned about marginal students, White needed them to beat Southern Cal. Maggard assigned budgetary limits, White had alumni willing to contribute at his call.

It couldn't work and it didn't. Maggard held his ground and fired White for insubordination. For public consumption, it was called a clash of personalities.

Now White is back and the rehashing is under way, complete with references to 1983 "cheap shot" plays born at Southern Cal in the mid-70s and right on through the NCAA's current inquiry into White's Illini football program.

White responds as best he can. He won't discuss the NCAA business and he flinches when his California firing is broached.

When Donahue discusses the "terrifying dominance" of Illinois in the Iowa game, White reminds that just a few weeks earlier the Illini failed at Missouri, and needed a blocked punt to put away Stanford, 17-7.

In the game of words, White rates with the best. But this is a contest he cannot win because, from L.A. Times columnist Jim Murray to the corps of UCLA students, this is a game which the Californians rather expect to lose.

It will be Illinois' task to win in spite of this.

Neale Stoner was correct is seeing UCLA's psychological advantage. The Illini left their game on the practice field, fell behind 28-3 at the half, didn't score a touchdown until the fourth quarter and lost the 1984 Rose Bowl, 45-9. Game star was Rick Neuheisel (new UCLA coach in 2008) who threw four TD passes.

HARRY COMBES WAS A HOMETOWN HERO
DECEMBER 26, 2002

A driving, intense Harry Combes rose from his Monticello roots to serve as one of the UI's greatest players and coaches.

"We need to make history a bigger part of our lives."
— Broadcaster John Madden

CHAMPAIGN — Combes Gym at Champaign Central is named for a man who, for more years than anyone in these parts, wore the cloak of athletic greatness.

The misfortune is that some faculty and many students aren't aware of the sky-high, multicolored rainbow that Harry Combes rode.

So here, on this Christmas holiday, is your mandatory history lesson.

It begins in the late summer of 1927 — three quarters of a century ago, the era of all-white college quintets, underhanded free throws and a center jump after each basket — when Combes transferred to Washington Grade School in Monticello, joining fellow seventh-grader Bob Miller in a friendship that lasted until Combes died 25 years ago.

Yes, that's the same Bob Miller for whom Miller Gym in Monticello is named. Like Combes, he attended the UI. Unlike Combes, he returned home. Bob and Dorothy Miller still attend Sages games in "their gym" in designated seats at midcourt. They were right there Monday night in St. Joseph when the Sages bumped Unity in a showdown of unbeatens.

"Harry and I played together for six years," recalls the 87-year-old Miller, the only Monticelloan who served as pall bearer at Combes' funeral.

"He was the most intense player and person you'd ever meet. He never wanted to be beaten, from grade school on up, whether it was basketball or cards or whatever."

Simply put, of all the young men who grew up in this section of the state, Harry Combes is unmatched in terms of his athletic accomplishments and contribution to the greater C-U sports community.

Monticello went 20-5, 25-2 and 27-2 in Combes' three seasons (he also starred as a quarterback and a pole vaulter), his late-season leg injury probably costing the Sages a spot in the IHSA Sweet 16 in 1933.

He was a two-time All-Big Ten basketball player and, on teams that were predecessors to the Whiz Kids of the early 1940s, he led Illinois to Big Ten co-championships in 1935 and 1937.

He took the basketball helm at Champaign High in his second year out of college, won 84.7 percent of his games during nine campaigns and reached the state championship game three straight years with records of 34-2, 38-1 and 34-4, winning the crown in 1946.

He was 32 when the UI moved him across town, and his early run of success was the stuff of legend. Three of his first five teams reached the NCAA Final Four — Illinois since has returned once, in

1989 — and his teams in 1951 and 1952 were two-point losers in the NCAA semifinals. In his first nine seasons at the UI, Combes' teams never finished lower than third in the Big Ten.

Adding it up, in a meteoric 25-year run — and discounting his freshman year of ineligibility at Illinois and his first year at Champaign High (before he succeeded Les Moyer) — Combes' record as a player and coach was 532-114, or an 82 percent rate of success.

In those 23 campaigns — until the 1956-57 season, which turned his career in another direction after tall center George BonSalle was ruled ineligible — he averaged a fraction less than five losses per season. At his peak, he was called the Paul Brown of Basketball, successful beyond Hollywood believability standards.

And if Combes, in failing health and losing key recruiting wars with the George Wilsons and Cazzie Russells in Chicago, was counted out in the 1960s, he rode Dave Downey and Bill Small to a Big Ten title in 1963 and had pieced together another splendid squad before the infamous "slush fund" felled Combes and the Illini in December 1967.

We'll get around to that, but first the good years. The great years.

HIS MONTICELLO HOME

Now understand, Combes wasn't the only hero in the family of Hester and Harry Sr. Four grades behind came Linden, smaller and less tenacious than his brother but a bombardier and navigator who flew 66 missions over Europe in World War II, earning a Purple Heart, two Distinguished Flying Crosses and 13 Air Medals.

Retired and residing in Monticello (he died in April 2008), Linden recalled seeing German anti-aircraft shots destroy a plane directly in front of him, snapping it in two.

"I watched it like you would watch a movie, the plane in two pieces with the props still going," he said. "And our pilot was killed on another mission. The co-pilot brought the plane in."

That's Linden, as unassuming as Harry was determined, as relaxed as Harry was high-strung. Linden was the youngster keeping score while Harry racked up the baskets. Linden was there cheering when Harry played infield for the Champaign Plumbers in the Eastern Illinois League. As a freshman at the UI, Linden lived with Harry during the latter's first year at Champaign High. They always were close.

"As soon as Harry reached high school, he played sports the year around," Linden said. "I went to all the games. He wasn't big (maybe 5-11 at his peak) but he was quick, and he always seemed able to get his shot. He and Bob Miller were pretty even as scorers. We always believed the Sages would go to state in his senior year if Harry hadn't gotten a knee in the thigh.

"I never doubted Harry had the ability to make it at Illinois. He was so determined."

Miller recalls the 28-22 sectional loss to Hutsonville at Casey, when Harry "was almost hysterical" wanting to play in spite of his severe thigh bruise. Harry tried but had to be taken out. And Hutsonville, with a 6-8 center, prevailed by getting virtually every tip after every made basket.

It was the disappointing culmination of a run that began early in their sophomore season when coach Carl Lutman broke his own rule of not starting sophomores after his seniors fell short in several early Monticello losses.

"We were in the lineup long before Okaw Valley play, and we only lost one Okaw game each year," Miller said.

"I was more of an outside shooter, and Harry had the ability to drive to the basket. He used his elbows and cleared his own path. That was his specialty. He shot a lot of free throws.

"He was somewhat frail, never weighed more than 150 pounds in high school. Looking at his build, you wouldn't think he'd be that great. But he was also very good in football and as a pole vaulter. He had a do-or-die attitude."

Combes enrolled with the UI's "best freshman class in a decade," new coach Leland "Slim" Stilwell fielding a group that included Pick Dehner, Benton's Wib Henry, Tolono's Bud Riegel, Chicago pitcher-forward Hale Swanson and Morton's Jim Vopicka. Combes was named freshman captain, and, after some uncertainty whether he should be a forward or guard, cracked the varsity lineup early in his sophomore season and sparked an 8-1 finish that earned Illinois a share of the Big Ten title — the championship coming after coach Craig Ruby had gone a mediocre 55-53 in Big Ten play in the nine previous seasons.

"Who said sophomores couldn't play basketball?" wrote The News-Gazette's Eddie Jacquin. "Who said Champaign County (Riegel) and the Okaw Valley didn't turn out cage stars?"

This came after an early 37-36 triumph against Purdue at a time when Purdue's Ward "Piggy" Lambert was regarded the nation's No. 1 coach.

"That kid Combes beat us with those two dizzy shots," Lambert was quoted after Combes ignited a rally from a 27-19 deficit. "Does he always hit 'em like that?"

Combes contributed 12 points in a follow-up 44-23 triumph at

Ohio State, playing every minute. The Combes saga was rolling in full force. He was a star. Two days later, in mid-January, Jacquin called Combes "the most dependable boy on the team right now."

And on he went through the typical ups and downs of a fierce title run. The 34-22 win against Michigan wasn't impressive, several Wolverine regulars remaining at home because, as it was related, "they couldn't resist the wiles of the Wisconsin co-eds last Monday night" ... whatever that means.

Purdue later got revenge, but the Illini won their last five games to tie Purdue and Wisconsin for the 1935 title. If 1936 went less impressively (13-6), Lou Boudreau was waiting in the wings as a freshman and joined coach Doug Mills' first UI team in a flashy, undersized run for the 1937 crown. Combes had a slow start because of another leg injury, but he returned in time to make the Big Ten's first all-star quintet for the second straight year.

Of a 42-28 rout of Iowa, Urbana's Bert Bertine wrote: "The lads from tall corn country were reputed to have a stout defensive club, but all their efforts availed them little ... (because of) the brilliant play of Louie Boudreau and Harry Combes."

Combes added 16 points against Indiana at Huff Gym, with a reported 7,000 on hand. The Illini were filling the gym, and Harry was becoming the UI's most recognizable name since Red Grange.

Swanson's tipin at Purdue broke a 14-year losing spell in West Lafayette, the 38-37 result precipitating a riot in which Mills and Combes were knocked to the floor, Jacquin noting, "The attack on the (UI) team was inexcusable and added another black chapter to the long list of poor sportsmanship charges against Purdue followers."

Combes racked 19 points in the next win against Chicago, but Purdue gained revenge, 61-34, in Champaign. The Illini needed to win their last four games to share the crown with Minnesota, and they did.

BORN TO LEAD

Combes received the Big Ten Medal for proficiency in scholarship and athletics, and Champaign veterans believe he had an agreement to succeed Moyer when he signed on as assistant basketball coach (and head baseball coach) for the Maroons.

The intensity and razor-sharp intelligence that were always his carried Combes to immediate heights as a coach.

"He was so competitive," said Ted Beach, who played three years for him at Champaign High and three years at the UI.

"He was tough in practice, and his players would do anything for him. He was innovative, a student of the game. From the first day, he said we were going to do something different, something that would give us floor burns and blisters. We pressed all over the court. We stole the inbounds pass more than once."

Combes' attacking, freelance style terrorized the opposition as Champaign High ruled after World War II. The bitter disappointment of a title-game loss to Decatur in 1945 — with a seven-man squad because Jim Cottrell, John McDermott and Del Cantrell were sidelined — was followed in 1946 by a convincing title-game win against Centralia, setting off a wild community celebration.

The Maroons lost the title game to Paris in 1947, completing a three-year run into the IHSA title game. No Champaign-Urbana team has reached the IHSA's final game in the 55 years since.

Although it took a while for the decision to be formalized, Combes was the natural successor to Mills in the UI's post-Whiz Kids era.

Although Combes said "the floor is bigger and college kids are so much better ball handlers that we can't go all the way pressing," he implemented a fast-break style that set a record for Big Ten points in 1948, a mark his Illini broke numerous times thereafter. His first two UI teams featured a slick pivot passer in Wally Osterkorn, the slashing Bill Erickson and the majestic Dike Eddleman, Big Ten MVP on Combes' first Final Four team in 1949.

Those three in particular stand out like giants for this high school senior who was fortunate to attend a few games in sold-out Huff Gym. Combes, reaching rock star proportions, had hot dice in his hands again and he kept rolling. He matched Don Sunderlage with Champaign's Beach and Rod Fletcher and super-sophs Clive Follmer, Irv Bemoras and Bob Peterson in 1951, reaching the NCAA semifinals before Kentucky prevailed 76-74. He added Red Kerr and inserted Jim Bredar for Sunderlage in 1952 when, for a second year in a row, the Illini lost a semifinal two-pointer, this time to St. John's.

"Some of those early players weren't much younger than Harry (when he started)," said Judge Fred Green, who hit the winning basket in a 46-45 win against Indiana in 1948. "But he had no difficulty. Harry was a straight shooter and a devoted student of the game ... an innovator in high school who brought his free-wheeling game to Illinois."

Expanding his racehorse style through the years, Combes saw his athletes top 100 points for the first time in 1955. The 1963 co-champs beat Indiana 104-101 at home and lost at Indiana 103-100. In 1964-65, the Illini topped the magical 100 mark nine times, beginning with a riotous 110-83 rout of No. 2 UCLA.

"Harry had a powerful idea about offense," Downey said. "It was like when Mike White came to Illinois and all the receivers were suddenly getting open. Harry had a way of getting his shooters clear for open shots."

But the pressure, the personal demands, the long hours were taking a toll. Illness forced Combes to miss several games through the years, including the end of the 1962 season when he turned over a 12-3 team to Braun and, after two more wins, the Illini sagged into a five-game losing streak.

Combes ultimately was diagnosed with diabetes. Miller saw what was happening to his long-time friend.

"Harry demanded perfection, both of himself and his players," Miller said. "I met him one day at the airport, and he told me, `This is becoming a rat race. Some of these athletes are almost impossible to deal with. They want to know, 'if I come, will I play?' That's something I can't promise. This is wearing me down.'

"I could see what was happening. I'd take him fishing after the season, and he had become a chain smoker. He (like Mills) did a lot of social drinking. I was afraid he'd become an alcoholic. He lived life at a very fast pace.

"I stayed here all my life and ran a dairy. I've never had a cigarette, and I've never tasted beer or any alcoholic beverage. I know that's unusual. We took different paths."

BEGINNING OF THE END

Caught up in his "rat race," Combes saw his majestic career crash suddenly for his involvement in an illegal "slush fund" that struck down the UI basketball and football programs. It hit like a bombshell in December 1966 when assistant director Mel Brewer, embittered because "a Michigan man," Pete Elliott, was to replace Mills as athletic director, handed the UI administration records he had been keeping on three illegal funds.

A winless football season in 1961 probably inspired the official formation of an organized under-table plan. From April 1962 until December 1966, the football fund received $15,354.77 and disbursed $14,378.99. The basketball fund began in February 1964, receiving $10,520 from supporters and disbursing $7,043.96. Some $600 was transferred to a third fund — the Mills fund — and $220 was used for administrative travel expenses.

This money, obtained from alumni privately and at gatherings, mostly was used to distribute monthly payments of less than $50 to needy athletes. This was considered a routine approach employed by several Big Ten schools desirous of meeting recruiting challenges from nonconference schools that were permitted to hand out $15 per month in spending money, but it was illegal under Big Ten rules.

Future pros Rich Jones and Steve Kuberski and standout center Ron Dunlap were declared immediately ineligible. Combes, assistant Howie Braun and football coach Pete Elliott, bowing to a Big Ten "show cause" edict, ultimately were forced to resign.

If Combes brought east central Illinoisans some of their grandest sports moments, he wound up in the epicenter of the greatest trauma the university sports program has ever known. The Neale Stoner scandal was minor compared to this. Combes had grown up here, had a huge following and had waved the baton of success for more than 30 years. Elliott was the most popular man in three states. The groundswell of torn emotions grew to earthquake proportions.

To this day, townspeople who knew Combes personally aren't clear how much he knew, or how much he left to his take-charge recruiter, Braun, and to close friends like late insurance man Cy Vaughn.

Combes' integrity was such that he declined radio-TV overtures and wouldn't accept a free car, living modestly and stepping down in 1967 with a salary of $16,200. When it came to recruiting, he let Braun do it.

Said one who was close to the program: "Howie was the one out in the field, dealing with the competition. Harry seldom attended a high school game. When prospects came to campus, Howie brought them to Harry's office, sat them down and took them out again. Harry would never have mentioned anything like that (monthly payments) to a player."

When the story broke in Chicago, where the team was scheduled to play, Combes appeared stunned and confused by the magnitude of it.

Huge scandals also marked the careers of two of the greatest coaches of all time, Combes contemporaries Adolph Rupp at Kentucky and John Wooden at UCLA. And if historians will agree they should have known, and couldn't have been completely in the dark, the debate will continue as to how much they actually participated.

Best guess is that Combes had tunnel vision when it came to coaching, that he understood in a general way what was happening, that he had been assured by Mills that this was the way the game was played in the Big Ten and that he elected to let others handle the details. Some say he followed the advice of a recruit-expert friend who told him, "Harry, you coach 'em, we'll do what it takes to get 'em."

Said a former UI athlete: "Several of us were prepared to file affidavits stating that other Big Ten schools made similar offers, but that was discouraged. It wouldn't have accomplished anything to say that everybody was doing it, so we didn't."

Forced out of coaching, Combes' influence remained so strong that his support for Harv Schmidt made the next coach a done deal. But if Combes brooded about basketball defeats, imagine how much deeper this bored into his soul. He had absorbed a body blow from which he never fully recovered. No one suffered more through the "slush fund" ordeal.

Into the 1970s, he split time between the physical education department and the Department of Plant and Services where he handled civil defense responsibilities. He never returned to the whirl, retiring in 1973, and might have felt some bitterness at being, for the first time since his early teens, out of the mix.

In increasing bad health, he died in 1977 at 62. And to those who knew him best, he left this Earth as a gentleman of integrity, fierce intensity and utter reliability.

Name another who was raised here, starred here, coached here, reached Hall-of-Fame heights and stayed here. That's Harry Combes: Monticello's finest. Champaign's finest. The UI's finest.

Harry Combes was a man caught up in the culture, the abnormalties of the time. His commitment to Illinois was such that his life should have ended better.

BRUCE WEBER HIRED AT ILLINOIS
MAY 1, 2003

Illinois got a bargain in hiring Bruce Weber to succeed Bill Self as basketball coach.

CHAMPAIGN — Nobody, not even first choice Shirley Temple, could have tossed a nation on its ear singing "Over the Rainbow" the way replacement Judy Garland did in "The Wizard of Oz."

Then there was Danville's Gene Hackman, perhaps the 12th choice to play Popeye Doyle, who turned up the brim on his undersized hat and won an Oscar in making "The French Connection" the best picture in 1971.

It's all about casting. Just because Tom Cruise can demand $20 million doesn't mean he's perfect for a certain role — or that someone less ostentatious can't do it better. You don't suppose Tom would like to try "Sling Blade" ... uhmm ... do you?

Which brings us to Bruce Weber, a choice of substance over glitz. Offered $500,000 a year to coach Illini basketball, he has doubled his Southern Illinois salary. But that's merely half of what his predecessor, Bill Self, received here ... and a third of Self's anticipated $1.5 million deal at Kansas when camps and other outside revenue are figured in.

What does it mean? On one hand, you can say the Illini, as represented by Ron Guenther, elected not to run with the antelopes. Salaries have gone berserk, and Illinois has returned to a degree of sanity.

So when Weber himself, on two occasions, labeled Illinois among the "top 15 programs," it was time to nod in agreement and recognize that, until more returns are in, that's about right ... not top 10 ... lodged in a Big Ten pack behind Michigan State again ... not ready to join the arms race with Kentucky, Arizona, Florida and Duke, not geared to engage in the same monetary overemphasis as North Carolina, Maryland, Memphis and Louisville.

The national media came off underwhelmed.

With the story breaking early Tuesday afternoon, everybody who cared knew Weber was Illinois' pick well before suppertime. Yet USA Today had no one tracking it and had no story about it in Wednesday's editions. Compare that with Self's ballyhooed move to Kansas.

AOL Sports led with T.J. Ford's likely intention to leave Texas and the trials of Iowa State's Larry Eustachy, and ESPN did pretty much the same thing. Compare that with Self and Kansas.

Guenther, meanwhile, caught criticism from two major columnists for not acting faster, disregarding two important facts:

(1) Guenther reports to Chancellor Nancy Cantor, a stickler on diversity, and protocol prevented him from making any offers in less than seven days — and certainly none before he talked to at least one minority candidate. Guenther didn't move faster because he couldn't. He started the search on a Monday and had it wrapped up the next Tuesday, roughly one day longer than it took North Carolina to hire Roy Williams and Kansas to hire Self.

(2) Just because our hard-working media brethren thought Guenther should want Marquette's Tom Crean doesn't mean he was a Guenther favorite. Talk about Crean was pure speculation, which, times 10, became overwhelming ... and probably speeded up Crean's new contract.

In fact, there was so much misinformation spilled during the eight-day search that it is downright discouraging to be a part of the business. Oh, well. If it started over again tomorrow, it would play out exactly the same way with all of us expanding our imaginations and tasting our flavor of the day. We must fill the same space whether we know anything or not.

With all that background turbulence, Weber didn't exactly ride in on a white horse. Rob Judson's supporters are still out there. And some can't quite get used to the idea of Purdue and SIU producing the next UI star.

But consider this. If SIU were located in Ohio or north Texas, had won consecutive Missouri Valley titles in the same league with on-rushing Creighton, had beaten NCAA runner-up Indiana and reached the Sweet 16 in 2002 and kept on rolling without Rolan Roberts in 2003, would you feel differently?

Isn't he about where Gonzaga's Dan Monson was in 1999 (one NCAA appearance before moving to Minnesota), about where Kent State's Gary Waters was in 2001 (two NCAA trips in five years before taking the Rutgers' job)? Isn't he close to where Self was at Tulsa in 2000 (two NCAA appearances)?

We should cheer the fact he has roots in Illinois, has developed contacts in St. Louis, knows his way around Chicago. These are advantages. We should cheer the fact that he's down-to-earth honest, that the toughness of Gene Keady has rubbed off, that he knows all the subtleties of out-of-bounds plays and man-to-man defense, that he is renowned for "getting along" with players, fans and media.

"I truly believe I'm the right fit," he said Wednesday. "When I heard Ron list the criteria for the job, I told my assistant, 'If that's true, I'll be that coach.' I really believed that."

So the race is on. And, remember, the highest salary doesn't mean the best production. Imagine how the uniquely witty "Fargo" would have turned out if a high-priced blockbuster like Julia Roberts or Jodie Foster had been engaged in the role that won plain-looking Frances McDormand the Oscar in 1996.

She was the right person at the right time. These things happen all the time.

After a 3-3 start in the Big Ten, Weber's first Illini team won the school's first undisputed conference championship in a half-century with a 13-3 finish. The Illini went from there to a 37-2 season and the national championship game in his second season, and they were 26-7 in 2006 before slipping back in the pack.

RON TURNER LEADS ILLINI TITLE RUN
NOVEMBER 21, 2001

Illinois rolls toward its seventh Big Ten championship since World War II.

CHAMPAIGN — When Ron Turner's 1999 football team scored 178 points in the last four games of an 8-4 season, it was reasonable to assume the Illini would be a contender when 2001 rolled around.

After all, Kurt Kittner, Luke Butkus and Brandon Moore headed a crack sophomore class, Bobby Jackson was set to return from knee surgery and Turner had budding stars like Brandon Lloyd, Jerry Schumacher and Eugene Wilson.

However, a bumpy cobblestone path led them astray (5-6) in 2000. It was unexpected, then, by almost everyone except draft expert Mel Kiper Jr., that they would find their way aboard a magic carpet of wondrous finishes in 2001.

These Illini have climbed to No. 8 on the most comprehensive rating system (BCS) ever devised, and with a Thanksgiving victory against Northwestern — a result we never should take for granted — they could slip in among the half-dozen greatest Illini teams since World War II.

Following are the UI's only six Big Ten champions in that span:

— 1951, No. 4 in final AP poll: After a late letdown — 0-0 tie with Ohio State and a 3-0 win against Northwestern — the 9-0-1 Illini became the only undefeated UI bunch since 1927 when they routed Stanford 40-7.

— 1963, AP No. 3: The Butkus-Grabowski club tied Ohio State 20-20 and lost to Michigan 14-8 but made the Rose Bowl with a 13-0 Thanksgiving shutout of Michigan State and defeated Washington 17-7.

— 1946, AP No. 5: The war returnees revved it up from a 2-2 start, rallying to edge Wisconsin 27-21 and squeezing past Michigan 13-9, Iowa 7-0 and Ohio State 16-7 before splintering UCLA 45-14 to finish 8-2.

— 1983, AP No. 10: After a 28-18 loss at Missouri, Mike White's athletes beat No. 4 Iowa, No. 6 Ohio State, No. 8 Michigan and No. 19 Michigan State. The team would rank higher but for a 45-9 collapse vs. UCLA in the Rose Bowl.

— 1953, AP No. 7: After an opening 21-21 tie with Nebraska, the Caroline-Bates duo stood the Big Ten on its ear, but a late 34-7 loss at Wisconsin dropped the Illini into a title tie and out of the bowl picture.

— 1990, AP No. 25: The 8-4 team shared the Big Ten title but wasn't as good as the year before, when Jeff George sparked a 10th-ranked 10-2 club that lost only to No. 8 Colorado and No. 3 Michigan.

WHAT DOES IT MEAN?

First, even if Michigan beats Ohio State on Saturday, the Illini have clinched at least the Citrus Bowl. And with Ron Guenther and Jim Delany emphasizing the value of TV sets in the Chicago market, a 10-1 Illini club would, with help, have a shot at the Sugar, Fiesta or Orange bowls, that eighth BCS slot being worth more than $500,000 to each league member if Illinois is chosen.

Second, Turner is a cinch to win Big Ten Coach of the Year honors and should contend nationally.

Third, an Illini team that might have had only one all-league player (Wilson) at midseason has, under the winner-gets-the-spoils theory, put at least a half-dozen under serious consideration.

WHAT ABOUT THE FUTURE?

We have learned that one season does not a dynasty make.

The 1946 champs lost close ones in 1947 and tumbled to 5-3-1.

Illinois rode a toboggan in the early '50s, going from 9-0-1 to 4-5 in 1952, and then from 7-1-1 to 1-8 in 1954.

Butkus returned in 1964, but the Illini fell to Ohio State, Purdue and Michigan, finishing 6-3.

White had high hopes after 1983, but probation hit and the Illini slipped steadily in the mid-1980s.

Where will Turner's Illini go from here? Much depends on the nature of Big Ten competition. The league has seldom hit such a low: with only two Top 25 teams; with Michigan State's defeat of Notre Dame and the UI's win against Louisville standing as the league's quality wins vs. outside opposition; with Ohio State facing loss No. 5 at Michigan; with Penn State just recovering from its worst slump under Joe Paterno; with Purdue and Wisconsin falling from recent highs; with Michigan State returning to mediocrity after upsetting Michigan; with Northwestern picked to win the league but not even bowl eligible.

The league will come back. It always does. And if Illini eggs appear healthy, they're much too fragile to start counting the chickens.

Only about 45,000 fans turned out as Illinois defeated Northwestern, 34-28, to capture the undisputed Big Ten title. Thus ended a fortuitous seven-game win streak, Kurt Kittner coming through in the clutch while several rivals had problems at the quarterback position.

MACKOVIC COMBINES DUAL ROLE
AFTER 1990 SEASON

Coach-AD John Mackovic leads Illinois through turbulent times while winning 14 of 17 Big Ten football games.

CHAMPAIGN — John Mackovic has spent two harrowing, incredibly pressurized years in the dual role as athletic director and football coach. In addition to routine business, and while winning 14 of Illinois' last 17 Big Ten games (three straight bowl appearances), Mackovic has:

— Overseen the complicated merger of the old UI Athletic Association into the university;

— Joined in a critical administration decision to drop investigator Mike Slive at midstream in the maddening, 17-month NCAA investigation of basketball, a move that led to elimination of all major charges in the NCAA Official Inquiry;

— Operated the department budget in the black for two-plus years (after inheriting a $2.7 million deficit and while paying more than $1 million annually in debt reduction);

— Participated at the Big Ten level in bringing Penn State into the Big Ten, and now in creating 1993 football schedules with the Nittany Lions included;

— Hired fund raiser Steve Greene to resume the capital building project, while working with the university toward a long-range $30 million renovation of Memorial Stadium;

— Gotten a stalled tennis facility moving toward an August completion ... cleared up the financial problems of the baseball stadium when Lou Proano became unable to make pledged payments ... ordered the formulation of a point system for preferred seating of season ticket holders, still a year off ... upgraded Huff Gym for volleyball and other future uses... approved a new Armory running track.

Mackovic and others in athletic administration have been working 24-hour days.

And yet there was Mackovic bright and early Monday morning, looking as scrubbed and fresh as ever, embarking on what he calls "a new three-to-five-year program" as combination coach-director.

"I'm happy," said Mackovic. "I like what I'm doing. And I like what I see in the future.

"Personally, I look at life in five-year blocks. When I took the dual job, I said I'd evaluate the situation in three to five years. I'm now pushing that back to another three to five years."

Mackovic states the merger of the Athletic Association with the university went easier than the administration anticipated.

"There was great cooperation," he said. "We didn't go kicking and screaming. And we were able to create financial order quickly in the face of the $2.7 million deficit. We're on course, and this summer will mark our third fiscal year in the black. And now, with Steve Greene coming on board April 1, we'll have someone to handle our long-range building plans and help coordinate our endowment drive."

In the next five years, Mackovic would like to see an administration building (costing $5 to $7 million) move from dream to reality. At the same time, he intends to finish work on the track, and create a fund for lights at the baseball field.

"Coaches are talking of moving baseball back into May, so lights would be a nice addition." he said.

Mackovic reminds that his regime was aided by the fact that baseball and track stadiums were built when he took over, and the air-supported bubble was up over the stadium. With both the bubble and the AstroTurf expected to last until nearly 2000, consideration of a return to grass at the stadium won't come up until the turn of the century.

That would come during Mackovic's third five-year segment.

John Mackovic was successful but aloof, and was wearing down under the dual role with the NCAA investigation taking up so much of his time. A year later, after falling to 4-4 in the Big Ten, he was ready to give up his administration chores and, receiving football offers from Arizona State and Texas, departed to lead the Longhorns.

FIRST OF THREE COLUMNS ON LOU HENSON
MARCH 11, 1991

Lou Henson engaged Bob Knight in a classic locker-room confrontation after a 70-58 Indiana victory.

CHAMPAIGN — Illini basketball coach Lou Henson is at a disadvantage in a shouting match.

First, it isn't his nature to look for trouble. Second, he never, under any circumstances, swears.

So, when he's hit from behind with crude profanity that would repel a drunken sailor, his strongest response is an appropriate: "Classic bully!"

"When," Henson was asked Monday, "are you going to lay all this stuff behind and engage in normal basketball competition?"

"I had that attitude Sunday," Henson replied, referring to the season-ending 70-58 home loss to Indiana.

"I don't want to carry this on forever. I never feel good about something like this, and in 36 years I've never had an incident like this after a game.

"But what do you do when the opposing coach attacks you? All these past years I've never had a problem with opposing coaches. I've always tried to avoid this sort of thing and, now, here we are in the center of it. At my age (59), I just want to finish my career and become a good grandfather. I don't want to be in the middle of constant controversy.

"I'm concerned about this. I've gone back and re-examined this to make sure I'm not the problem."

In his self-analysis, Henson elected to shake hands with coach Tom Davis at Iowa even though his feelings toward Davis and his staff are not positive.

Henson said he entered the Assembly Hall locker area with the intent of congratulating the Indiana coaches, just as he had done in a 109-74 loss at Indiana. He said he had actually passed the Indiana locker room — which was open — when he was showered by a wave of the worst-kind expletives from the rival head coach.

"I've never looked for trouble," said Henson. "That's why people say I'm boring. If somebody writes negative things about Illinois, I let it go, I don't challenge people.

"But there are times when you're forced to defend yourself. I was being verbally attacked. What else could I do? Some say you should turn the other cheek. I don't know what you should do."

What Henson did, believe it or not, was make his "class bully" response and dare his overweight rival to "step outside."

"I'll probably get a letter of reprimand from the conference," said Henson. "You're not supposed to make disparaging remarks about other coaches and schools. But I wonder, do other people who knock coaches and schools receive letters (from Big Ten commissioner Jim Delany)?"

In attempting to analyze what set off the anti-Henson explosion, Henson pooh-poohed the belief that it was a violent reaction to his "conspiracy theory" — that negative-recruiting rivals cleverly spread false "street talk" of Illini misdeeds in recruiting. This would date back through the Indiana-initiated claims that Illinois cheated on Lowell Hamilton, the first Henson-recruited player that the Hoosiers really sought in this state and didn't get.

Henson, instead, pointed to releases by the Illinois sports information office.

"It wasn't the fact that we are promoting players for postseason honors. That's not it." said Henson. "It's that our SID office has been sending out material showing our accomplishments over the past 10 years, showing Illinois rated No. 7 nationally in winning percentage (73 percent) and Indiana 13th (71.7), and other stats casting us in a favorable light."

Publicity departments routinely mail such material, hyping All-America candidates and promoting their programs. Pondering the reaction, Henson said:

"I've seen a lot of top coaches, but I haven't seen any who are out to belittle other coaches who haven't been as successful as they are. It's like a big bully picking on a smaller kid, or kicking someone when he's down. We've been down here at Illinois. We've been suffering. And then we have someone come along and further complicate things with this kind of a put-down.

"It's because I'm not accepting 'my proper place,' accepting the intimidation. What was said at the postgame press conference is just another way of making it appear that I'm doing a bad job. There are coaches who are always involved in tearing down somebody else's program."

Henson described it as "nothing new," recalling that Illini fans, including wife Mary, were insulted and embarrassed by postgame remarks on the public address system at Indiana a year ago.

"I'm not going to speak about this any further to the media," said Henson. "But I'll be interested to see what happens. I'll be interested to see what kind of report is filed by (referee) Tom Rucker. You're not supposed to berate an official after the game."

Henson has gained many fans for the performance of his job under difficult circumstances the past year, and he gained many more by his combative response to Sunday's stunning developments.

Lou Henson never looked for trouble but couldn't avoid it when Bobby Knight erupted on him at the Assembly Hall. Knight often ridiculed and made accusations against Henson, both publicly and privately, throughout the years. This was just one more example of Knight's crude behavior.

MARCH 14, 1996

Lou Henson retires in the wake of another three-point loss in postseason play, this to Alabama in the NIT.

CHAMPAIGN — Perhaps Lou Henson used up all his good fortune in winning 14 of Illinois' last 16 overtime games.

Lady Luck never smiled on his Illini in the postseason. Never.

Going back to 1980, Illinois has been eliminated by consecutive margins of 2, 5, 3, 3, 3, 8, 2, 1, 3, 2, 2, 17, 7, 6 and, Wednesday night, 3 points.

Just one frustrating, mind-searing setback after another ... a lone double- figure loss out of 15 outings, that to Vanderbilt in 1993 ... the Illini seemingly snakebit when it counted most.

Even if we philosophize that virtually everyone except the NCAA and NIT champions wind up on a sour note, it's nevertheless tough to accept such a lengthy string of postseason disappointment.

How long did it take to outlive the 68-67 NCAA fiasco with Austin Peay in 1987? Or the inability to make free throws while Villanova rallied with eye-popping three-pointers in the closing minutes of 1988? Or upset losses at the hands of Dayton in 1982 (61-58) and 1990 (88-86)?

Three years ago Illinois had Georgetown on the run, 73-67, with Kiwane Garris on a breakaway, but the game turned suddenly and the final five minutes were all Georgetown, 84-77. Last year Illinois performed efficiently against Tulsa, but a 60-56 lead evaporated in the last four minutes into a 68-62 defeat.

And the biggest hits of all were the 54-51 grinder with Kentucky in Lexington in 1984, and the 83-81 Final Four loss to Michigan on a rebound putback in the last two seconds.

In fairness, the Illini were 17-15 in postseason play since 1980, but they did not get their share in wins against opponents of equal caliber.

Wednesday was all too typical. Alabama caught a refreshing breeze of inspiration, breaking the back of the Illini team with an incredible streak of three-point shots to turn a 42-32 Illinois lead into a 72-69 NIT triumph.

The Tide drained 9 of 13 treys during a game-deciding 35-15 run.

From assistant coach Dick Nagy's view, it was more than an Alabama hot streak. It was the case of one team playing with passion, and the other unable to reach back into a reservoir that had gone dry.

You can cite various reasons. There is always uncertainty within the ranks when a coach retires (the team is 1-4 since he made it public). Jerry Hester was never the same after spraining his ankle. Kevin Turner, whose season never measured up to autumn promise, had that stunned look after a quick trip to Chicago where his 23-year-old brother, Kenny, had been killed in an outbreak of gang war. Jerry Gee battled through another game in which his leaping rival had a one- foot reach advantage.

So the new head coach, whoever he is, inherits a club that couldn't win the close ones in a 7-for-11 final tailspin, and he takes over a program with a distressing postseason record.

It still boggles the mind to think back on the number of narrow NCAA losses during the Henson era. It seemed like something always went wrong, and that includes 1989 when the Flying Illini lost to a Michigan team that they had defeated 96-84 and 89-73 before Bill Frieder was replaced as coach.

JULY 25, 2007

Lou Henson displays the power to persevere as he battles abdominal cancer.

CHAMPAIGN — It is appropriate, perhaps, that a higher power tests our sturdiest members with the most severe challenges.

The car-accident loss of an adult son is beyond anyone's ability to comprehend.

Nor was it enough that Lou Henson had to stand erect after dealing with Michigan's third-time's-a-charm upset in the 1989 Final Four, the unlikely rallies by Iowa and Purdue and the devastating NCAA setbacks against Villanova and Austin Peay. He somehow handled the persistent insults of Bobby Knight and a vengeful NCAA which, after a long and excruciating investigation, used "lack of institutional control" to apply sanctions when little of significance was uncovered.

Now, darn it, he's under the care of Carle Hospital's Dr. Kendrith Rowland due to the return of abdominal cancer (non-Hodgkin's lymphoma) that popped up four years ago. Before you overreact, know that the 75-year-old Henson will bounce back. Resiliency is his specialty. This episode was uncovered in the early stages through a routine physical. You might see him on the golf course this week in Savoy.

But Tuesday found him at Carle taking four doses of chemotherapy in an eight-hour stretch: Cytoxan, Vincristine, Rituxan and the steroid Prednisone. At the same time, he received nausea medication and soon he'll get a shot of Neulasta to strengthen his cells from Tuesday's attack. He is obliged to continue shorter treatments every three weeks for eight to 10 months.

It's not nearly as serious as four years ago. It is the kind of cancer that can be successfully treated. But, at the same time, it might never completely disappear. Even in remission, it's always there.

Henson is not easily thrown off course. After 21 seasons and 423 triumphs at Illinois, he coached again at New Mexico State where, accepting an emergency assignment for $1 per month, he ultimately signed a contract that led to four 20-win seasons in his last seven. And he finished with 779 career victories despite losing 18 wins due to recruiting infractions imposed on his Aggie predecessor. The NCAA denied an appeal to reclaim those 18.

He would have made it to 800 anyway if not for health issues. Four summers ago in a checkup at Carle, Dr. Jeff Kyrouac suspected cancer by, in Henson's words, "poking around in my abdomen." Tests confirmed non-Hodgkin's lymphoma at Stage 4 and spreading back near the pelvis. The bulldog in Henson wouldn't let him retire, and he coached the Aggies while taking chemotherapy that season. But the following September, in a likely reaction to his complicated medication, a weakened Henson was struck down by viral encephalitis (inflammation of the brain).

That was the truly difficult time. Henson dined with a recruit, couldn't eat and put off discussions until the following morning. He has no recollection of the next 3 1/2 weeks. In and out of consciousness, he "woke up" in El Paso with his weight dwindling from 183 pounds to 136 and no movement in his right leg.

Once while watching golf on ESPN with a blind-like stare, he suddenly asked daughter Lisa: "What club should I use? What club?"

Lisa replied: "How far out are you?"

Which drew laughter from wife Mary who joked: "Way, waaayy out!" Lou doesn't recall the incident. He was hallucinating.

Henson has gradually advanced from bed to a wheelchair to a cane and now is walking with a slight limp. Golf course directors allow him to drive his cart right up to the ball wherever it is (except on the greens).

An early riser (how about 4:30 a.m.), who now admits to an occasional afternoon nap, Henson strides out of his south Champaign home as the community's most popular septuagenarian.

Admittedly, he was once the object of catcalls by bitter critics (be thankful, Lou, you missed the real Internet era). Now everywhere he turns he is greeted with wide smiles and eager handshakes.

Lou spans the local culture. He's just as relaxed with the university president as the guys on the softball field. Bridge is a favorite evening pastime, and he's nearly impossible to beat at checkers. He enjoys golf regardless of his score, and whether he's kicking up the sunrise dew with Jim Terry and Bill Vaughn at Savoy, or tackling Champaign Country Club with George Shapland and Tom Harrington.

The memory recalls 1989 when, at the peak of his career, he declined a special breakfast with the nation's top coaches and network broadcasters to sit down with an old geezer who once loaned his program a car many years before.

Henson's popularity isn't restricted to his "permanent address" in the heart of Illinois. Whereas a street was named for him in Champaign, New Mexico Route 28 between Las Cruces, N.M., and El Paso, Texas, a stretch lined with onion fields and pecan groves, is now Lou Henson Highway.

The Pan American Center, which he helped build long ago as NMSU athletic director, now features a court named in his honor. In a gesture to his alma mater, the Hensons made a $100,000 endowment gift in the name of Lou Jr.

Lou and Mary plan to spend roughly half their time here. If this is a tough six months, they'll battle through it just like they always do. It's a bumpy ride, but this isn't their first rodeo.

Lou Henson continues to forge ahead, spending half his time in Las Cruces and the other half in Champaign. He watches basketball on TV during the winter, and calls friends here every week to discuss the Illini. One of my most memorable experiences was watching Lou and Mary work the crowd on a warm Saturday night in downtown Champaign.

SCHMIDT POSTS MEMORABLE WIN
DECEMBER 22, 1968

Illinois pulled off one of its premier victories under Harv Schmidt in snapping Houston's home win streak at 60.

HOUSTON — It was just 12 years ago in December that Harv Schmidt captained Illinois to a triumph over San Francisco, snapping the longest winning streak in modern collegiate basketball history: 60.

The Frisco club had just lost Bill Russell and K.C. Jones through graduation and Illinois absolutely tore the visitors apart in Huff Gym, and made like a national title contender until 6-foot-8 George Bon Salle was lost through ineligibility.

Last night Illinois stopped another 60-game streak, the long home victory string of Houston which was established through the era of Elvin Hayes. Obviously, Houston is not the same club without Hayes but the Cougars are nevertheless physically formidable and it took a courageous performance by an inspired Illini club to pull it off, 97-84.

There were several ironies to the outcome. Not only the two 60-game figures, but the fact that Notre Dame, which beat Houston here back in January 1965, also lost its luggage on the flight in.

Actually, the Illini didn't lose their luggage, it was just late in arriving Friday night and, coupled with a minor traffic accident involving Schmidt, prevented the Illini from practicing. So Schmidt bought a ball at the Shamrock Hilton Hotel and sent the team through a practice in a room there. It was reminiscent of the triumph in Chicago last season over Texas Western, the only difference being that Illinois employed a 1-3-1 zone to beat Western and tore up Houston's 1-3-1 zone in Delmar Gym.

Mediocre shooting by Illinois (.384) kept this result from being more decisive.

Houston had more physical ability but Illinois was sounder fundamentally ... and more important, said Schmidt:

"Did you ever see such character on the court? We fought them off. We wouldn't let them catch up. I've never been happier. Imagine a victory over Houston in Houston."

It was, without question, a fantastic Christmas present.

Harv Schmidt was at the height of his popularity, drawing standing ovations at the Assembly Hall, with the unit of Dave Scholz, Fred Miller, Mike Price and the late Jodie Harrison and Greg Jackson. That Illini team went 19-5, trailing only Purdue in the Big Ten. It was a fun group to be around.

FIRST OF TWO COLUMNS ON LON KRUGER
MARCH 18, 1997

Lon Kruger's athletes get blamed for something they didn't do.

CHARLOTTE, N.C. — Losing in the NCAA's Southeast Regional was difficult enough, but having it stuffed up your nose by an ever-growing fabricated postgame story left Illini coach Lon Kruger with a sour taste Monday.

"Whatever works," he conceded with a touch of despair.

Please explain, they're asking at WMAQ, ESPN and elsewhere, why Illini basketball players would intentionally disrespect Chattanooga's team?

The answer is obvious and has been oft-repeated: They weren't.

Why, then, did the Chattanooga contingent react so sharply after defeating the Illini 75-63 in Charlotte on Sunday?

First, you have to understand the mind-set. These Tennesseans make Rodney Dangerfield look like he's bubbling with self-esteem. Their every press conference in Charlotte was marked by stories of how these underdogs get no respect, how good teams won't schedule them, how the Southern Conference is overlooked in the polls and downplayed in the NCAA seedings.

The coach, Mack McCarthy, was recently on a committee that changed the Moccasins to Mocs — please don't call them Mockingbirds — and altered the school name from UT-Chattanooga to Chattanooga (remember, just because you're paranoid doesn't mean somebody isn't out to get you).

"They were celebrating (beforehand) and yelling things about the Final Four like we wasn't even there," said Mocs' ungrammatical point guard Willie Young.

Responses:

"They need to get their ears checked," responded Illini forward Brian Johnson. "Do you think we're dumb enough to look past a game in the round of 32?"

"We never mentioned the Final Four," said UI senior Chris Gandy.

"We heard the hoopla when they found out Providence had won (over Duke). We wanted to send them a message," said Southern Conference MVP Johnny Taylor.

Responses:

"I came into the locker room and told the players that Providence had the game won with 15 seconds to go," said Kruger. "There was no reaction."

"We didn't care who won," said Johnson.

"Our kids took offense at what they heard. They were singing the CBS song, the ESPN song, the Illinois song. They were singing every song in the world. It was like a pep rally," said McCarthy.

Responses:

"There was no singing of any kind," said Kruger.
"I don't even know how the CBS song goes," said UI junior Bryant Notree.

That's because there are no lyrics to it. Filled with victory, McCarthy was becoming an exaggerating jokester.

Irritated by the unfortunate postscript to Illinois' final game, and aware that ESPN was using McCarthy's sound bite over and over, Kruger talked to his players Monday and called McCarthy.

He did not appear entirely satisfied with the response, although he said McCarthy agreed that the Illini players were not disrespectful, and felt the matter had been blown our of proportion. On Monday's statewide radio show, Kruger said he was told that a Chattanooga team manager walking past the Illini locker room heard the UI's customary pregame ritual and carried the message two doors down.

What happened after that is pure speculation but, said Kruger, "There was no singing. There was no rapping. There was no reference to the opponent. There was no mention of the Final Four. There was no reaction when Providence won. It was just Jerry Hester challenging each guy to tell what he'd bring to the table in the game Sunday, and the players responding individually. It can get a little loud, but it's their way of getting charged up.

"This is all very unfortunate. It's entirely at our expense and it makes us look foolish. Our players are really hurt by it."

If McCarthy and Chattanooga had any class, they would publicly apologize for this silliness. They could not have heard what did not happen.

That said, there's nothing wrong with internal pretending in order to get fired up, as long as it stays internal. But they're apparently so caught up in their "no respect" motif, so consumed by their underdog, us-against-the-world theme that it probably hasn't occurred how childish and lacking in sportsmanship their postgame revelations were.

No wonder they get no respect. They don't deserve any.

Once the ball gets rolling on ESPN, there isn't much you can do about it. This was a clever ploy by Chattanooga to emphasize their Rodney Dangerfield situation.

MARCH 2, 1998

Overlooked coach Lon Kruger deserved a Coach of the Decade award.

CHAMPAIGN — Heaven save us from our impatient brethren who can't wait until the regular season is over to fill out ballots for award winners: MVPs, Heisman picks, all-stars, Coaches of the Year.

Too often we take the easy way out in honoring coaches. We pick the champion. He is always deserving.

Thought processes should go deeper, but they seldom do. Illinois' Lou Henson, whose 11-7 Illini finished far behind Indiana (17-1) and Michigan (15-3) in 1993, is the Big Ten's only non-champion to receive the award in the last seven years.

League voters chose another champion this year: Tom Izzo. He did a superb job but, face it O.J. fans, these are bad times for juries. And this was clearly a fouled vote. Even as the deadline on the sheet mistakenly was dated March 9, many ballots were filled out before key late-season games were played.

So, I say: OK, Izzo is Big Ten Coach of the Year. Illinois' Lon Kruger is Big Ten Coach of the Decade.

In the modern era, not even Purdue's Gene Keady in 1996 matched his act.

This is, remember, a league dominated by future pros. Steve Smith led Michigan State champs in 1990. Ohio State ruled twice with Jimmy Jackson. Indiana had Calbert Cheaney, Alan Henderson and Brian Evans. Glenn Robinson ignited Purdue's threepeat. Minnesota had two 1997 National Basketball Association first-rounders.

The Illini have been overlooked by NBA scouts, had no preseason All-Big Ten pick and wouldn't have had anyone on the all-league quintet if deep thinkers hadn't seen Illinois up top and reasoned: "My goodness, the co-champ should have an all-star ... and Kevin Turner scored the most points."

While the NBA awaits the Spartan ringleader (Mateen Cleaves), an innovative UI coach manufactured an effective offense with minimal points in the post, without a dominant rebounder (the UI outrebounded 3 of 16 foes), with inconsistent bench scoring, without a penetrating, beat-your-defender point guard, with a nonshooting former walk-on (Brian Johnson) at power forward, and with a Simeon afterthought (Turner) as his scoring leader.

The Illini won with defense, leading 16-game stats in three areas: points allowed (62), field goal defense (41 percent) and three-point defense (29 percent). This is a team thing, stemming directly from the coach. And they did it without anyone in the top 10 in blocked shots or steals.

But essentially, my argument is this: When you think of the Bulls, you think of Michael Jordan. When someone mentions Duke, it's Mike Krzyzewski. In some cases, a player overshadows the coach. In others, vice versa.

Tell me who you visualize when Michigan State is mentioned. Outstanding as he was, it isn't Izzo. Cleaves is the man at Michigan State. He is the quarterback. At Illinois, Kruger does everything except take the snap.

Yes, Michigan State was great in Sunday's 99-96 loss to Purdue. But the Spartans also were mediocre in edging Northwestern in OT and nipping Wisconsin. And they were fortunate to catch Michigan (which won early) the second time when Maceo Baston was out.

In direct meetings, the UI won 84-63 in Champaign and saw a 16-point lead in East Lansing destroyed not by some clever team strategy, but by Cleaves' unstoppable long-shooting binge.

Perhaps the biggest factor in Kruger's favor was the consistent readiness of his club. How many years would you need to research through the archives to find a Big Ten team that never trailed at the 10-minute mark of any league game?

The Illini were steady on the road (six wins) and finished without a loss to Michigan, Indiana or Iowa for the first time since the 1943

Whiz Kids.

We're talking history here.

Kruger primed the pump, getting maximum output, without demeaning his athletes, without badgering refs ... really, without offending anyone.

"Most coaches take a negative approach with their players," former DePaul coach Joey Meyer said during his one-year sabbatical. "I have studied 15 coaches this season, and Kruger is by far the most positive."

That alone is worth the 1990's Coach of the Decade.

Kruger's clever matchups and his strategy in using different defenses on the same possession gave opponents fits. Illinois wound up sharing the championship, and it was based on a coaching performance matching any in Illini history.

LOU TEPPER WAS A GRITTY COMPETITOR
OCTOBER 4, 1994

Diabetes forces football coach Lou Tepper to lead a disciplined lifestyle.

CHAMPAIGN — Lou Tepper is a disciplinarian because, out of necessity, he is so disciplined himself.

"When you 'shoot up' (with insulin) at least three times a day, and you test your sugar count four times a day, it is rare that you put it out of your mind," he said.

"There is always the concern that you might lose control. If you were unable to discipline yourself, and do things with regularity, you could have a serious problem."

The 49-year-old Fighting Illini football coach discovered he had diabetes when he was a 22-year-old physical education instructor and coach at New Hampshire. He was just one year out of Rutgers, where he led the football team in interceptions as a junior and tackles as a senior.

"I had been warned that I had an 85 percent chance of having diabetes because my father was diabetic, and there was diabetes on my mother's side," he said. "The doctor didn't have to tell me. I knew immediately because of the symptoms. When the blood stream gets full of sugar, you become sluggish and urinate constantly. I went to the doctor and told him."

For 11 months, Tepper took a pill that prompts the pancreas to produce insulin. But for more than a quarter of a century, he has given himself the sugar-consuming protein hormone hypodermically. I became aware of it several years ago when he routinely removed a kit from his desk and gave himself a shot during an interview.

"No, I'm not squeamish about the needle," he said. "It's been with me all my life. My father was found to have diabetes about a year after insulin was discovered, around 1926 or 1927. Prior to that, diabetics generally ate very little, lost weight, went into a coma and died. When my father started taking insulin, it had to be refrigerated and the needles kept in alcohol. It was a problem to travel anywhere, and he had to keep it cold at work.

"And, at that time, the only way to test the blood sugar was with a urine strip, which was color-coded and would tell you what your count was 30 minutes ago."

Presently, Tepper tests himself four times a day by pricking his thumb or middle finger for a blood sample. The digits remain sore all the time.

"I try to keep my blood count between 90 and 120," he said. "And I weigh every morning. I was 177 as a senior in college, and I'm at 173 now. For me, 180 is the high-water mark.

"I jog 20 miles a week during the offseason, and I jog roughly 12 miles (four miles on three occasions) a week during the season. When I jog at noon, I don't have to take insulin because the exercise essentially does the same job of working off the sugar."

Game days are the toughest. Tepper eats four hours before kickoff, and lets the blood sugar run a tad high before going onto the field. He carries crackers with him on the sideline, not always eating them. He tests again after the postgame press conference.

"Actually, my physical condition is probably better because I am a diabetic," he says. "I'm active and I exercise, and I'm not going to let it beat me. My heart rate is 38 and my blood pressure is 120 over 70. Insurance agents tell me what great shape I'm in, and then my premiums come back three or four times higher than anybody else's. That part is frustrating."

Tepper's strong religious convictions do not stem from his problem.

"I committed to Christ in 1965 when I was a college sophomore," he said. "I was at a physical peak with no health worries. There is no relationship."

Nor, he believes, did diabetes have anything to do with his recent eye (detached retina) problem.

"Genetically, I have weak and thin retinas," he explained. "When the season is over, or at the conclusion of recruiting, I'll probably need to have laser surgery to reenforce the retina of the surgery I just had."

Tepper is too much of a disciplinarian to let a pressing problem drift out of control. The fact is, he must be attentive to his own special needs every four to six hours, every day of every month of every year.

Lou Tepper, who ran defense for John Mackovic, might have been successful as head coach at Illinois if he could have kept Greg Landry as offensive coordinator. But that relationship blew up and the program turned south. Tepper still has a wonderful forgiving nature. When we had our differences, he prayed for me.

PLAYERS

FIRST OF TWO COLUMNS ON DEE BROWN
DECEMBER 1, 2002

Dee Brown's third game as an Illini indicated an ultra-bright future.

CHAMPAIGN — Dee Brown is a tad under 6 feet tall.

That's a statistic we can be most thankful for because (1) it's all the better to outrun you, my dear, and (2) if he was 6-6 with that speed, he'd be joining Charlie Villanueva — and perhaps a couple of those North Carolina youngsters you'll see here Tuesday night — as a prospect for next year's NBA draft.

So, for those of us planning to hang around these parts for the next four years, ain't it nice to know — I say, ain't it nice to know — you've got a friend ... for the duration?

In two exhibitions and three games, Dee has established himself as the fizz in Bill Self's drink, as the energy propelling a restructured Illini basketball team.

"Dee dominated the last nine minutes of today's game," said Self after Illinois, with the collar starting to tighten as Brian Cook sat down with his fourth foul at 9:01, turned a 54-46 lead into an 85-56 drubbing of Western Illinois on Sunday.

"There wasn't much energy in the building, and what energy there was, Dee created."

Brown had two steals and a near-steal to extend the lead back into double figures, and classmate Deron Williams caught the idea with a steal that he turned into a three-point play. Then Brown forced an over-and-back miscue, and the rampaging Illini led 76-54 by the time Cook returned.

During this stretch run, Brown served up five assists among six UI baskets, capping it with his own trey. He closed with 10 assists, a number topped by current New York Knick Frank Williams once last year, when he handed out 11 against Minnesota in the Big Ten tournament.

"I thought Dee and Deron were duds in the first half," Self said.

"They were passive. They didn't play to their intangibles, and I was on them pretty hard.

"We had Brian back, and he played fine, but when the ball went inside to Brian, everybody stopped. We ran better offense in the first two games without Brian. I anticipated that this might happen. There was too much standing and not enough ball and body movement."

Believe it or not, this is Brown's team. He brings it up, sets the tone and stokes the fire.

"His personality," Self said, "is the whole deal. He doesn't have to make shots to be effective. When he's bubbly and playing with energy, it impacts everybody.

"I've never seen him not bouncy, but I've seen him more bouncy on some occasions than on others."

It is not unusual for Illini teams to fall under the direction of freshman point guards.

The first since the NCAA ruled freshmen eligible was Derek Harper in 1981, and he joined forces with another rookie playmaker, Bruce Douglas, in 1983. Douglas holds the UI career record for assists with 765 (roughly six a game).

Steve Bardo was limited to 10 starts in 1987 on a team with experienced guards Tony Wysinger, Doug Altenberger and Glynn Blackwell. Rennie Clemons stepped in as a rookie regular in 1991 but had a cushion with Larry Smith returning for a fifth season. Then came Richard Keene in 1993, and he relied heavily on Clemons until another crack freshman, Kiwane Garris, arrived for a four-year stint. Cory Bradford was a second-year "freshman" in 1998 when he was forced to play out of position at point, and Frank Williams was likewise in school a year before he became eligible in 1999.

So Brown follows an impressive line of freshmen who have taken over Illini teams. And he might be the swiftest of the bunch.

When Self referred to him as "the Tasmanian devil," it was with a smile. Brown has speed, skills and the personality to handle the pressure.

And, thankfully, he's not 6-6 or we wouldn't see him for very long.

Dee Brown always had a harder edge than his fans realized, and his level of confidence allowed him to start at a higher level than most rookies. Newly into the Top 25, Illinois rocked North Carolina 92-65 two days later and rolled to a 25-7 season.

DECEMBER 29, 2004

Dee Brown becomes the "face of basketball" for Illinois and the nation in 2004-05.

LAS VEGAS — "Dee for threeee!" is music to Illini ears. And the vibes are sweeping through a newly attentive nation.

With a flashy, flamboyant style and a personality to match, UI junior Dee Brown has captured lightning in a bottle. He is riding herd on a stampede that includes 26 victories in the UI's last 28 games.

His trademark braids and white headband are copied by youths, wildly popular with his female following and readily accepted among the elders of Illini Nation.

It takes talent to excel, but this story is not exclusively about talent. Arguments can be made in support of several members of the nation's No. 1 basketball team. The UI's smooth-working guards depend on each other. This is about personality, charisma and the ability to uplift more than just a basketball program.

With Brown, there is none of the controversy that clouded the career of backcourt predecessor Frank Williams.

And if Cory Bradford drew a nation's attention by draining treys in a record 88 consecutive games, Brown draws a greater audience by making his teammates better (13 assists Monday against Longwood). Bradford brought fans to their feet in Chicago's United Center with a last-gasp three-pointer to edge Indiana. Brown brought Chicago fans to their feet with a dive that failed to save a ball from going out of bounds.

"Dee is our poster child," predicted his former coach, Bill Self, when Brown was recruited out of Proviso East High School. High-scoring Brian Cook might have been a senior and the first option, but that Big Ten champion was led by a freshman.

"Dee has always had that quality," UI publicist Kent Brown said. "And he is very approachable. It helps us immeasurably when a student-athlete enjoys and understands that role. Frank didn't have that kind of outgoing personality and didn't give himself to the role of being interviewed, and that may be part of the reason he was misunderstood by the media and the fans. Dee recognizes that he can use the media to shape his perception.

"The attention can get overwhelming at times, particularly around Christmas. There have been so many autograph requests that Bruce (Weber) had to call a halt to it. And Dee is approached more than anyone."

Standing in the baggage line Tuesday morning at O'Hare International Airport, Dee was hailed by a worker who recognized no one else. Everywhere he goes, people point to him. We can argue who is the best player — Dee or Deron Williams or Luther Head — but nationally, Dee is the face of this team. Kids see the white headband and want to imitate him. Fans swarm to him.

Smiled Brown on Tuesday: "I never really knew what poster child meant. It was kind of a joke. But now I'm beginning to understand what it means."

He is, Mr. Barkley, a role model. And there he was at the Las Vegas airport, signing again and posing for pictures in front of an orange-clad welcoming party shouting I-L-L, I-N-I.

Said UI fund-raiser Shawn Wax: "Dee has a magical presence. He emits a pizzazz that transcends youngsters, students, faculty and fans in general. He is bringing Illini people out of the woodwork."

Wax is in Las Vegas to meet potential contributors, some of whom are traveling from California to see the top-ranked Illini. Wins might not elicit gifts, but a No. 1 ranking doesn't hurt.

Brown understands his position in the scheme of things and what it can mean to his future.

"I just try to avoid problems, go to class and give off a positive image," he said. "I love the kids. They are by far the most important. And it's special to get the love of the older fans. I'm just trying to use basketball to my advantage. I grew up around violence on the West Side. A lot of my guys are involved with gangs and drugs. I'm trying to stay out of trouble. I came to Illinois for four years and to graduate."

Nor did he come alone. Dee helped to recruit his summer teammate, James Augustine, now a third-year starter. And when Texan Williams questioned the advisability of coming aboard as a second point guard, Dee soothed him with words of confidence.

"I called Deron's mom and told her it would work out. Deron bought in, and there has never been any jealousy. Recruiting for Illinois, that's what I do," he said.

The fans recognize his passion and loyalty, and they are forming a mountain of support. The Illini didn't pack the United Center for games against Cal, Clemson and Arkansas, much less Bradley. But, with Brown spearheading a No. 1 team, they had standing room only for Oregon this month. This meant thousands of dollars to the

UI program.

There are routinely empty seats in the Assembly Hall for meaningless games during the Christmas break when students are gone and the faculty is on vacation, but seats were filled Monday for a Longwood opponent that most fans never heard of. That's more income for Ron Guenther, who now calls some of these big basketball games "small football games" in terms of the gate. Contests in Indianapolis, North Little Rock, Ark., and Washington drew larger orange-colored turnouts than originally projected.

Two key games set up Illinois for its No. 1 ranking. Brown already had been named Big Ten Player of the Week when he sparked back-to-back routs of Gonzaga and Wake Forest. In those games he made 13 of 22 shots, gathered nine rebounds, served 15 assists and had no turnovers. Through 12 games, he is shooting 56.6 percent from the field and 45.8 on treys, with 20 steals and a spectacular 71-26 assist-to-turnover ratio.

This is not to say he is more of a perfectionist than gymnast Justin Spring, or more internationally famous than Canadian hurdler Perdita Felicien. But he, more than anyone else, has put a happy face on an athletic program that is struggling on the football side and, a decade before he arrived, was serving NCAA sanctions about confusing and fan-killing basketball charges.

The remarkable aspect was the way people of all ages and in all places migrated to Dee. He was the true rock star of the Illini group although other teammates contributed just as much on the court for a Final Four team.

FEBRUARY 7, 2005

Deron Williams had a fantastic run of assists for No. 1-ranked Illinois.

CHAMPAIGN — Something marvelous was happening, and not many in the raucous, orange-colored Assembly Hall realized it Sunday.

While prep teammate Bracey Wright watched in street clothes (sprained ankle), Illini junior Deron Williams dominated the game while missing every shot he attempted.

In an outpouring of gifts, he delivered the setup pass for all of Illinois' seven baskets in Sunday's 20-3 jump against Indiana.

What we're seeing, based on the numbers, is the most prolific setup man in Illini history. Pro scouts might have some doubts because of his erratic shooting — the entire UI team has them guessing — but not about his playmaking.

With Dee Brown and Luther Head pitching in, the Illini not only lead the nation in assists vs. turnovers, but have the best ratio (449 assists, 256 miscues) in the four seasons the NCAA has kept the statistic. There is no better way of judging the skill and unselfishness of this remarkable team. This knack, coupled with tight defense, is why the Illini prevail even when their shooting is off.

In Illinois' 9-0 Big Ten getaway, Williams has 71 assists (7.9 average), far ahead of runners-up Chris Hill of Michigan State and Jeff Horner of Iowa, each with 35 in eight league games. He had 12 against Penn State, 11 in the rout of Wake Forest, nine twice and eight on three occasions. He is the motor that makes Bruce Weber's halfcourt motion offense purr. The 6-foot-3 Texan is the only Illini starter not scoring in double figures, but he remains the most valuable member ... even if he shoots 0 for 7 as he did Sunday.

Illinois is averaging 80.5 points through 23 magical games, and when the fast break is muzzled, the Illini look to Williams. James Augustine should buy him dinner. Roger Powell Jr. should bring him drinks. Head should take him to a movie.

At his current pace, he will easily lead the Big Ten (league games only) in his specialty and will join Illinois' Bruce Douglas and Michigan State's Mateen Cleaves as the only players to do so three times. If Williams stays for his senior year, he'll have a shot at Douglas' seemingly unreachable record of 765 career assists. He already has Douglas' single-season mark of 200 (in 1985) in his sights, needing 39 more to top that. And with 492 assists overall, Williams could reach 766 with 84 more in the last third of this season and 190 next season.

His biggest booster could be Brown, who sometimes dons Williams' No. 5 jersey in public and says he does it "because Deron is the best point guard in the country, and he's my guy."

Brown went on: "Last year when we made that late run, we became tight as a family. We started getting in that family mold, and it has continued. We understand each other. You can't explain it. You can't explain why you fall in love with somebody, whether it's a guy or a girl. It's just something that happened."

Like many fans who were busier making noise than counting statistics, Brown was unaware of Williams' early run of handouts.

"I don't pay attention to statistics," he said. "I just try to do my job. Deron was doing his job, getting the ball to the right people. He understands the game. He is deceptively quick, he sees the court and he is unselfish."

Indiana coach Mike Davis echoed Brown's comments: "If you look across the country, Deron has got to be one of the top two point guards. He handles the pressure, makes big shots and is always looking to pass. He plays at a terrific pace on both ends of the court."

Said Weber: "Deron has a great feel for the game. He knows how to penetrate and find the open man. He had 11 assists today, and he could easily have had three or four more if we had converted. We didn't shoot very well today, particularly from the perimeter.

"When Deron is in the flow, he draws people to him. And he's particularly good at feeding the post. And he's very good on the defensive end as well."

It took awhile, after seeing Dee Brown and Luther Head for several years, to realize that Deron Williams' playmaking was the special part of a special team. Williams was extremely smart, and he got better ... and he continues to improve as he stars for Utah in the NBA.

1992

Centralia's Dike Eddleman was the state's greatest athlete of the first half-century.

CHAMPAIGN — A half-century has passed but Thomas Dwight Eddleman remembers that March moment as though it was yesterday, "Thirteen points down with five minutes to go," he smiles. "That's what it was."

Huff Gym, cobwebs and all, still reverberates with that shocking finish. There has never been a rally in the championship game to match it. Suddenly, Dick Foley, Max Norman and the Paris Tigers, 39-0 at that juncture, lost it to a whirlwind.

Here's how Don Schnake described it in his book: "Trout — The Old Man and the Orphans."

"Paris inflated its lead to 13 and (Centralia's) Farrell Robinson fouled out. As the red-eyed little Orphan walked to the bench, the hopes of Centralia went with him."

Remarkably, the Orphans caught fire. Jim Seyler scored twice and, when Paris tried to stall, Eddleman broke it up with a steal. Suddenly, the Paris lead was eight, and then it was four.

"Eddleman, with a fury-filled drive, brought the Orphans within two," wrote Schnake.

Seyler tied it with two free throws, but Tiger star Dave Humerickhouse matched them. Then Eddleman, fouled on another scorching drive just under the one-minute mark, knotted it again with a pair of his patented two-handed kiss shots.

"An overanxious Warren Collier missed everything (for Paris)," wrote Schnake. "Centralia had the ball with 30 seconds to break the tie. Eddleman missed. Humerickhouse rebounded, but couldn't hold on. Eddleman pounced on the loose ball and dropped it in at the buzzer. Champions! Champions! Champions!"

This was just one moment in the career of the greatest all-around athlete in the first half-century in this state, and perhaps the nation ... an individual called "the most publicized high school athlete in world history" by Nelson Campbell, author of "Grass Roots and School Yards."

Today, as Fighting Illini fund-raiser Eddleman and wife, Teddy, look forward to his Dec. 31 retirement date — he'll return in the spring of 1993 in a part-time capacity — Dike gazes back on a stretch of athletic versatility that would now be considered impossible.

Yes, he won 11 varsity letters at Illinois, five in track and three each in football and basketball.

Yes, he quick-kicked the football 88 yards against Iowa in 1948, the same year he led the NCAA and set the UI record of 43 yards per punt.

Yes, he was a three-time Big Ten high jump champion, captured the NCAA high jump title in 1948, and cleared 6-7 1/8 at Evanston's Dyche Stadium to advance to the Olympics in London.

Yes, he was Big Ten MVP in basketball in 1949, the UI's Male Athlete of the Year in both 1948 and 1949, and twice an NBA all-star.

Who else can you recall who made it to the Olympics in track, the Rose Bowl and the Final Four?

But none of these accomplishments surprised anyone in Centralia, where he was a folk hero by the time he entered high school.

If athletics came easy for Dike, life did not. His mother died of pneumonia before he was 2. With his father a 45-year railroader, Dike was raised largely by an older sister, Mrs. John Lichtenfeld.

Dr. George Ross, Marion County historian, quoted Eddleman: "I can remember when I was 10 years old, we got a hoop and nailed it to the side of a barn. Even in freezing weather, we'd go out and shoot until dark."

Inspired by Centralia's Lowell Spurgeon, a two-time IHSA high jump champion who became Illini football captain in 1937, Eddleman dug a pit and hauled sawdust so he could practice high jumping. According to Mike Eisenbath of the St. Louis Post-Dispatch, Eddleman was offered a scholarship by an eastern university when he was in seventh grade, the same year he high jumped 5-feet-8 3/4 in bare feet and street clothes.

Even though he suffered a severe knee injury in football as an Orphan freshman, Eddleman persevered through the basketball season with his right leg taped to the hip, and scored a state tourney record 24 points against Champaign in the 1939 Sweet 16.

His state record of 2,702 points held up for 16 seasons as he led four Arthur Trout basketball teams to a 136-27 record. The success of 1942 came just one year after four Orphan seniors and Eddleman — called the Wonder Team — saw their 40-game win streak end in an upset by Morton of Cicero, 30-29, in the semifinal at Huff Gym.

"For overall athletic ability, Dike was probably the best of his time, and for a long time afterward," said Foley. "He was quick, and the spring in his legs was greater than anybody of that era."

By 1942, he was featured in newspaper and magazine articles from coast to coast. One metropolitan writer came to Centralia for a day and stayed two weeks. On Feb. 10, 1942, two months after the outbreak of World War II, he was featured in the same Look Magazine that carried a Mussolini-Hitler cover story.

"In 44 basketball games last season, he scored 969 points," wrote Tom Meany in Look. "He was an outstanding high jumper, broad jumper and quarter miler. Last fall, in 11 football games, he scored 73 points, gained 1,210 yards from scrimmage, kicked, passed and called the signals. To the local kids, he is the biggest hero in sight."

That senior year, after two years away from football, Eddleman sparked a 13-7 opening win with an 80-yard run, a 65-yard run and a drop kick for the extra point ... and saved the game with an interception on the goal line.

Wrote Meany: "Dike was elected president of the students almost without opposition. His clothes set styles. Stores advertise 'Eddleman hunting caps.' A year ago, Dike turned up his trousers 4 inches above the ankle. Within 24 hours, so had every other youth in Centralia."

The war interfered with his Illini career, as it did with the basketball Whiz Kids. After three years away, the senior quartet of Gene Vance, Andy Phillip, Ken Menke and Jack Smiley returned, and the 6-foot-2, 180-pound Eddleman found himself a reserve on Doug Mills' last Illini team.

When Harry Combes replaced Mills, Eddleman's driving style fit perfectly with Champaign's run-and-shoot coach.

"I believe we'd have won the Big Ten that first year (in 1948) if Junior Kirk hadn't turned pro," says Eddleman today.

The Illini won it in 1949 on a team featuring Jim Marks, Bill Erickson and Wally Osterkorn, and Eddleman earned Big Ten MVP honors. He led Illinois to the Final Four where Kentucky's champions, featuring Alex Groza and Ralph Beard, prevailed 76-47.

In his first UI football game as a junior in 1947, Eddleman was listed as a No. 2 halfback.

"With Eddleman on the bench, Centralians huddled in dejection at their radios while an underdog Pittsburgh team held the Illini scoreless for a good part of the game," wrote Jerry Thorp later in the Saturday Evening Post.

"Eliot finally ordered Dike to take over one of the halfback spots. His name had barely been announced when Dike smashed through tackle and sprinted to a touchdown. A few minutes later he turned in the only other touchdown run of the day, thereby assuring himself of a starting assignment for the rest of the season."

Illinois won 14-0.

By today's standards, Eddleman would have left the university to become an immediate millionaire. As it was, he played four years in the NBA, two with Quad Cities in Moline and two with the Fort Wayne Pistons, with a peak salary of $28,000. When the Pistons attempted to trade him to Baltimore, Eddleman, already 31, retired to go into business. In 1957, he moved to Gibson City where he worked in personnel until 1969.

"Gene Lamb and Red Pace talked me into joining the Athletic Association as a fund-raiser," said Eddleman, climbing aboard a scholarship program that was taking in approximately $135,000 at the time.

"It's at $3 million annually now," he reminded.

If he didn't become a millionaire, the program did. And Dike has many millions in memories.

For me, as a teenager in the 1940s, Eddleman was bigger than life, a true superstar. I saw him in a restaurant once and still remember it. Like Red Grange, that popularity never went to his head. In the end, he was a friend.

OCTOBER 5, 1994

Despite coach Lou Tepper's misgivings, linebacker Dana Howard backed up his prediction that the Illini would defeat Ohio State.

"The big lug's heart is in the right place, but not his tongue."
— Illini coach Lou Tepper

CHAMPAIGN — Nearly a century ago, the media was already into its "Yost fears whoever" pattern in headlining Michigan games.

And the phoniness carries right through the fearful fancies of Lou Holtz, who cleverly overstates every rival while only occasionally facing anyone with football talent comparable to that on Notre Dame's bench.

Silly as it is, it's the unwritten rule. No matter how confident you are, never predict a victory. There is only one Joe Namath, and only one Babe Ruth. Mere mortals shouldn't be so brash. And by all means, don't give rivals anything to pin on their bulletin board.

"We counsel our players prior to the season in that regard," said Tepper, chagrined that star linebacker Dana Howard forgot and, heavens, actually told the Ohio press corps Monday that Illinois will beat Ohio State on Saturday.

"Dana rocked my establishment," said Tepper. "I was upset and I showed it. He's not a bad kid. But we can't have a guy guaranteeing victory. He doesn't have the right to guarantee anything but his best effort. He apologized to the team."

Aw, lighten up Lou. That's just Dana, reacting predictably, with candor, to the Purdue loss. He forgot to lie. Besides, he never used the word "guarantee." What he said was: "We're going to Ohio State and we're going to play them tough and win the game."

When asked if he was predicting a win, he took the challenge, adding: "I'll predict a win. If you want to tell them, you can. I don't care if it's locker room material or whatever, we'll win this weekend."

"That's over the line," fumed Tepper. "If he had stopped with the first sentence, if he hadn't embellished it, it wouldn't have been so bad. Sure, that's probably the way he feels. But we can't have that sort of thing."

After practice Tuesday night, Howard backed down only slightly.

"What's the big deal?" he questioned. "I always think we're going to win. I thought so last week, and if you ask me next week, I'll feel the same way. We intend to go to Columbus, be physical and show them that we come to play. It's the same way any coach or player feels."

In Columbus, Ohio State running back Eddie George said the Buckeyes were aware of Howard's statement.

"Dana can say things like that because he can back it up," said George. "I respect his confidence. I wouldn't expect him to feel any other way."

OK, Eddie, would you predict a win?

"I don't want to get into that," was his careful reply. "The game is on Saturday and we're not going to win it through verbal confrontation in the media. I will tell you that we're not going out there to lose."

The truth is, all these young athletes have supreme confidence. They think they're going to win every game.

And the Illini may feel stronger than usual with their recent success against Ohio State. Since Howard and the other fifth-year seniors were juniors in high school, the Illini have beaten Ohio State five of six times.

What is sillier than coaches and media making a big deal out of players' predictions? They all think they're going to win but aren't supposed to say so. Howard backed his prediction as he made a key interception in Illinois' 24-10 win at Ohio State that Saturday.

AUGUST 25, 1994

Simeon Rice never played linebacker although he was listed there.

CHAMPAIGN — With the aid of a Butkus-Nitschke reputation and heady promotional work, a quartet of Fighting Illini linebackers have been billed two years running as best in the country.

This is not entirely out of line with their production.

Dana Howard is a deserving All-American for his run-play defense, his 420 career tackles moving him within 152 of the Big Ten record of 572 by Ohio State's Marcus Marek (1979-82). Howard's inside mate, John Holecek, was recognized at the UI banquet last year as the team's best defensive player.

Going into the 1994 campaign, the trio of Howard, Holecek and Simeon Rice received preseason All-Big Ten status.

All of which brings us face-to-face with two major myths that must be exploded.

— Rice is not now, nor was he ever a linebacker. He attacks from a down stance as a defensive end, the position being called "rush linebacker" because coach Lou Tepper finds it easier to recruit players when you call them linebackers. Thus, Illinois is known for its 3-4 defense even though it is obviously a 4-3, with Rice joining Chad Copher, Tim McCloud and Mikki Johnson in the line.

— Kevin Hardy, the so-called fourth linebacker, does not take a back seat to anyone.

At 6-foot-4 and 239, Hardy is equally at home on pass defense or crashing in from the corner. The Evansville athlete's mobility is such that he came back 10 pounds heavier, increased his bench press from 325 to 360, ran the same 4.6 time in the 40, and bested the entire team with a 3.88-second time in the jingle-jangle, a change-of-direction drill. Yes, he outsped the running backs, receivers and defensive backs.

But let's concentrate on Rice because that's where the most obvious misconceptions have grown.

Understand, now, there may not be a Big Ten player in his size range (6-5, 243) who can match the 40-yard dash he ran on opening day. He was clocked in 4.52 seconds, faster than many UI running backs. Because of his reputation, he has forced opposing game planners to make adjustments in their pass protection to keep him out of the quarterback's hair. Truth is, much of Rice's value is in forcing opponents to react to his presence.

Rice gained early notice as a raw freshman in 1992 when he shattered the Houston protection for nine tackles, including four behind-the-line stops, earning ABC-TV Player of the Game honors in a 31-13 loss. But game records show that, in the UI's eight Big Ten games, he didn't start a single game (he was backup to Todd Leach) and had just four more behind-the-line tackles in league play.

Based on his early-season notice, Rice was named Big Ten Freshman of the Year even though he was eighth on the UI's 12-game tackle list with 33 solos, with nine sacks.

Because of his freelance rushing style, and his late-game fumble recovery that set up Johnny Johnson's winning TD pass at Michigan, his reputation grew in 1993. He joined Howard and Holecek as consensus All-Big Ten players even though he again shared time with Leach, and his season numbers dropped (in one less game) to 29 solo tackles and eight sacks.

It is no secret that a major concern of the defense this year is whether Rice is strong enough to repulse running plays down after down against Big Ten rivals.

"Based on his techniques and strength development, Simeon should be better against the run this year," said assistant coach Greg Colby. "We've stressed that so much. He's been protected in the past (by Leach), and he knows he must be better."

It will be a part of everyone's game plan to test Rice with runs directly at him. If problems develop in that regard, Colby may start looking for a Leach type.

Simeon Rice was a late pickup from Chicago Mount Carmel and immediately shocked line coach Denny Marcin with his pass-rushing ability. As he gained strength at his "School of Hard Knocks," Rice became adequate against the run, and his pass-rushing specialty gave him a long career in the NFL.

OCTOBER 12, 1999

Illini basketball standout Matt Heldman is killed in an auto accident.

CHAMPAIGN — Oh, no! Not the poster boy for hard work and eternal optimism. Not the young man pictured next to "overachiever" in Webster's. Not the decade's runaway winner of the "grittiest competitor" trophy... the guy with a future too promising to even speculate on.

That future was altered in a split second Sunday night when Matt Heldman, the cohesive factor on Lon Kruger's 1998 Big Ten basketball champs, was killed in a horrible automobile accident that took his father, Otis Heldman, and two others.

Flashbacks produced the memory of similar crashes that took popular UI grads Don Sunderlage and Jodie Harrison in the prime of life.

Drive carefully, friends.

Lon Kruger, whose successes in his first two Illini years were linked to Heldman, was ashen as the news swept the state Monday.

"It's tough because sometimes it doesn't make sense," said Kruger. "We just have to wrestle with that. I hope that somehow we can benefit by appreciating the things we have, and not take anything for granted.

"Matt was a guy who took great satisfaction in investing himself, getting in the best condition and challenging people who on the surface were more talented. As far as realizing his own potential, he certainly did that. He was himself without reservation. And I don't recall a negative thought."

Aware that Michigan State had made an early offer to Heldman, then-Illini coach Lou Henson watched Heldman closely in summer camps.

Others were ranked higher that year but King's Michael Hermon toted so much baggage that UI recruiter Jimmy Collins backed off, Peoria Manuel's Brandun Hughes had grade troubles, Westinghouse's Mark Miller didn't like the idea of competing against old teammate Kiwane Garris, and Carbondale's Troy Hudson was set for SIU-Carbondale.

Heldman's stats at Libertyville, particularly in big games, told a glistening story. In the clutch, he was sensational. But Henson wasn't convinced until he saw Heldman at a summer camp in Normal where the stocky athlete burned the nets with an arched-back jumper that big defenders couldn't block. From that day, Henson waged a hot duel with Michigan State for Matt's services.

By midseason of his sophomore year, the persevering sub was demanding double-figure minutes. He peaked with 20 points in a 74-71 loss to Purdue and filled at point guard when Garris was hurt. But when Henson stepped down, Heldman had to prove himself all over again to a new coach, and Matt would play just four and five minutes against TCU and Louisville in Hawaii the following November.

"He had a good game (18 points) against Virginia Tech in the consolation game in Hawaii," said UI assistant coach Robert McCullum, "and his game just took off from there. We had a lot of questions about who would be our three-point shoooter next to Kiwane, and who would support Kiwane at the point. Matt was the guy."

Challenges grew even greater in Heldman's senior year. Garris was gone, Cory Bradford was ineligible, and BYU transfer Robbie Reid chose Michigan after giving UI coaches what they thought was a verbal commitment. But if everyone else had doubts about Heldman's ability to play the point, he didn't.

Heldman provided the missing link as five seniors bonded to win a Big Ten co-championship that no one expected. He joined hands with former walk-on Brian Johnson, Kevin Turner (a throw-in on the

Byrant Notree recruitment), Jarrod Gee and redshirted Jerry Hester (recovering from back surgery).

In the stretch, the durable Heldman played at least 35 minutes in 19 consecutive games. He hit 14 straight free throws against Clemson, was deadly in late-game situations, and closed with the No. 2 career FT percentage (84.0) in UI history, trailing only assistant coach Rod Judson (87.5). He held turnovers to a minimum (81 in 33 games) even as opponents targeted his playmaking and three-point efforts.

Illinois lost one of its favorite sons Sunday. It is our nature that we never reach full potential. Matt Heldman came closer than almost anyone.

The UI's Matto Award for commitment and hard work was named after Matt Heldman. He was the ultimate overachiever, always performing a little better than anyone thought he could.

DECEMBER 17, 2004

Luther Head carried some of the "street" with him from Chicago, but he overcame physical and personal problems to spark the UI's 2005 run.

CHAMPAIGN — Bruce Weber made his most important decision a year ago, sticking with a then-aimless Luther Head.

The world was tumbling around Head's shoulders. First, he was involved in a late-night apartment burglary. He sat out the UI's first two games as punishment. When the aggrieved students declined to bring charges, neither did John Piland, a decision that Julia Rietz used in a heated campaign to unseat Piland as Champaign County state's attorney last month.

Later, Head was benched for two games at the outset of the Big Ten season for multiple traffic violations and for driving on a suspended license.

Head was ready to give himself the door.

"If I'm too much of a distraction ... if you want me to leave, I will," he offered.

Weber's response set the stage for what is now the hottest basketball program in the nation. The first-year coach, feeling pressure from all sides, could have said, "OK go."

But he saw something worth saving.

"It wasn't just me," Weber said this week. "The administration had a say, and the police and the state's attorney. Luther made some mistakes, and he knew he had to change. I could tell it bothered him because he showed such remorse. It embarrassed him so much. You see NBA guys who make mistakes, and they show no remorse. Luther was different.

"I can remember discussions when I was on Gene Keady's staff (at Purdue) and we had problems. The assistants might vote 4-0 to get rid of a player, but Keady's vote outweighed us all. He had learned to offer an extra chance because he had been given an extra chance himself.

"Later on when we played at Purdue (March 3), Luther made a great play at the end. He threw a lead pass and then he had the instincts to run down the court past several players and put back the winning basket in overtime. That reminded me that if you don't give up on players, they won't give up on you."

Head is now in the midst of another controversy. But this one is fun. Who deserves the most credit for Illinois' 9-0 start? Which of three spectacular guards is best? What about Roger Powell Jr.?

Head has slightly more minutes (31.9 a game), would receive Weber's nod on defense, is tops in scoring at 16.3, has the most steals (14) and the best free throw percentage (92.9), is shooting 48 percent on threes and has the best assist-turnover ration (45 to 18).

This is, you see, the first season Head has played unencumbered.

Said the Chicago Manley senior: "I had a lot to learn as a freshman. Just being a freshman was a problem in itself. It was like starting over."

He started twice in the first 23 games and went scoreless in five of them. It was a team directed by Frank Williams and Cory Bradford, but the lean rookie cracked the lineup when the Illini won their last eight games to share the Big Ten title. He proved the three-guard lineup could work.

But his sophomore season was limited by a stomach muscle ailment. He missed four nonconference games and three Big Ten games. Seldom able to practice, he started eight times alongside freshmen Dee Brown and Deron Williams.

"I sat out about 75 percent of the practices that season and all of them at the end," Head said. "I'd try to build back up, and the pain would start. It was like something was holding me back in the groin area. I couldn't go up strong. It affected everything I did. The only good thing is that it helped me become a better set shooter. When I couldn't run, I practiced shooting."

Then came last season, one Head doesn't want to talk about.

"I was ready to give up," he grimaced. "Coach stayed behind me and told me not to worry. I don't ever want to think about it."

Fans of the Kingdom of the Orange now see the real Luther Head. Offseason surgery corrected the stomach problem. His ball handling skills improved and, with slashing speed, he gives the Illini a third creator. He is a key cog in a machine that has its eye on reaching Jan. 1 undefeated — and going from there.

With all five starters performing at such a high level, health is emerging as a critical issue. There have been too many problems in the past with Head, Robert Archibald and Damir Krupalija, to name a few, to take this for granted. Veteran fans still grimace when the Flyin' Illini are mentioned because of tournament injuries hampering Kenny Battle and Lowell Hamilton in 1989. Other fans can go back to 1984, when Efrem Winters was barely able to go against Kentucky.

"We can keep this going if we stay healthy, stay on the same page and keep praying for each other," Head said.

Early last season, with all of Head's problems, Weber sought to use Powell at small forward. It didn't work. This is the first season that an Illini coach has thrown size out the window from the beginning, Weber settling on the 6-foot-6 Powell strictly inside and the 6-3 Head lining up opposite the rival small forward.

"That is a sign of today's game," Weber said. "At SIU, we had no choice. We had to use three guards. That's how we won the Valley. That's how we beat Texas Tech and Georgia (in the 2002 NCAA tournament).

"Everybody is looking for a 6-foot-7 small forward, but it's better to have speed and shooting ability."

That's what the Illini have in a fresh and focused Head.

For a time, it appeared the administration might force Weber to dismiss Head. Certainly, if Piland and the students had brought charges, it would have turned out differently. To his credit, Head made full use of his second and third chances.

MARCH 14, 1983

Derek Harper corrected his shooting release and became one of Illinois' legendary players.

CHAMPAIGN — Hey there, you national experts, look over here. Illinois has a basketball All-American on its hands.

Yeah, I know. You guys haven't really been serious about an Illini player since rising junior Rich Jones was declared ineligible in December of 1966.

You gave Dave Scholz, Mike Price, and the Dawson brothers a nod, and Nick Weatherspoon drew recognition just below the superstars a decade ago. Eddie Johnson, the UI's first consensus All-Big Ten player since Spoon, was completely overlooked.

But this time it's for real. That guy who slugged Minnesota with a 25-foot shot to end Sunday's stomach-wrenching 50 minutes is the genuine article. Don't spit out old scouting reports to me. I don't care if he used to spin his shots like a top, this winter they went in at a 56.7 rate in 18 rugged Big Ten games. Only a few centers shooting dunks and 5-footers bested him, and they didn't launch 24 three-pointers (making 13) from beyond 21 feet.

Now that we've discussed his weakness, let's move on. From a pure physical standpoint, he can fly with the eagles and dash with the deer. If he isn't the best defensive guard in the country, he is at least the best these eyes have seen.

That 3-for-15 audit Sunday alongside the name of Minnesota's prize outshooter, Tommy Davis, isn't coincidental. You won't find quicker hands this side of Pickpocket U. He led the Big Ten in steals for the second straight year. He accumulates more deflections than a bumper car.

And Sunday, when that delirious Illini fandom poured down onto the Assembly Hall court, it was Derek "Sweet D" Harper they lifted above their swarming bodies for a shoulder ride he will carry in the Harper memory bank forever.

Yes, it was only a second-place finish in the Big Ten, only a 21-10 season.

But look at Derek's supporting cast. The season began with two centers just below the standards thought necessary for Big Ten play, two willing guys who drew mindless boos from their own fans, one of whom could have bypassed his redshirt year without so much as a sigh from so-called supporters. There were two small forwards, sophs Anthony Welch and Jay Daniels, one of whom was trailing in age and experience and the other about to be sidelined for the season with a stress fracture. And there were four key freshmen, two of whom had to start whether the coach liked it or not.

"No, we didn't talk about the NCAA tournament back there in December, not with the guys so young," said Harper on Sunday. "I knew we had a lot of ability, but I knew it would take awhile before Anthony and Efrem (Winters) and Bruce (Douglas) would be ready. I'm really thrilled we made it. It was a tough grind."

A deeply caring individual, Harper put a governor on his boiling point and withstood the early disappointments in grim silence. Finally, when Illinois opened the Big Ten season with a 75-49 loss at Minnesota — the UI's second 26-point loss in four games — he called the players together and laid down the law according to Harper. Chests were cleansed in that private affair in Madison, Wis. Each came out fully understanding his role ... rebounder, feeder, sub, etc.

From that moment, through 17 skirmishes, the Illini lost only twice by more than three points, both to veteran Big Ten champion Indiana, 69-55 and 67-55, wilting in the face of incredible 70 percent field goal shooting in the latter contest.

But the last-second losses hurt. Harp had the final shot in a 63-62 setback at Purdue but it bounced off. He had the last poke at a three-pointer, however rushed, in the 68-66 back-breaker at Iowa. He had a chance to break the final tie with Purdue here, but Ricky Hall deflected his jumper and set up the Boilermakers' lucky bell ringer. And Harp had a three-footer at the end of regulation Sunday, but it also missed.

So the tug-of-war with Minnesota went on and on. And finally, it was the end of the second overtime, and Harper brought Illini fans out of the stands, off their living room couches and indoors from the sunshine.

"I really didn't flip the first one at the end of regulation," he reflected. "The last one felt good. I asked God to put it in and he heard. I just knew it was going in."

Actually, Harper was disappointed that he wasn't given the opportunity at the end of the first overtime. That's when Bruce Douglas tried to penetrate and had his jumper blocked to hold the score at 59-59.

"I think it's my job to take charge in a situation like that," said Harper. "That's why I had one coming. It was confident I could make it. I had good balance and the ball came off my hand just right. It was a great feeling."

Thus did the 6-4 UI junior make his final pitch for the Big Ten's MVP award. He's in against two talented seniors, 7-3 Randy Breuer of Minnesota, the league's most dominant inside player but for a 9-9 club, and Indiana's Randy Wittman, who began to draw serious consideration only after forward mate Ted Kitchel underwent back surgery at the end of February.

Whoever prevails, Harper is certain to join the Kansas City Kings' Eddie Johnson as the UI's second consensus All-Big Ten player since Weatherspoon. He'll receive some All-America consideration this year — he's on the Basketball Weekly third A-A quintet — and he'll make EVERY preseason A-A team worth its salt in the fall.

But that's next year. The Illini have a new season in between, and it's a comforting feeling to have Harper leading the way to the 12,583 seat Boise State Pavilion for Thursday's showdown with Utah.

Harper surprised Henson by turning pro early. Based on his junior year, he could have stamped himself as the best UI basketball player up to that time. Illinois never had a better defender.

OCTOBER 27, 1983

Red Grange spoke about Michigan from his Florida home in 1993.

Sometimes during those endless eras when the Illinois tradition has been trampled down by Michigan and Ohio State, Red Grange seemed like a myth to the modern generation.

A ghost story.

But the ghost is taking form again this week.

As the octogenarian spoke from his home in Indian Lakes, Fla., he brought a shocking realization. No Michigan-Illinois game has directed such attention on Memorial Stadium since Grange dedicated the $1.7 million structure with five touchdowns in 1924.

In 58 intervening years, Illinoisans have seldom, if ever, let their imaginations run so wild over a game.

Speaking specifically of the UI-Michigan series, only a few games have approached Saturday's in significance. The past half-century can be all too easily capsuled in one paragraph.

From 1930-45, Illinois fielded a string of mediocre teams (57-73 with 7 ties), except for the 7-1 club in 1934. The Rose Bowl team in 1946 had lost early to Notre Dame and Indiana, and Michigan had lost to Army and tied Northwestern the two weeks before Illinois beat the Wolverines, 13-9. Illinois' 9-0-1 Rose Bowl team in 1951 beat a 4-5 Michigan club that was out of the running. The 1963 Rose Bowl team lost to a 3-4-2 Wolverine team here, contributing to Michigan's current 23-for-24 win streak against Illinois, and in many of those years the UI was barely competitive.

Last year? Nope. Illinois had already knocked itself out of the Rose Bowl by losing to Iowa and Ohio State. Face the facts. This is the first time in 20 years that Illinois has gone to the wire in the Run for the Roses. Both rivals are 5-0 in the conference, and that's an infrequent occurrence.

And, with all the live-wire atmosphere, the NoMoBo buttons, the influx of media (AP is staffing from New York), the ticket scalping, the network television, the campus excitement ... well, we feel the closeness, the greatness of Grange as though nearly six decades of time had not elapsed.

The old redhead will watch Saturday's 11:30 a.m. contest on his TV set at Indian Lakes Estate. Now 80, he declined overtures from UI coach Mike White to make the trip.

"I stay pretty close to home these days," he explained. "It's monotonous at times, but that's the penalty you pay for the good weather down here. I feel pretty good but I'm not up to traveling. I don't really give any consideration to leaving here."

Grange blames "travel and tension" for his one bout with ill health. Worn down by business (insurance) and NFL television broadcasts, he suffered a heart attack in 1951.

"I called it exhaustion more than anything else," he reflects. "I learned to take it easy."

But there was a day when Red Grange, the Galloping Ghost, the Wheaton Iceman, stole the spotlight of a nation. He made the great names of the Roaring Twenties, Jack Dempsey and Babe Ruth, take a back seat.

In his very first game as a sophomore in 1923, he gained 208 yards and scored three TDs against a Nebraska team that served Notre Dame and the Four Horsemen their only 1923 defeat. He went on to score 12 TDs and make All-American on an 8-0 club.

"But we didn't play Michigan that year, and we tied them for the Big Ten title," recalls the famed No. 77. "That 1924 game had a year-long buildup, and it was chosen as the dedication game for the stadium. People talked about it all summer."

Illinois' little Dutchman, Bob Zuppke, and arch-rival Fielding Yost of Michigan took potshots at each other in the press. But, as is sometimes forgotten, Yost traveled to Europe that summer and stepped down as Michigan coach after 23 unbelievably successful years.

Perhaps Yost's absence contributed to what happened Oct. 18, 1924. Others say Michigan was psyched out because Zuppke had his players remove their wool socks in the 80-degree heat. Grange himself cites two factors, (1) Zuppke's carefully planned cutback strategy on the sweeps and (2) exquisite blocking by every member of the UI team.

"That game has had more written about it and been diagnosed more than any in history," said Grange. "You'd think the fate of a nation depended on it."

The crowd was 67,000-plus, and twice that number would have attended. The Chicago Police Department, at the request of Champaign Police Chief A.V. Keller, dispatched 35 patrolmen, nightsticks at their side, to help with the influx of fans into the community. Flags fluttered and bunting draped every lightpost.

And the clever Dutchman, Zuppke, had a plan.

"Zuppke had talked to me all year about cutting back," said Grange. "My tendency was to use my speed to get to the outside and run to the sideline. Zuppke planned the blocking for me to cut back, and when I made my moves, our blockers had perfect angles on them. All I had to do was run."

Grange dashed 95 yards on the opening kickoff, his early path cleared by Earl Britton and Wally McIlwain, the redhead exploding out of a pile of players at the 35 and into the clear. His only recollection of the play was escaping the Michigan safety, Tod Rockwell.

"The only man in front of me was Rockwell and I remember thinking: 'I'd better get this guy because after coming all this way I'll sure look like a bum if one guy tackles me.' I can't tell you, though, how I got by him."

Behind 7-0, Michigan elected to kick off again. This Wolverine team, the record shows, had played 22 consecutive games without defeat and had permitted just four touchdowns in that stretch. More than that, after Oct. 18, 1924, Michigan was to permit just 50 points in the next 25 games. This was a devastating squad of tacklers, and they used a strategy of kicking their opponents deep and pouncing on them.

But on that day, the most famous in Illini history, Grange would make four long TD runs in less than 12 minutes, and would return in the second half to run and throw for two more scores.

What happened was totally inconsistent with the Michigan record in the early part of the 20th century. These Wolverines were unbeaten and unscored upon in Yost's first year, 1901, and beat Stanford 49-0 in the Rose Bowl. When the 1905 team lost to Amos Alonzo Stagg's Chicago club, 2-0, it snapped a non-losing string of 56 games.

Yost continued to field outstanding teams through the teens and into the Grange period, and the 39-14 result stood as the most points scored against Michigan in this century until 1935.

"It was the blocking," Grange has repeated over and over. "Every man did his job."

This isn't just the modesty of the man speaking. One year later, with Yost returning as head coach, Michigan returned to the same Memorial Stadium to get its revenge.

The signs of trouble were already out. Five of seven Illinois' linemen were gone. McIllwain, called by Zuppke the greatest open-field blocker he ever saw, had graduated and quarterback Harry Hall had a collarbone injury. Zuppke moved Britton up front to bolster the line.

And it was an autumn of persistent rainfall, turning grass fields into mudbowls. The green Illini line failed in the opener against Nebraska, 14-0. It was Illinois' first loss in the stadium, and one story read, "The red of Nebraska was mightier than the Red of Illinois." Illinois barely edged Butler, 16-13, as Grange went 70 yards on a punt return, and lost at Iowa, 12-10, despite his 83-yard dash on the opening kickoff.

Michigan came seeking revenge the next weekend. Again 67,000 UI homecomers were on hand, but Grange couldn't get free on the slimy, chewed-up gridiron. He had the ball 28 times but, including kick returns, gained but 126 yards as ends Bennie Oosterbaan and Bill Flora kept him like a caged lion. Bo Molenda intercepted five UI passes and the Illini never penetrated Michigan's 25-yard line. Michigan won, 3-0.

Grange's senior year was by no means a total loss. He played one of his most famous games at Pennsylvania the next weekend, scoring three times and rolling up 363 yards (including kick returns) to assure his third All-American selection.

After a season-ending 14-9 win at Ohio State, he immediately turned pro and played a whirlwind five games in 10 days with George Halas' Chicago Bears. Beginning with a Thanksgiving Day game against the Chicago Cardinals, he attracted large crowds from Chicago to Philadelphia to New York, and received two checks amounting to $100,000 within the month. This focused attention on a new pro league that was just gaining public acceptance.

Through it all and to this day, Grange seems almost embarrassed by the emphasis on his role in a team game.

"It was the blocking," he repeats. "When we had the blocking in 1924, we did fine. When the blocking slipped in 1925, we had problems."

I met Grange in the 1970s while doing TV for Channel 15. It was his nature then and always to praise his teammates and play down his own accomplishments. This wasn't an act. For all his accomplishments, he was as modest as anyone I ever met.

DECEMBER 31, 1990

Illini star Howard Griffith is granted a memorable opportunity to meet an ailing Red Grange prior to the UI's date with Clemson in the Hall of Fame Bowl.

TAMPA, Fla. — Galloping Ghost, meet Galloping Griff.

White-haired, frail and impaired by Parkinson's disease and a bout with pneumonia, an 88-year-old Red Grange has resided in a Lake Wales, Fla., nursing home since July. He won't be able to join his beloved Illini in Tuesday's Hall of Hall Bowl date with Clemson.

But Grange, a product of the Roaring '20s who has far outlived such legendary peers as Jack Dempsey, Babe Ruth and Bobby Jones, agreed to meet the UI's record-breaking Howard Griffith this afternoon less than 24 hours before Tuesday's noon (CST) kickoff.

"It's a great thrill for me to meet a living immortal," said Griffith on Sunday.

"I began learning about Red Grange when I first came to Illinois. I don't know what I'll say. I'll just walk in and see what happens."

Today's trip and Tuesday's game are the culmination of a magical season for Griffith, whose life story reads like a Hollywood script.

Adopted as an infant, he wasn't made aware of it until his mother died of cancer during his junior year at Chicago Mendel, precisely when his dream of a football career temporarily crumpled due to a broken ankle.

Operating on the fringe of the drug-infested South Side, Griffith transferred to Chicago Julian at the outset of his senior year, joining forces with J.W. Smith, a coach who had a huge impact on his decision to enter Illinois without either the qualifying grades or a scholarship.

If he isn't the Big Ten's only Proposition 48 walk-on, he is at least the most successful. He sat out a year alongside close friends Nick Anderson and Ervin Small, retaining four years of eligibility because he wasn't on scholarship.

He first drew attention as a special teams dynamo in 1987, and made his peace with new coach John Mackovic in becoming an adept receiver and a blocker for Keith Jones in 1988.

By 1990, when most were talking about Moe Gardner, Darrick Brownlow, Mel Agee and the veteran defense, Griffith won the player-voted MVP award in a storied season in which he:

— Broke Grange's career and season TD records with 33 and 15 scores;

— Scored an NCAA record eight TDs and 48 points against Southern Illinois University;

— Rushed for 263 yards vs. Northwestern, breaking Jim Grabowski's single-game record, and pulling him to No. 3 on the UI's all-time rushing list with 2,426 yards.

All this after a shaky beginning with the discipline-oriented Mackovic.

"The way I was brought up, when I got into conflict, I took care of it physically," said Griffith. "I wasn't very mature and I was involved in some incidents that I shouldn't have been.

"I think it all turned around for me when he came out on the field that first year and said, 'I understand you don't like me, and I'm not sure I like you either. But we're going to do it my way, whether you're with us or not.'

"Mike White (former UI coach) had been more lenient in the social aspects. Mackovic was stern. He knew what he wanted. I've changed. I don't even get in arguments anymore."

Griffith takes out his aggressions on the playing field. And Mackovic leaned on him increasingly at season's end, using him not only at fullback but at tailback and in the "ace" position as a lone back.

"Howard has become an outstanding person," said Mackovic.

"I think he was going to make progress under any coach. He's a solid young man who had to earn everything he's had. He has carried it well and been a great team person. He paid his dues, and all the nice things that have happened this year haven't changed his attitude about work and effort.

"I'm pleased he has the opportunity to see Red Grange. I think it's more meaningful for him to go down than for me to go again. We had a nice visit last year, and Red struck me as a person with great recollections of his career and as a genuine individual without a large ego. He sent his congratulations this year when Howard broke his records."

If one element is missing for Griffith this season, it is a big rushing game against a defensive powerhouse like Clemson. With the UI line getting whipped up front, he didn't come close to 100 yards in the losses to Arizona, Iowa and Michigan, and also failed to reach triple figures against Ohio State and Michigan State.

"We need the running game Tuesday," said Mackovic. "We have to move the ball to have any chance to win, and we need a good mix between the run and the pass."

Griffith said he likes the tailback opportunities - he left Mendel in 1985 seeking more ball carrying and less blocking - because he can cut to the soft spots from 7.5 yards back.

"Our offense showcases what I do best," said Griffith. "We'll try different formations and use what works best. But there are no weak links in the Clemson defense. We've had a nice time down here but Tuesday will be all business."

Grange died less than a month later, leaving a legacy of collegiate greatness unparalleled in American football history. Illinois was no match for Clemson, falling 30-0 in the Hall of Fame Bowl.

JANUARY 1, 1994

Kiwane Garris missed clutch free throws against Missouri but he produced great offense as a freshman.

CHAMPAIGN — He missed 10 free throws.

He charged with the score 79-79 and :04 left in regulation. He failed at the line twice with the score 97-97 and :00 on the second overtime clock. He launched some off-balance shots and committed five turnovers.

No, this wasn't Magic Johnson or Isiah Thomas, who did those sorts of things as freshmen at Michigan State and Indiana. This was Kiwane Garris in the 108-107 triple-overtime loss to Missouri, and Illini fans should get aboard for some of the thrills of a basketball lifetime as a youthful, explosive Garris bounces along between his unpredictable peaks and valleys.

He is only a freshman with eight pre-New Year games under his belt, but the 1994 Illini basketball team is Kiwane's. It isn't Deon's, because the Thomas personality is as feather-soft as his shooting touch. It isn't Shelly Clark's, although the JC transfer has the character to lead if he can relax and play to his capabilities.

It is the freshman's because Kiwane combines speed, toughness and durability, one of which is missing in each of his teammates. Kiwane controls the tempo, Kiwane cracks the press, Kiwane runs the break, Kiwane is setup man, and the only one who penetrates consistently off the dribble. At halftime or when the game is tied, four teammates head for the baseline and Kiwane goes one-on-one.

The team's destiny is in his hands.

It won't always work out. But the old checkers expert, Lou Henson, knows how to maneuver his pieces, and he has concluded that Kiwane is the UI's best bet. The rookie played 51 of 55 minutes against Mizzou, and shot more free throws (22) than any player in Illinois history. He scored 31 points. He had seven rebounds and six assists. Will he be traumatized by those two free throws when the world stopped and everybody watched him miss? Yep, about like a runaway freight train will be halted by a no-passing sign.

For that moment, the pressure got him. He was tired and he had lost his stroke along the way. It happens. That stroke was worth 26 straight free throws earlier in the season, almost certainly a UI freshman record.

He'll get it back. And he'll continue to get better because, for this sturdy Chicagoan, that was just one blip on the master plan, just a stepping stone to where he's going. Basketball is his life. He'll be right back at home against those visiting streaks from Texas Sunday afternoon.

Now, understand, there are those of us who would like to see better "situational" basketball. We'd like it to be more neat. We'd prefer no turnovers, two-handed passes and maybe some underhanded free throws.

But controlling what Garris does is like giving Emmitt Smith instructions on what to do with the football. Oh, by the way, Emmitt, would you remember to break to your right, straight-arm the linebacker, and give a limp leg to the safety. This is the correct way, Emmitt.

Sure. Tell the creator how to create. Hey, the Cowboys' Smith has no idea what he's going to do when he puts the ball under his arm. No great back has ever been able to explain it. What he does is react. And no great dribbler can submit a map in advance of the route he'll take to the hoop. It's pure instinct, and that's why you take a Garris aside, you wind him up, and then you turn him loose, hoping he'll take the right fork in the road and praying he won't get lost among the trees. You wait for experience to up the percentages.

And you do it with the realization that the old school has never had a rookie who can do it better.

That's not to say he's a superior all-around freshman guard than Derek Harper. With his long arms, Harper was the best defender who every donned the UI uniform. Bruce Douglas had superb all-around skills, and was a coach on the court. But neither could shoot or play the offensive game with the skills of Garris.

Kiwane's mistakes are the mistakes of aggressiveness. He'll bore in sometimes when he shouldn't, but that's better than never going in at all. He has attempted 57 free throws already. His running mate at guard, Richard Keene, has shot four.

Get used to Kiwane. The Illini basketball future is in his hands.

Kiwane Garris was the most underrated player in UI history. As the No. 2 career scorer, he should have been named to the 20-man all-century team. It was an oversight to leave him off.

AUGUST 1, 2000

Jack Smiley, who earned his reputation on defense, was the first of the great Whiz Kids of the 1940s to pass away.

CHAMPAIGN — Personal toughness doesn't always project into longevity.

And so it happened Sunday that the rigors of advancing senior citizenship waylaid one of the Fighting Illini's original musketeers ... Jack Smiley ... the guy whose picture is next to the dictionary definition of "hard-nosed."

Between zones and switches and scrambling substitutions, we quickly lose track of who's covering who these days. Not so in college basketball of the early 1940s. The top opposing scorer was Smiley's job, and he made a lifelong reputation out of it. Not the leading scorer nor most clever passer, Smiley anchored the legendary Whiz Kids as they captured Big Ten titles in 1942 and 1943 before World War II prevented them from confirming their No. 1 ranking in the NCAA tourney.

As reported by late News-Gazette sports editor Eddie Jacquin, the Whiz Kids "sounded a clarion note around the far corners of the conference" when, in their first Big Ten game, they defeated defending national champion Wisconsin 55-40 before 7,000 disbelieving Badger fans in Madison.

This was a Wisconsin team on a 19-for-20 streak and featuring All-American John Kotz, tournament MVP for the 1941 national champs, Big Ten scoring leader and MVP in 1942.

There was no hint of "stage fright or buck fever" expected of 19-year-old sophs engaged in their first Big Ten game, wrote Jacquin. Smiley, Ken Menke, Gene Vance and Andy Phillip — running Doug Mills old-fashioned weave around alternating centers Art Mathisen and Vic Wukovits — were described as "traveling at a mad pace" as they met expectations from two years earlier when they were four of the classiest athletes in the state.

"These four sophomores will have a merry three years if the war doesn't catch up with them," said Wisconsin coach Bud Foster.

That was the catch: the war. But before their junior season ended due to military call-ups in early March of 1943, they went 12-0 in the conference and blistered Wisconsin twice more with Smiley holding Kotz scoreless in a 50-26 whitewashing at Huff Gym.

"Kotz got so frustrated that Foster finally took him out," Vance said. "Jack was the kind of defender that you simply couldn't get around. Oh, we switched on occasion. We were the same size and we helped each other. But only as a last resort."

It was a different picture when Mathisen and the four younger members met for golf in Savoy last August. Eighteen holes were reduced to nine by unanimous agreement.

Health problems in the form of tumors were overtaking Smiley. Mathisen has had both hips replaced. Phillip has a pace-maker. Menke is feeling the ravages of time, most recently encountering foot problems. And Vance is the Six Million Dollar Man with two new knees and two makeshift hips.

"When I go through the metal detector at the airport, I tell them to get out their wands," said Vance. "I set off every alarm in the place."

So the July reunion was called off a couple of weeks back. Smiley couldn't make it. They planned to hold it another time, when he felt better. But he died in his sleep Sunday.

But theirs is a wondrous feeling of accomplishment carrying with it the memories of a loving fandom and a fellowship that grew over the decades.

They did it the hard way, without benefit of scholarships. They waited tables at fraternities for their "freebies," handling three meals a day and a pileup of dirty dishes when they arrived late from practice. They had no orthopedic experts, no academic adviser checking attendance, no strength coach.

Still, guards Smiley and Vance, in particular, were muscular in a naturally sculpted way. And they were ornery-tough. Call them Butch and Sundance without chaps.

Oops, did someone say "guards?"

That's a mistake! There was no point guard, no small forward ... just four rangy (in 1942, 6-foot-3 was rangy) athletes who raced each other to lead the break, to get back on defense, to spear the loose rebound. All four had the ball-handling skills of guards and the athleticism of forwards.

There is now a gaping hole in the lineup that formed the most storied team in Illini history. Smiley made us smile, and we will continue to do so when we think about him.

Doug Mills' Whiz Kids were ahead of their time in terms of speed and flair, and a great bunch to be around. Smiley was the steadying influence as the defensive stopper. He was named Illini MVP in 1947.

JULY 30, 1994

Memory Lane is better because of the great athlete and friendly judge Fred Green.

URBANA — He was taller then ... taller than anybody around ... long before osteoporosis and the ravages of 80 summers took their inevitable toll.

In the parlance, he has scaled the mountaintop and seen the elephant. He remains, right there alongside the good guys, the John Cribbets, Byron Vedders and Bob Eisners, as a lasting community treasure ... a giant who dug in and reached heights that few ever did or ever will approach.

Fred Green, 80, spent 42 years as a judge elected by the people. He is the third of four generations of lawyers, his father graduating from Harvard and serving on the University of Illinois law faculty.

It challenges the imagination now, as he moves slowly through prostate and back problems, to visualize a day when Fred was a 6-foot-7, rebounding-scoring scourge, when he was pictured every week in these pages, when "Green for Governor" signs abounded, when the angular center led Urbana High on a six-game tournament run that remains the Tigers' greatest basketball moment.

Later on, he would lead the fight for law and order. But return with us now to those thrilling days of yesteryear ... the tall Tiger rides again ... and the story is too remarkable to leave in the dustbin of history.

Green was a force as a junior in 1940 when Urbana won the Big 12 basketball title, but the Tigers fell in the sectional. Champaign High's Maroons had become something of a jinx, dominating football for more than two decades and ruling in basketball. Urbana had, to that point, never enjoyed the exquisite pleasure of eliminating Champaign from the basketball playoffs under the old format.

Slumping in February 1941, Lew Stephens' Tigers were throttled 67-27 by Centralia and Dike Eddleman (then a junior on the Wonder Five) before falling to Tuscola's Okaw Valley champs, 45-36 (coach Al Kish triple-teamed Green), and for a second time to Harry Combes' streaking Maroons. It was inconceivable after that 47-30 rout to imagine the result would be reversed later.

But that's part of the most astonishing tournament turnaround in Twin City history. It didn't begin until undefeated Homer dumped the Tigers 41-31 in the regional final. The regional runner-up was allowed to advance, but it didn't look good. To stay alive, the 10-loss Tigers needed a makeover, a total rejuvenation ... not once but three in a row.

"We weren't together as a team," Green said. "As we found better ways to pass the ball inside, I became a more effective scorer. We came together as the tournament went along."

The 47-34 win against Hoopeston was routine, but the next two weren't. A basket by Walt Franklin at the gun edged Indianola 32-31.

The newspaper report was overshadowed by the announcement that Ray Eliot had been named Illini head football coach.

But interest soon centered on a third Maroon-Tiger shootout with Combes' team heavily favored. Green erupted with 20 points in a shocking upset, the Tigers prevailing 42-38 by scoring the last nine points of the game. The Combesmen were stunned and devastated. Stephens said over and over: "I can't believe we did it."

Off to Springfield for the round of 16, Green was unstoppable in accumulating 51 points in decisive defeats of Collinsville (44-36) and Pittsfield (50-30). If Eddleman was the state's runaway hero, Green was close behind.

"I had my faults," Green said, "but with my height, I had the same advantages that 7-footers have today."

Back at Huff Gym for the Final Four, the Tigers spilled Canton's one-handed shooters 39-38 on a late bank by Leal Nelson (Green tallied 22), while the state reverberated with the shocking end of Centralia's 42-game win streak (30-29) at the hands of Morton of Cicero. The Orphans couldn't hone in on their famed kiss shot, making nine field goals in 65 shots.

Urbana might have won it all, but Green fouled out early in the fourth quarter with the Tigers ahead 28-25, and Morton rallied to take the 1941 title 32-31.

"They were always on me to be more aggressive," Green said, "and I made some mistakes that forced me to leave with seven minutes to go."

Thus ended the magical run, as close as the Tigers ever have come to the state championship. A few years later, in 1947, News-Gazette sports editor Pat Harmon named Green as his center on an all-time all-state team that included Eddleman, Lou Boudreau, Andy Phillip and Otto Graham.

Fred was bigger than life and wanted to enroll at the UI, but he didn't buck his father's decision to send him to Exeter (N.H.) Academy. He played football in the fall and then sparked the Exeter basketball team with a 22-point average that led all Eastern prep schools in scoring.

Green was back at the UI in the fall of 1942, saying: "Doug Mills more or less recruited me. There was never any question where I was going to go"

Green, Eddleman, Walt Kirk and Chester Strumillo served a year of ineligibility on a freshman team that sometimes practiced against the Big Ten champion Whiz Kids.

"I could rebound and get a shot off," Green said, "but I couldn't pass like Art Mathisen. He fit right in on a team where everyone could run and move the ball. The Whiz Kids were special passers. After the war, I was never able to give them the same qualities at center that Mathisen did."

The war snuffed out a potential national title, and Green entered the army along with the Whiz Kids. Actually, he was an inch too tall to be accepted but, like a good attorney, he pleaded his case and won it. That led him to such dangerous Pacific stops as Bougainville and Luzon (Philippine Islands) where, as a corporal in the field artillery, he earned a Bronze Star for heroic achievement.

According to the report, when a tarpaulin covering ammunition was set afire during a hostile artillery barrage, threatening a catastrophic explosion, Green and a sergeant ran amid the firing from their sheltered position and extinguished the flames.

"There were only a few tough days," Green said. "When we hit one of the beachheads, it was virtually undefended. I was able to return in December of 1945 and played in three Illini games."

Always self-deprecating, Green said of the 1946-47 season, "It was great for me but probably a disaster for (the Whiz Kids). They expected to win again, but other schools were loaded with war veterans, and it didn't happen. They liked to cut off the post, and I wasn't particularly good at that. I wish I could have done better for them."

Phillip was below par healthwise, and Mills' last team dropped its finale at Indiana 48-41 to finish one game behind Wisconsin in the standings.

Green was the only returning starter in 1947-48 and shared time at center with the appropriately nicknamed Wally 'Ox' Osterkorn. It was Combes' first season, and the Illini struggled to a 7-5 league finish, Green being credited with "the finest game of his college career" in a 52-51 triumph at Indiana.

But it was the early run of Big Ten games in the title season of 1949 that solidified Green in the UI history book. He was the late-game hero of three straight league wins against Indiana (44-42), Ohio State (64-63) and Minnesota (45-44).

"Harry put me in late in the Indiana game with the idea that perhaps I could get an offensive rebound," Green said. "I feinted out before cutting back to get position. I was briefly open, and unexpectedly someone threw me the ball. There were only four seconds left, so I shot a hook. Really, it was unconscious. I'm just happy it went in."

At Ohio State, Osterkorn and Green combined for 30 points. Afterward, Buckeyes coach Tippy Dye singled out Green as the "best Illini" ahead of such dashing stalwarts as Eddleman, Bill Erickson and young Don Sunderlage. So impressive was Green that Buckeyes fans gave him a hand.

"That was the greatest road trip I can imagine, a real highlight," Green said.

Then came Minnesota, with Green playing 37 minutes as a defensive stopper against 6-10 Jim McIntyre.

As the championship march progressed, Green was little noticed in the 80-point runups against Northwestern, the 80-49 rout of Iowa and the late 91-68 bashing of Indiana. The speed boys piled up the points in those. But Combes would talk later about "five games in which Fred turned defeat into victory."

Said the ever-honest Green: "I had some good moments but, in truth, Osterkorn beat me out, and I mostly served as his backup, and on occasion we played together."

Illinois was one of eight teams invited to the NCAA tournament, and a 71-67 defeat of Yale gave the school its first Final Four appearance. The Illini were no match for Kentucky (76-47), and Green played only briefly in independent circles, preferring to concentrate on his law career. That's another story for a man who served 42 years as an elected judge, the last 24 (1974 to 1998) on the State Appellate Court.

Reflecting, he smiles: "It's kind of funny. My father looked askance at sports participation. He was in his 60s by the time I played, and he thought it was a waste of time. But later on, having the reputation as an Illini basketball player was a tremendous advantage in getting me elected. It's strange how things turn out sometimes."

To which let the chorus ring: "Green for Governor." We could do worse. Truth is, we probably are.

It has been difficult to watch this wondrous Urbana man lose his health and physique, but he has done it with immense courage and grace. The world is better because of Fred Green.

AUGUST 10, 2001

In the midst of a spectacular beginning at the UI, Lou Boudreau was declared ineligible.

CHAMPAIGN — Just as there was one Joltin' Joe and one Say Hey Willie, there was the one and only Good Kid.

Lou Boudreau, the Good Kid, was legendary in multiple ways. With baseball enjoying a Golden Era on the event of World War II, he was named manager of the Cleveland Indians at the unheard-of age of 24. His innovative mind would fashion the "Williams shift" to confuse Boston slugger Ted Williams. He would squeeze whatever was left from an ageless Satchel Paige. Lou was at the cutting edge. He led, others followed.

As a shortstop, he led AL fielders throughout the era, setting a league fielding record of .978 in 1944, and .982 in 1947. He led the league in hitting in 1944, thrice topped the league in doubles, collected more hits (1,578) than any player in the 1940s and sparked the Indians' most revered team to the championship in 1948, batting

.355 that season and hitting two homers in 8-3 playoff win over the Red Sox.

How ironic that the state's premier athlete of the 1930s (Boudreau) and of the 1940s (Dike Eddleman) should pass away within a 10-day span. A two-sport whirlwind, Boudreau was honored as Varsity "I" Man of the Year in 1987 and saw his No. 5 retired at Illinois Field April 18, 1992.

"We've lost another legend," said UI athletic director Ron Guenther. "He never lost touch with the university. Whatever we asked, he would participate in. He was a gracious man."

While middle-aged fans recall Boudreau as Cubs manager (1960) and WGN broadcaster for more than 20 years, he laid a rich foundation many years earlier. The first name on The News-Gazette's initial All-State basketball team in 1933 was the sophomore leader of Thornton's Flying Cloud. A flamboyant playmaker-scorer, Boudreau led the Harvey quintet into three straight IHSA championship games, winning in 1933 and finishing second to Quincy (39-27) in 1934 and Springfield (24-19) in 1935.

Moving on to the UI, he led scoring in 1937 as he joined late teammates Harry Combes, Bud Riegel, Tommy Nisbit, Jim Vopicka and Wib Henry in winning the Big Ten title, and he batted .347 that spring in sparking the UI's Big Ten baseball champions.

If Red Grange was big man on campus in the 1920s, Boudreau assumed that role during his sophomore year in 1936-37. Even more great things seemed around the corner.

Thirty years before the "slush fund" scandal would shatter Combes' 1966-67 basketball team and force the resignation of Combes and football coach Pete Elliott, the campus was rocked by the midseason loss of the UI's favorite athlete.

During the semester break of Boudreau's junior year, a Harvey resident reportedly informed Big Ten commissioner Major John L. Griffith that the Indians were providing Boudreau's mother $100 monthly payments under a contractual agreement assuring his signature with the Indians after completing his education at the University of Illinois.

A January vote by the Big Ten eligibility committee declared Boudreau a professional. The league's faculty representatives at first voted clemency to Boudreau at the end of the year, but this was later changed to declare him permanently ineligible.

Frank Richart, UI faculty rep, said at the time: "I am convinced he was wholly unaware this payment to his mother constituted a violation of amateur rules. The fact the money was not delivered to Boudreau is of small moment."

Eddie Jacquin, writing for The News-Gazette, noted that it was "common practice of some major league clubs to 'sew up' young players in this manner."

Boudreau signed with the Indians in May. He spent two years in the minors, batting .331 for Buffalo in the International League in 1939 and playing shortstop for the first time. He arrived at Cleveland in 1940.

Through it all, he remained particularly close to his college coaches, Doug Mills and Wally Roettger. He assisted in coaching the UI freshman during the winters of 1939 and 1940, was instrumental in recruiting Whiz Kid star Andy Phillip, and earned his B.S. in education in 1940.

Lou Boudreau is a name for the ages. Other records will be broken but no one will ever be named a major league manager at 24. The Good Kid will carry that through eternity.

Boudreau always felt close to the UI. He and I were officers for the Illini club in the Chicago Heights-Hammond area in the early 1960s. Lou was OK on radio, but sensational in telling baseball stories to banquets and small groups.

EARLY JANUARY 1991

Andy Kaufmann was undoubtedly the most contradictory star in Illini basketball history.

CHAMPAIGN — A Springfield writer noted that Andy Kaufmann is a basketball star who has been cheered and booed, loved and hated by Illini fans ... and all on the same play.

For this bull in a China shop, it's almost routine to hear, in a single gasp, "Oh, no, don't try it ... wow, great play!"

Sometimes Steve Bardo, Kendall Gill and Marcus Liberty, under their breath, stopped after the first portion of that sentence. Last year's Illini was "their team" and, even as Kaufmann started the first 16 games, he didn't fit in. Some observers said the team needed a second basketball.

"Yes, to be perfectly honest, I think I offended them with my offensive attitude," Kaufmann said this week. "It's just the way I play. I don't realize I'm shooting a lot. It may look like I'm trying to be selfish, but I'm not."

Kaufmann is an extemporaneous, non-jumping scoring machine. He does it any way he can — drives, treys, free throws, double-pumps, anything. He is a fullback in shorts, boring, twisting, spinning, faking and careening to launch his shot.

Averaging 24 points midway through his junior year, he's maintaining a figure topped only by past Illini greats Don Freeman (27.8), Red Kerr (25.3) and Nick Weatherspoon (25.0). Holder of a national high school record for most free throws made (918), he has converted 88 of 104 one-pointers this season. When the Illini missed eight of their last 10 against Purdue on Saturday, he made the two.

In coach Lou Henson's mind, basketball is an intricate, five-man game built on strategic picks and cuts. Kaufmann simplifies it. Give him the ball and he creates his own offense. The coach accepts the fact that he is adjusting more to Kaufmann's style than Kaufmann is to his.

"We wouldn't be 11-4 without him," Henson accepts, "and this year, every victory is appreciated."

Like a breakaway halfback who can't explain how he evaded the linebacker in the excitement of the chase, Kaufmann tends to forget the planned play when the ball comes into his hands. He does what comes naturally, advancing goalward by air or land.

No amount of failure discourages him. When he went 0 for 9 at Memphis State, the best bet was that he would shoot on the next opportunity. And he uses devises that don't always work, leading to a team-high pileup of turnovers.

"We're trying to get Andy not to spin around against a set defense. They are double- and triple-teaming him as soon as he starts to drive," said Henson.

"He's even faking out the referees. They think he's traveling when he isn't. They see the bodies collide in there, they don't know what to call, so they whistle traveling.

"We don't want to discourage him because he has so many positive assets. We're just working with him to try to get him to avoid turnovers and to get the ball to the open man when he is double-teamed."

Early this season, Kaufmann became the only Illini ever to have back-to-back games of 40 or better. Then he went to Penn State and hit a brick wall of defenders. Secretly, he likes the idea of taking on two or three defenders. It's irresistibly delicious.

"Sometimes I'm too stubborn. That's my mentality. I don't want to be so stubborn. At Penn State, I was still learning what I could and couldn't do," he said.

Then, at Memphis State, he got his first three shots blocked and went 3 for 17. Even in victory, he felt empty.

Understand, this athlete lives to score. It is his life. He skims through his school work, always needing summer classes to stay eligible. He has minimal sideline interest, no deep thoughts about Chief Illiniwek or Iraq, no earthly idea of what his life will consist of beyond basketball.

"I'm pretty boring," he shrugged. "When I have free time, I like to work out."

To upgrade his scoring skills, he leaves hard practices, eats and then holds private shooting sessions at the IMPE building.

There is method to everything he does. He eats for the purpose of maintaining the right weight — around 224 pounds — to overpower rivals. Loading up at his favorite cafeteria, he is said to top even Jens Kujawa in the consumption of food.

He lifts weights diligently to increase his strength around the basket. Returning home at 2 a.m. after the Memphis State trip, he immediately put his weary body through his personal routine of push-ups and sit-ups.

"I don't lift anything over my head because of the blood clot that knocked me out during my freshman year," he said. "But I do four or five sets of about 40 push-ups. I do them until I can't do them any more. I don't feel right if I miss workouts. I felt really lazy when I had to stop training as a freshman, and that really hurt me last year."

Lurching forward with spurts of power, he likes the feel of contact. When he gets a defender on his hip, when he can feel the other body, he is in total charge. Some say he isn't fast but, in that situation, he has an advantage.

"His first step is unbelievable," said UI assistant Mark Coomes. "Nobody can stop him one-on-one."

And his hands. So quick and strong. If the ball falls to the court in his area, see who gets it. If the rebounds carom below rim level, see how many he picks off. He's averaging six boards, quite a feat for a non-jumper.

"I try to make up for my poor jumping ability," he said. "My body takes up space and I have good hand strength. I could jump better as a high school freshman, and I dunked the ball as a sophomore. But I've never dunked in a college game. I guess it's my weight."

He employs other means to take advantage of his broad-backed size. He still remembers how, before his sophomore year at Jacksonville High, when he first led the state in scoring, he whipped Chicago King's sensational leaper, Levertis Robinson, in the one-on-one finals at Henson's summer camp. His eyes light up with the recollection.

"I always took pride in beating someone one-on-one," Kaufmann said. "Levertis was a stud of an athlete, and I admired him. He was older and bigger and stronger. It was a super thrill. I had a sense of accomplishment.

"That's how we played back on the concrete courts in Winchester (his home, 12 miles south from Jacksonville, throughout grade school). I'd take the ball in and spin to get open. I'd feel the contact and spin away from it.

"I work on those moves even when I'm alone. I pretend there's a defender, and I work myself to the spot where I know I'll be open. Then I go up quick and shoot. I never practice anything I don't use. I never shoot for recreation."

But nothing hones him into the hoop like the finish of a close game. His two game-turning treys in a 32-point effort against Purdue last Saturday are typical.

"I focus better at the end," he said. "I see everything so much more clearly then. The first one (against Purdue) was a set play for me, and I turned and shot just like in practice. You never know for sure whether it'll go in, but it felt good. I had a terrible feeling before I hit that one. I don't recall winning a game that was so far gone (Purdue led 59-52)."

Now, Kaufmann thinks of playing smarter, of passing in certain situations, of avoiding the mistakes that Henson harps on.

"When I want to discuss things, I talk to my brothers, Kevin (24) and Chad (19)," he said. "They know my game. Kevin says I've always done it on physical ability, that I need to think more, use my head, penetrate and pull up for the soft jumper."

But influencing a thoroughbred to alter his course isn't easy. As he says of himself:

"I should study more. I know that. But I'm addicted to basketball. It's high and mighty for me. I want to be the best I can be. I dream of the NBA. I don't think about anything else but basketball."

Driving and spinning and scoring, Andy Kaufmann enjoyed some incredible highs as an Illini. He was solo player in a team game, his 46 points in December of 1990 ranking second only to Dave Downey's record 53. But it is sadly true that he and Lou Henson were ready to separate by the time he played his last game.

FEBRUARY 5, 1993

Andy Kaufmann's long shot defeats Iowa in a miracle finish at the Assembly Hall.

CHAMPAIGN — In an instant, the Assembly Hall was hushed, stunned, confused.

Was someone heavenly looking out for Iowa's Hawkeyes?

In one mind-boggling moment, it was as though the spirit of the late Chris Street had just lifted the caroming basketball off Deon Thomas' shoulder and remarkably ... unbelievably ... deposited it in Iowa's basket to break a 75-75 tie.

And what mystic power, just seconds earlier, had caused ref Phil Bova to choke on his whistle when 250 pounds of Acie Earl landed full atop Andy Kaufmann as he shot a three-pointer? Instead of Kaufmann going to the line with three free throws to tie, the contest proceeded through the final minute while Illini coaches screamed bloody murder.

But in those traumatic last seconds, as the deflected ball magically found the hoop (supposedly hit by Iowa's Jim Bartels), Rennie Clemons was alert enough to call time. Clemons wasn't sure his plea had been recognized, and when the clock ran to :00, he disgustedly heaved the ball away.

Inspired, spiritually driven Iowa had apparently won again.

"The officials turned away from Rennie," said Illini athletic director Ron Guenther. "If it hadn't been for that monitor, they wouldn't have been able to determine how much time to put back on the clock."

At first, it read :00.5, not enough to catch the ball and shoot it. The discussion continued at the timer's table. Then a second was added. It read :01.5. Just enough for a coach with the "Nick Anderson shot" up his sleeve, with former prep quarterback T.J. Wheeler to play the Stephen Bardo role, and with a steelwilled gunner on the receiving end.

"We had another play in mind at first," said coach Lou Henson. "But then Mark Coomes recommended the Nick Anderson play."

It was Anderson who, at Indiana in 1989, took Bardo's long pass, dribbled and sank a bomb just after Hoosier Jay Edwards popped a remarkable baseline looper to tie it 67-67.

"We wanted to make sure they didn't tip the in-bounds pass," said Henson, "because that would start the clock, and then the game would be over. So we used Rennie to screen while T.J. ran the baseline and threw it long. We had the deep man set a pick for Andy (Kaufmann), and he did a great job just catching the ball. Without a perfect pass and a perfect catch, there would be no shot."

Said Wheeler:

"We had worked on that play. But at first we weren't going to run it. Then I started yelling 'Let's do the play for Andy where we've got the two big guys picking.' We changed to it before we came out of the huddle.

"I saw Andy breaking. I led him. I threw it as hard as I could."

Andy went up to grab it near the sideline, turned with a dribble and popped wide open about 3 feet beyond the arc. When the ball swished the net, the roar was deafening. Whooping celebrants erupted onto the court in a wild melee.

This was Christian Laettner drilling Kentucky. This was North Carolina State shocking Houston. Clemons tackled a running, jumping Kaufmann, and everybody piled on. It was a mob scene.

Mentally, you see, this one had been lost. The spirit of Chris Street, which rallied Iowa from 15 down with 3 1/2 minutes left at Michigan State, had taken almost visible form. He willed in their free throws. He turned Wade Lookingbill into Superman.

But wait, did Kaufmann get the shot off in time? The human eye couldn't tell, although stop action later showed it departed his hand with two-tenths of a second left. Yep, the refs guessed right on that last one.

"I've stayed up at night with my feet sweating, thinking about something like that," said the ever-quotable Kaufmann.

"I remember back in our early practices at Huff, we must have gone over that play 15 times, 20 times. I was thinking back then, 'You know, are we really ever going to use this?' It got old for me at the time but now I see that it paid off.

"The one dribble allowed me to feel a little more comfortable, and I was surprised at how open I was."

Later, Thomas pondered it all.

"That's the second time a ball has deflected off me into the basket. It happened against Princeton too. I was pretty discouraged.

"But the finish, well, that's the wildest thing I've ever been involved in. I stayed out of the pile, and then I went in and picked Andy off the floor. It was amazing."

Andy Kaufmann never, ever felt pressure. He had ice in his veins. The Iowa shot was bigger than Anderson's at Indiana because the Illini were trailing and had seemingly lost, and the animosity toward Iowa was enormous at the time.

MARCH 4, 2002

Frank Williams' driving basket gives Illinois an improbable comeback and the Big Ten basketball crown.

MINNEAPOLIS — Welcome back, Rod Serling! In a return to The Twilight Zone, Illinois was lying face-up as the grave diggers began flipping dirt on the casket when Frank Williams, Cory Bradford and a never-say-die squad came roaring back to the surface.

Down 66-57 with three minutes left Sunday at Minnesota, distressingly error-prone and severely punished by the Gophers' offensive rebounders, still trailing 66-62 in the final half-minute with the Gophers in possession, Bill Self's miracle workers forced three late turnovers to polish off a 10-0 run that allowed Illinois to win 67-66 and share its third Big Ten basketball championship in five seasons.

"I've been involved with some crazy finishes, but never anything more crazy than this," Self said.

"Their length really bothered us, they killed us with offensive rebounds (23), and with all our turnovers (20) and missed free throws (Robert Archibald missed six in the last 10 minutes), we shouldn't have been in the game. The deck was stacked against us ... but somehow we managed to hang in. I have questioned our toughness in the past, but never again."

There have been numerous Illini mini-miracles in football through the years: the clock-beating 29-28 win in 1982 at Wisconsin; the improbable triumphs against Ohio State in 1983 (17-13) and 1992 (18-16); the 14-13 surprise at Southern Cal in 1989; the 24-21 rally in 1993 at Michigan; memorable comebacks against Indiana and Minnesota; and all those clutch fourth-quarter rallies orchestrated by Kurt Kittner last fall.

But this stacks up as the most unlikely UI basketball victory since the 78-77 home win against Iowa in 1993. That one had flown away on angel's wings until the refs put precious seconds back on the clock, giving Andy Kaufmann time to catch T.J. Wheeler's baseball pass and drain a long game-winning trey.

Sunday's thriller appeared gone until Williams, who said he "reached in with both hands," tore the ball from Kerwin Fleming, rolling it out for a Bradford trey that made it 66-65 with 17 seconds showing.

In Gopher lore, and in The Word as it is spread by veteran Minneapolis columnist Sid Hartman, the melee around Fleming will go down with Ty Douthard's "nonfumble" at the Gopher goal line in 1994. Did Ty reach the goal line before fumbling? Was Fleming hacked before he turned it over? Opposing sides will offer different versions.

Fleming, who claimed he was screaming for timeout in the din of 14,612 roaring voices, said: "Three guys trapped me, and they were fouling the mess out of me."

Offered Hartman: "You guys had a horseshoe on your backside."

Which brings this retort: "Well, Sid, that's better than a pitchfork."

So it shall be reported that no whistles blew, Bradford's trey was good and Minnesota still had the ball and a one-point lead. Then, with Self calling for Luther Head to foul at 0:10, Kevin Burleson avoided contact with a reverse pivot in the backcourt and threw the ball wildly out of bounds with seven seconds left.

That set the stage for a classic Williams burst down the lane as Minnesota, having employed a zone almost throughout, switched to man-to-man.

"When I saw that, I told Sean (Harrington) to throw the ball to Frank and let him drive," Self said.

It sounds easier than it was. Williams sped past long-armed Travarus Bennett and banked in a flying semi-hook with Bennett all over him. It was his only basket of the half and came right in front of CBS analyst Billy Packer, who criticized him so severely Feb. 3.

"I'd rate this No. 1," Williams said.

For this injury-hampered team, the 67-66 win capped a season that began 0-5 on opponents' courts and ended 5-0 on the road, that started 4-5 in the Big Ten and finished 11-5 with an eight-game win streak that was ignited by overcoming a 27-14 deficit at Michigan, an awful 27-11 start vs. Purdue and was capped with another comeback from 27-14 deficit Sunday.

Double-digit deficits mean nothing to Williams & Co. Criticism flows off their shoulders. They miss shots, and they keep shooting. They commit turnovers and make it up somewhere else. This was one of the UI's all-time great stretch runs, no Illini quintet in the last half-century (since 1951) closing the regular season with an eight-game win streak.

Can they repeat this act Friday against Minnesota or Penn State in Indianapolis? Looking at Sunday's first 37 minutes, you wouldn't think so. But that overlooks the 10-0 run in the last three, when the Illini turned their own graveside visit into a Gopher funeral.

The picture of a wide-eyed, open-mouthed Williams Arena fandom, watching in shock as Frank Williams soared for the final basket, told the story of this remarkable finish. They couldn't believe it. Neither could I.

APRIL 12, 2002

Brandon Lloyd, Walter Young and their buddies comprise the UI's best receiving corps.

CHAMPAIGN — Best Illini receiving corps ever? As Brandon Lloyd, Walter Young, Greg Lewis and Aaron Moorehead perform brilliantly this spring, pushed by quality backups Eric McGoey, Kendrick Jones and Ade Adeyemo, have they reached the all-time best level?

That's covering acres of territory. That's sliding around greats of the UI past — John Wright Sr., Garvin Roberson, David Williams — until historical digging brings a realization. If Illinois has been prominent in producing linebackers and quarterbacks, few major college programs have turned out fewer big-time receivers.

You'd think it would be the opposite. Wouldn't receivers here draw more of a spotlight than at, say, Michigan or Ohio State? Didn't Bo Schembechler resist the pass wherever possible? Yet here is Michigan with an incredible array dating to the great Anthony Carter and roaring through the 1990s with Desmond Howard, Amani Toomer, Mercury Hayes, David Terrell, Tai Streets and most recently Marquise Walker.

And there's Ohio State with the grind-it-out tradition of Woody Hayes, Archie Griffin and Orlando Pace, flashing a quality list of receivers on NFL rosters. There were eight in 2001 including Cris Carter, Jeff Graham, Joey Galloway, Terry Glenn and David Boston. Illinois trails badly. Not even Mike White and John Mackovic could attract preferred choices, a trend that carries into today when the state's top-rated pair, Centennial's Marquis Johnson and Dunbar's Jason Avant, chose Texas and Michigan, respectively.

Illini Mike Bellamy reported with the Indianapolis Colts in 1992 but never appeared in a game. Williams had a bangup Canadian career, but no Illini receivers have played in the NFL since 1989, when the careers of Mike Martin and Darryl Usher ended.

Lacking the receivers to gain separation in the secondary, Ron Turner inherited an easily defended UI offense. And it didn't change until walk-ons Moorehead and Lewis (upcoming seniors) began to develop, Lloyd was moved from the defense and Young gave up quarterbacking.

Yep, what might be the best-ever corps was woven out of irregular cloth. Now, all receivers return from a group that participated in 226 receptions and 29 TDs for the most prolific Illini offense in history (32.5 ppg.). Lloyd had 65 catches, Young 50.

"We didn't have anything when we started," fourth-year receivers coach Robert Jackson said. "That first spring, we were totally stuffed at the line. We were playing extremely slow. We're at a point now where we'd love you to play man against us. Bring it on! No question, we see ourselves as the best receiving corps in the Big Ten. We have that talent. Now we have to prove it. We intend to be a big-play team."

Best ever? Shawn Wax, UI director of development who caught 102 career passes, calls this group "1-B" behind the "1-A" corps of Williams, Usher and Steve Pierce in 1985.

"A year from now, that might change," Wax said. "I believe Lloyd is, without doubt, our all-time best receiver ahead of Williams, Bellamy, Pierce and Martin. Those are my top five. Lloyd has great ability, and Young is an exceptional playmaker, much like Jason Dulick (169 career catches). Of course, as a corps, our tight ends used to catch a lot more passes."

Indeed, Tim Brewster caught 52 and 64 in his two seasons.

Lewis looks at Lloyd and Young as "something for the rest of us to shoot for." He said:

"I think we have four starters, and those top guys give us something to focus on. Brandon is our most remarkable athlete. I can't believe what he does day after day. Walter isn't razzle-dazzle, but he makes big plays. But I won't lay down and say I'm a backup. Coach Turner has a lot of formations that need extra receivers. When our opportunities come, we have to make the most of them."

Moorehead chimes in, seemingly including Lloyd as a senior because, like basketball's Frank Williams, Lloyd will be in his fourth year (redshirted in 2000 with a broken leg) and figures to turn pro after next season.

"Our goal is to leave as the best corps in Illinois history and the best in the country," Moorehead said. "You have to set high goals. Personally, I finished strong last season, and I'm using that as a steppingstone. We all want to make the QB transition easier."

Lloyd has a natural flair and was the UI's best-ever in terms of catlike reactions on long bombs. He caught 65 passes again that year and Young added 56 as the team amassed 3,388 in the air, just 10 shy of the UI record set in 1981. This was clearly the UI's best group at the wideout position.

SEPTEMBER 11, 2002

J.C. Caroline's legacy as a great Illini lives on at Memorial Stadium.

CHAMPAIGN — J.C. Caroline drives from Champaign to Urbana, passing within eyesight of Memorial Stadium every workday. But the former Illini and Bears great hasn't seen his large, illuminated picture connected to the new stadium videoboard. Nor is he exactly sure when he will.

"On Sundays, church comes first," Caroline said. "I played 10 years of Sunday football and I appreciate the game, but I don't worship football. I've rearranged my priorities. Even if the game started at 1:30, it would still be hard."

Don't worry. Caroline will attend several Bears games this season. If he isn't in a hurry, it's just part of his relaxed, low-profile lifestyle. Unbelievably, J.C. will turn 70 in January. Less than a year later, we'll be celebrating the 50th anniversary of a bust-out 41-20 rout of Ohio State that led to a 1,256-yard season and a Big Ten co-championship. It is now 39 years since Caroline and the Bears intercepted five Y.A. Tittle passes to hand George Halas his final NFL championship in 1963.

There are tinges of gray in that dark hair, but Caroline looks trim and muscular. At 205, he's only about 10 pounds over his pro playing weight.

"I don't work out, and I haven't played golf for a few years," he said. "I don't go out much. I've never been a person to change my environment. I've lived in the same house since 1970. I eat the same things over and over."

Caroline still teaches physical education at Urbana Middle School, remaining in the system 19 years after his five-year stint as Urbana football coach. He said he has no thought of retiring.

A member of the College Hall of Fame and a former Pro Bowler (last Bears salary: $23,000), Caroline originally enrolled at the UI on the recommendation of friends and businessmen in South Carolina, where the state university was segregated in 1952.

"My high school, George Rogers, was right on the university campus, and I couldn't go there," said Caroline, a prep sensation with some 50 career TDs. "I didn't know anything about Illinois. I thought the university was in Chicago. I took a train to Cincinnati, and then I came to Tolono and took a bus in."

All freshmen were ineligible in those days. When his time came, Caroline made the biggest splash ever by a first-year UI player. He led the nation — the nation — in rushing and, as a virtual unknown, finished seventh in Heisman Trophy voting even as he nearly doubled the rushing output of the 1953 winner, John Lattner of Notre Dame. Illini regrets? There were several.

Caroline thought a 7-1-1 Illini team deserved to go to the Rose Bowl after tying Michigan State for the 1953 title, but the Spartans were riding a high wave of sentiment, were undefeated national champs in 1951 and 1952 and were in their first year in the Big Ten. They got the vote.

Then came 1954, when Illinois couldn't replace its departed linemen and finished 1-8.

And, finally, came 1955 when Caroline suffered the greatest setback of his career: his lost senior year. If he is not talkative on other subjects, this one sets him off. Scheduled to be the UI's first black captain, he relates his version of the half-century-old story as though it was yesterday.

"It was one of those situations where the head of the physiology department wanted to get back at the football program because he couldn't get a seat on the 50-yard line," Caroline said. "He took it out on the team.

"I had a C in the course, and I passed the final. He wasn't even the teacher, but he came in and changed the grade on his way to Germany. Out of the first 50 papers graded, 30 flunked, so they stopped right there and started going over the papers."

When the professor returned, Caroline said his grade was changed to passing, but he already had departed for Canada, where he played professionally for one season before joining the Bears.

Years later, Caroline completed his degree at Florida A&M and became an assistant on the UI staffs led by Jim Valek and Bob Blackman. Dropped by Gary Moeller in 1977, Caroline said: "Moeller felt I had too much influence with the players and didn't want to compete with that."

Thus ended Caroline's UI career. But, hopefully, he'll get back there soon to see the memorial of himself. He's right up there with Halas, Grange and Butkus ... mighty good company.

I was in service when Caroline exploded at Illinois, but I watched him when he was a crashing tackler in the Bears' secondary. When called on to carry the ball, he was a slashing, north-south runner. He still looks like he could play.

MISCELLANEOUS

OCTOBER 9, 2007

Fighting Illini make dreams come true with strong finish in 2007

CHAMPAIGN — What is life if you can't dream?

How shallow is your hum-drum daily existence if you can't roll back your eyes and imagine the thrill of the chase?

Well, anyone who dared to dream about Illini football in recent years found himself in a constant state of disappointment. Dreams die if they never come true. It's too painful. It's better to count sheep and avoid thinking about it.

For Illinois, it wasn't happening. The team struggled through four consecutive seasons with a Big Ten audit of 2-30. Ron Turner's last team in 2004 beat Indiana 26-22. And Ron Zook's second team in 2006 edged Michigan State 23-20. That was it. A little ray of hope and then, kaput! It's easier to enjoy the tailgate. Or watch a real game on TV.

But there are cycles in this business. And the recognized evolution of Illini football is that the program tends to rise sharply from time to time, not for long periods, to steal the show. Traditionally, when the Illini catch a rare wind in their sails, they've shown a unique ability to ride it through seemingly uncharted waters.

Consider that Illinois has won or shared the Big Ten title seven times since 1946 and finished second twice. That computes to a conference championship roughly every decade, which is the fair share for a nine-, 10- or 11-team league.

But runner-up? That has happened twice in 78 years. You see, championship contention has been shamefully infrequent. And yet, in those special years where Illinois evolved into a legitimate challenger, their dreams came true ... whether it was Pete Elliott capturing a Rose Bowl despite an 0-11 (one tie) record against Michigan and Ohio State from 1960 through 1965 ... whether it was Mike White making a Rose Bowl team out of a program with one positive record (6-4-1) between 1966 and 1980 ... whether it was Turner starting at

0-11 in 1997 and reaching 10-2 in 2001 (only to fall back again).

That's what a 3-0 Big Ten start does to Illini Nation. It allows the fandom to dream, maybe even fantasize. In this case, the possibilities are hitting us almost overnight. Even if Ohio State goes undefeated, chances are the Buckeyes will find themselves playing for the national championship in the Louisiana Superdome, leaving the Rose Bowl open for — dare we dream — a team like Illinois.

OK, so it's a long shot. OK, in that case, the Rose committee wouldn't have to take the Big Ten runner-up. And worse yet, Michigan survived an ineligible player and stands like a mountain in the way. But Illinois has a chance in just the next two weeks (at Iowa, home vs. Michigan) to stake a claim that would be difficult to dislodge.

The attitude at this juncture is extremely strong. Juice Williams and Arrelious Benn apparently have rebounded from their second bout with minor injuries. Zook is rotating huge numbers on defense. Rashard Mendenhall is playing for monster NFL dollars.

"We took a lot of butt whippings to reach this point," Zook said. "We're not yet where we want to be, but we're rounding the bend. We're not satisfied. We know how close it is to be back where we were."

Fame can be fleeting. Check out Saturday's host. After 11-2, 10-3 and 10-2 seasons, Iowa coach Kirk Ferentz could have run for governor. The Hawkeyes' win streak reached nine in early 2005. Shockingly, the worm turned that September, and Iowa is 14-16 overall since that time with eight consecutive Big Ten losses. That's right, eight failures in a row, including two apiece to Indiana and Wisconsin.

Just when the world seemed brightest, dark clouds swept over Kinnick Stadium. Rather than achievers, the Hawkeyes have been reduced to spoilers.

Just a reminder. That's how the world turns.

A sidelight to the Illini quest is whether it can be maintained over time. The last 10 Illini coaches saw their fortunes receding before their mostly forced departures. Two of the 10, Ray Eliot and John Mackovic, left on a winning record. Eliot was 5-3-1 in 1959 but only 21-29-4 in his last six campaigns. Mackovic dipped to 6-5 in 1991 before leaving for Texas.

The difference in 2007 is that Zook's aggressive recruiting is putting an ever-increasing level of talent on the field, and early indications show him heading toward possibly his best recruiting class yet. With January enrollees counting back, Illinois might attract more than the NCAA limit of 25 this year and is drawing look-see visits from several young stars who have made oral commitments elsewhere.

Hang on, you dreamers. This whirlwind could turn into a tornado.

The Illini didn't beat Iowa and Michigan in the next two games, but they rallied to finish second in the conference for only the third time in nearly eight decades, and they reached the Rose Bowl after a remarkable series of events lifted Ohio State into the national championship game. In this case, the dreams came true.

2000

Michael Jordan gets the vote here as the greatest athlete of all time.

As our experts settle on Muhammad Ali as the Athlete of the Century, let me explain why he's not.

Boxing, once a national pastime, has for many years produced boxers from an ever-decreasing pool. You don't see thousands of youngsters turning out for the boxing team because, in 99 percent of our towns and cities, they don't exist. There are only a few pockets. And only a fraction of young boxers are heavyweights.

Ali was a wondrous fighter and a striking personality, but he dominated a sport that few elect to participate in. He ruled a tiny kingdom ... and one that is often suspect.

If the turnout of young football players is many times greater — and how many prospective boxers are on those rolls? — the basketball numbers are off the charts ... in the millions.

Parents build basketball goals in their driveways, not boxing rings. Everybody wants to be Michael Jordan.

Imagine, for a moment, the quick hands and strong muscles of Sergio McClain in a boxing ring. And is there anything about a 220-pound Cleotis Brown's athleticism that would prevent him from floating like a butterfly and stinging like a bee?

Well, multiply those two, McClain and Brown, by thousands, and imagine the kind of elimination competition you'd have in boxing if it had evolved as the popular sport of choice.

The numbers factor enhances the standing of Jordan as the century's greatest athlete.

He is the No. 1 player in the most popular sport ... better than Oscar Robertson, superior to Magic Johnson, offensively spectacular and defensively one of the all-time best.

Basketball is a team sport but, face it, Jordan was a one-man gang with the Chicago Bulls. He literally willed the Bulls to one title after another. They were nothing before he arrived and they're nothing since he left.

Repeating, Jordan forged this talent against the best athletes this country and all the other countries could produce. Unlike boxing, every U.S. teen-ager who might excel in basketball does.

What about Babe Ruth? You can't discount one who changed the game and was so much better than everyone else in his era. However, Ruth evolved (after his pitching period) as a power hitter without speed, and performed in a sport with restrictions. The great black athletes of the period, some of whom may have been comparable to Ruth, were non-participants.

Ever since Jackie Robinson broke the color line, African-Americans have dominated baseball's offensive statistics, creating the suspicion that this would have happened sooner if they hadn't been shut out.

In mentioning offensive stats, it's clear these are overemphasized in analyzing athletes of the past, and defensive prowess underemphasized ... even though defense (in Ruth's case, the ability to run) should be a major part of the equation. Examples are modern ratings putting Ted Williams over Joe DiMaggio and lifting Hank Aaron alongside Willie Mays (in some polls), even though DiMaggio and Mays were more complete outfielders, and ranked higher by many, at the time.

Furthermore, it should be noted that when votes were taken in 1950 for the greatest athlete of the half-century, Jim Thorpe won. Fifty years later, experts deciding this issue look on from a different perspective. Thorpe has slipped down the ladder.

No matter, Jordan is The Man. Not Ali. Not Ruth. Not Jim Brown.

Believe it.

One of my pet peeves is that so-called experts, in looking back over time, turn almost totally to offensive statistics, and don't put proper weight on an area where these athletes spend half their time, on defense. Another pet peeve is the extra weight given durability in all-star selections. Mays and Aaron? Willie was far better. Aaron wasn't even deemed strong enough defensively to play center field on his own team.

JANUARY 15, 2000

Michigan's cheating in basketball caught up with them when the feds became involved.

CHAMPAIGN — So you think Lon Kruger's Illini have problems? So, you're upset that a supposed Top 25 club has lost five basketball games?

Well, you don't know what trouble is.

How would you feel if published reports indicated a member of last year's team had received $50,000 from a booster, that a 1996 star had received $37,000, and another celebrated squad member had used the same booster's address as his home.

That's the hangover facing the University of Michigan — the Fighting Illini's opponent Sunday — as "Martingate" springs anew.

The Ann Arbor News reports that Ed Martin, an erstwhile gambler who attached himself to Michigan athletes, is trapped in an IRS inquiry ... and is expected to sign a plea bargain with the U.S. Attorney that would give the NCAA what amounts to the subpoena power that its investigators don't have.

In other words, the plea bargain would require Martin, who is charged with running illegal gambling operations in Ford plants, to come clean on everything ... to cooperate ... to fully disclose his relationships to the NCAA.

Due to a four-year statute of limitations, Fab Fivers Chris Webber, Jalen Rose and Juwan Howard appear out of reach. But not Louis Bullock, who reportedly received some of his $50,000 even as Michigan was already running its internal investigation and after Martin had been banned ... not Albert White, who transferred to Missouri after being financially linked to Martin ... and not Tractor Traylor, whose address was once listed as the same as Martin.

If the NCAA takes up this quest, the names of Bullock, White and Traylor will live far beyond whatever successes they brought to the program.

And the NCAA, which repeatedly backed down and softened its investigative attitude in the latter portion of the 1990s, will again have to wipe egg off its face after having accepted light sanctions that "pro-active" Michigan had imposed upon itself.

Michigan is paying an ongoing penalty in terms of basketball results, and, even though the statute of limitations saves Chris Webber, Wolverine wins have been struck from the books in five seasons. And no one was more critical of this episode than former Michigan athletic director Don Canham.

AUGUST 4, 2003

Hey, Tom, there is no profit in throwing out the good with the bad.

CHAMPAIGN — Tom Knott of the Washington Times is smarter than most of us.

But his head is deep in the egg when he blames an imperfect collegiate sports system for the death of Baylor's Patrick Dennehy.

Referring to NCAA leadership as "nitwits," Knott points out they have "objected to the most basic academic standards ... providing this or that street urchin with a second or third chance." He calls it a "rotten system built on lies and greed ... a system that might as well have an open-admission policy for athletes."

Knott concludes "you open your academic doors to the riffraff and you get ... those who commit the garden-variety police-blotter stuff and you get the football player who relates to his girlfriend by dragging her down the stairs by her hair. You also get the athletes who rape and pillage the community, and you get the sad-sack dimwits who would not be in college if it were not for those who do their work."

OK, Tom, this rebuttal won't be a Nancy Cantor speech on the values of campus diversity — or the list of comparable talent exemptions for singers, musicians and artists, or how brilliant mathematicians escape English requirements, or how the UI's summer bridge program (graduation is Saturday) helps those with portfolio deficiencies.

Nor will this be a recitation of appalling statistics showing legions of black men killed annually by other black men. What happened to Dennehy, presumably at the hands of an irrational Carlton Dotson, is replayed over and over in the margins of society.

No, the response is simply this: The NCAA's three divisions had 355,688 male and female participants receiving $25 million in scholarship aid in 2000-01. That's a lot of student-athletes being, at the very least, subjected to the values of learning and competition. And as we see each spring at the UI scholar-athlete banquet, overwhelming numbers emerge with degrees and embark on rewarding careers.

If there were 5,688 bad eggs — and that's a high number — that leaves 350,000 who profit immensely from the experience. For every Dotson who hears voices, thousands are receiving a clear message.

Admittedly, the 24-7 news cycle has poured out many stories about coaches or athletes who have gotten off good conduct. But take note. Businessmen who fudge, gamble and/or get caught in late-night escapades don't get fired. Rick Neuheisel, Mike Price, Larry Eustachy and Jim Harrick are out of work. And athletes who fall short are obliged to find a new avenue.

Like all enterprises, problems arise and demand constant attention. Pressure builds as basketball and football are asked to carry the financial load.

And costs are skyrocketing. The St. Louis Post-Dispatch reports that fans wishing to sit courtside at Missouri's new $75 million arena in 2004-05 will pay more than $30,000 a seat. Maryland's new arena requires a $100,000 one-time donation for courtside seating.

The remarkable aspect is that people and/or corporations are willing to make those investments even in difficult economic times. And there is vast seating, even if less desirable, filled by enthusiasts less fortunate.

What we see are major college arenas and stadiums packed from coast to coast with people who care. Big Ten football will average more than 70,000 this fall. Men's basketball and football are staples in the entertainment industry and use that income to support their nonrevenue brethren.

To blame the Dennehy-Dotson episode on the favored academic standards provided specifically talented student-athletes overlooks overall values. If Dennehy and Dotson are playing with guns and are involved with people who threaten their lives, the death of one or the other was even more likely outside the campus environment. It's a stretch to suggest that a "rotten system" led to this tragedy.

This isn't to say that some student-athletes shouldn't be rejected. This isn't to say there isn't cheating in the classroom. And we've heard new cases where counselors might be doing some of the homework. But every school has a compliance department these days, and as you saw with Bill Self and Rick Majerus, each one is nitpicking in a search to uncover the smallest infractions.

For all its faults, the system is working.

It isn't a perfect system to tie big league amateur sports with our universities. But it happened that way, and it is a faulty exaggeration to say it is all bad.

SEPTEMBER 11, 2000

Faced with a zero tolerance decree, Bob Knight saw his era at Indiana University end with a strange incident in which a student called him by his last name.

Indiana University officials were in denial for nearly three decades.

So it would have been inappropriate to oust the Classic Bully in May for outrageous activities that these very administrators had overlooked in the past.

The Classic Bully deserved, regardless of your point of view, a chance to start over.

To have done otherwise would not only have been a retroactive response but would have reflected negatively on board and administrative members who chose to overlook a long list of disgraceful acts — when they happened.

The CB couldn't have been offered a better second chance. All he had to do was act like the rest of us ... just be normal ... avoid confrontations ... mind your own business.

That was asking too much. A lifetime of defiant, intimidating and disrespectful behavior led to more of the same.

He disliked his former attorney, Clarence Doninger, too much to work with him as athletic director. He verbally abused a female school official. He was as foul-mouthed and insulting as ever.

And as the end neared, he called a news conference without notifying superiors, and appeared wild-eyed and over the edge in his televised explanation of the latest episode with a student waiting in the football ticket line at Assembly Hall.

If it was hard to make sense of his "Who's your daddy?" overreaction to student fans at Northwestern, it was doubly difficult to comprehend why he became so unhinged over someone calling him by his last name.

What, no Mister, no Sir, no Your Royal Highness?
We leave that unnecessary incident with one reaction: If the Classic Bully couldn't control himself over something so innocuous, how would he handle all the unexpected challenges next winter in West Lafayette and Iowa City?

The sad part is that, like the late Woody Hayes, whose prophecy proclaimed the Classic Bully would follow in disgraceful exit, he had the great intelligence and immense talent to be a glorious winner of his time ... only to see it overshadowed by one fatal personal flaw.

The irony, for one so roundly successful, is that the inspired innovator who changed the face of Big Ten basketball, who assembled the 32-0 team of 1976, who orchestrated three NCAA championships, mysteriously had become erratic and distracted on the bench ... strategically inconsistent.

Upsets in Big Ten and NCAA tournaments became routine. His Hoosiers were routed by Pepperdine in the most recent playoffs.

The Classic Bully mishandled late-game situations. He became Lon Kruger's pigeon.

His actions carried deeply into his squad. You don't see quality athletes like Luke Recker and A.J. Guyton go into a shell if they aren't feeling intimidation from the sideline.

Recker couldn't get out of there fast enough. And Guyton would have also left early if it had been in his best interests. The list of departures is long.

So, the reign of terror is over at Indiana. The Classic Bully too long had roamed without restraints. President Myles Brand recognized the hopelessness of the situation in 17 weeks of hostile fence-walking, and reacted appropriately.

It will be a different atmosphere when coach Bill Self takes his Illini to Bloomington for their only meeting with Indiana this winter. Something will be missing. But the Classic Bully, as Lou Henson so aptly described him, brought it on himself.

His successor?

Indiana is best advised to let the smell dissipate, to hire an interim coach for a year and thereby create a gap that will allow heated passions to cool down before the ultimate successor takes the helm.

After having a good relationship with Bob Knight for years, I refused to use his name in my column as a response to his shameful actions and, after the Lowell Hamilton recruiting confrontation, his claims that Lou Henson cheated. Knight should be ashamed of himself.

NOVEMBER 21, 1994

Basketball center Shelly Clark pays an extra price for domestic violence against his girlfriend.

CHAMPAIGN — Whatever mistakes University of Illinois senior Shelly Clark made in the early morning of Oct. 22, these truths should be self-evident:

— That university administrators (and his coach) are obligated to hand down penalties commensurate with similar first-offense cases in the past;

— That he not pay an extra price because UI officials are concerned about the unusual nature of the publicity and the school's image;

— That, as a prominent member of the basketball team, he not be spotlighted simply because certain interests see this as a grand opportunity to promote their legitimate crusade against domestic violence;

— That when all three persons agree in their testimony as to what happened that night ... even if it contradicts previous statements ... it may be appropriate to suspect they are fabricating, but you cannot formulate a judgment on anything other than their sworn testimony;

— That even though this junior college transfer changed majors and dropped classes last year when his mother died, and needed a successful appeal by faculty rep Mildred Griggs to gain eligibility this semester, his marginal academic situation should not be incorporated into the case. Face it, the UI would not be selling out the Assembly Hall if coach Lou Henson restricted his recruiting to scholars;

— That administrators should accept the innocent-until-proven guilt aspect of the American justice system, which they surely espouse, and understand that there are legitimate reasons why home invasion and battery charges against Clark were dropped.

The unnatural aspect of the case is that while Henson handed down the decision, he was obviously coerced by higher-ups who, in a series of grim meetings, sought a much larger chunk of Clark than they got.

The truth is, they needed Henson to make the announcement and take the heat because, with his special rights as coach, he was the only official source that attorney J. Steven Beckett wasn't willing to take to court.

If the student disciplinary committee had barred Clark from playing, Beckett would have appealed their decision and, at the same time, filed in court for a temporary restraining order that would probably have put Clark on the airplane for Puerto Rico on Wednesday morning.

Much as we ridicule lawyers, a lot of decisions wouldn't be made correctly if we didn't have them hovering over the deliberations.

As it is, everybody is grudgingly accepting the five-game suspension and going forward with their lives.

But this one leaves a sour taste in mouths on both sides, some factions wanting Clark's head while others, like this writer, seeing it as a case of certain individuals prejudging this high-visibility incident, protecting their behinds with politically correct posturing, and forcing a decision that is unjust in comparison to a long list of similar cases on record in Urbana.

"I've been stewing over this since midweek, when I realized what was going to happen," said Beckett.

"A five-game suspension is unprecedented, but this is the era of political correctness on campus, and Shelly's timing was very bad. These are trying times for traditionalists.

"The only reason this decision is palatable is because Henson made it."

Face facts. It is always difficult to get a level-headed decision when high-profile athletes are involved in misdeeds. These events nearly always turn into a political football and get kicked even higher by know-it-alls in the workplace.

MARCH 28, 2003

Whoever called for games to be stopped due to the Iraqi war forgot that diversions are healthy for the soul.

CHAMPAIGN — "March Madness has such allure that people finger-paint their faces in streaked school colors, rainbow-dye their hair, bedeck themselves in garish clothing, yell until they can barely summon a rasping whisper, stand and clap and sing and riotously shout taunts at the opposition like: 'You (stink)!'

"And that's just the faculty."

These are the words of Champaign's own Bill Lyon as he nimbly forms award-winning columns in the city where W.C. Fields would rather be, Philadelphia.

What Lyon describes is an annual way of life in which close followers turn basketball into a mini-vacation, distant viewers puzzle over office brackets and cage conversation everywhere offers a diversion from grim realities.

Yet there are those who say it is callous and insensitive ... yes, even unpatriotic ... to play games during wartime. No good-ol'-boy auto races. No sniffing the azaleas in Augusta. No Kobe, no Sosa.

William C. Rhoden of The New York Times, stunned by the TV images of Iraqi buildings being demolished and soldiers exchanging fire, says flatly: "The NCAA tournament should have been canceled ... (Myles) Brand made a mistake."

Rhoden quotes Utah coach Rick Majerus as saying the ground assault "should have been the end of the tournament."

This is a minority viewpoint. For the most part, we find ourselves in favor of proceeding normally insofar as new national security rules permit.

The solution is simple ... as uncomplicated as it has been since troops' morale became an issue in World War II.

Ask the soldiers. They're the collective boss. This is not about politicians or generals or corporate executives. This isn't a decision for those who cower in the corner and want everything to stop. This is about the dogfaces who'll go house-to-house in Baghdad.

So, as long as large assemblages aren't a security risk, as long as planes are safe in our airspace, let our bravest make the decision. They have earned the right.

Why them? At the risk of a mistaken paraphrase of something that flashed before my eyes, remember:

Newspapers aren't free because of brilliant editorial writers, they're free because of soldiers.

This nation's system of enterprise exists because of soldiers.

Terrorism is not on the run because of political hand-wringing, but because of soldiers.

Throngs of antiwar protesters and individuals like Michael Moore have the latitude to express themselves because soldiers forged that right.

And through a lifetime of periodic outbreaks of war, it has never come to my attention where, regardless of the dangers facing them in a far-off land, U.S. soldiers ever asked for the world to stop back home. Rather, and hopefully this perception didn't emanate from some Ronald Reagan movie, they have sought results in their spare time. What's going on with the Lakers? How are the Yankees doing? What happened to Duke?

By the way, isn't it presumptuous for those within the NCAA power circle, those who could halt competition, to place such importance on their event?

Is anything else being disrupted? Isn't it our responsibility to keep producing whatever it is we produce? Mitch Albom of the Detroit Free Press was on the money when he surmised the tournament "is just one form of nonwar life, like going to work or eating in restaurants."

Venture out tonight on North Prospect, and see if anything has changed. Are the waiting lines shorter?

On that subject, imagine what percentage of the $75 billion war budget we could collect if everyone coast-to-coast took his customary dinner-drinks bill, put it in a fund for Iraq and spent one Saturday night on bread and water?

Think that's too much of a sacrifice?

Then you're advised to watch "The Pianist."

Yep, you caught me at the movie Tuesday night. Me and lots of other people. We all need a respite from the constant bombardment on Fox and CNN. Too much of this is demoralizing to the human spirit. We can't help by watching all the time. What's important is that we understand the seriousness of what's happening and we keep living. Keep the games going. Diversion is good for the soul.

Even during the grim days of World War II, sports continued. Yes, the Rose Bowl was moved from Pasadena. And, yes, the 1944 St. Louis Browns were the worst pennant winner any living person ever saw, barely sidestepping their "first in booze, last in the AL" reputation. But the games went on and it never made sense for them to do otherwise.

1991

A national study tells a misleading story about UI basketball graduation rates.

CHAMPAIGN — My first inclination is to reject the significance of men's basketball graduation rates because:

(1) It's easy to finagle the numbers, and national reports are often incomplete and/or confusing;

(2) You can't make someone graduate if he doesn't want to;

(3) There may be more pressing things to do with your life, like using a supple body to earn $15 million in the next seven years playing in the NBA;

(4) Failure to graduate doesn't mean the individual didn't have a positive, rewarding and meaningful college experience.

Recently, Lou Henson's Illini program received a minor black eye because a national study of the enrolling 1984 class showed a 25 percent graduation rate at the UI. Only one, Jens Kujawa, graduated.

Actually, all four graduated. But Glynn Blackwell was a negative in the computation because he returned later to complete his degree, and two others — Scott Haffner and Olaf Blab — transferred to Evansville University and received their degrees there.

The percentage should have been 100 percent but came out 25 percent because of the particular limitations used in the study.

A more meaningful question than how many graduated would be: During the Henson years beginning in 1974-75, how many of the 45 freshman cagers who enrolled through 1986-87 had a positive, profitable college experience?

Terry Cole, director of academic services, offers to handle that question:

"I have a concern when anyone does not graduate because I feel this leaves a void. It's important to graduate. And when athletes leave without graduating, we encourage them to return.

"But I wouldn't say that lack of a degree means that it was a negative experience. Of the 45 freshmen we tracked, I wouldn't classify any of them as a failure."

For the record, 29 of 45 enrolling freshmen have received bachelor's degrees. A 30th, Phil Kunz, is graduating this spring at Iowa State with a 3.7 grade point average, bringing the graduation percentage to 66.7. A 31st, Curtis Taylor, is on line to graduate at Jacksonville. A 32nd, Tom Schafer, left Iowa State to play pro basketball but is now back in school there.

NBA squadmen Kendall Gill and Scott Meents, who left after four years at the UI, are within two courses and could accomplish that in summer school.

As it stands, Gill "counts against" the UI despite the fact he's headed for a multi-million dollar career in his chosen field.

Does it make any sense for Gill to be a negative? Isn't he a plus in the real sense, just as Magic Johnson is for Michigan State, and Michael Jordan for North Carolina?

And who is going to take the position that Dallas' "most popular Maverick" Derek Harper, who'll be 30 on his next birthday, has somehow failed because he left school a year early to join the NBA?

"That would be tough to say," said Cole. "I just hope he's been advised well and has used his money correctly. Was Illinois a positive experience for Derek? Based on the time I spent with him, that part was good, although there is a gap there and I'd still like to see him finish. But he may not feel that he needs it."

Of eight Illini in the NBA, only Eddie Johnson and Ken Battle have graduated. Gill and Meents probably won't. But a lot of folks with degrees are not nearly so successful. Barring atrocious investing, Johnson, Harper and Norman are already set for life, and several others are on line.

One problem in the national emphasis on graduation rates is the tendency of many basketball players to transfer. Two Wisconsin squadmen, Kass Weaver and Larry Hisle, have decided to leave in the last few weeks. Purdue coach Gene Keady has received word for the impending departure (to Rice) of Todd Schoettelkotte, latest in a swinging door group that includes such coming-and-going Boilermaker prospects as Woody Austin, Loren Clyburn, Rich Mount, Bill Reid, Keith Stewart and Sean Sutton in just the last two years.

In this sense, basketball can't be compared with volleyball and tennis. There is much more at stake, and cagers sometimes need two shots to find their proper competitive level. It is also a fact that a higher percentage of basketball players come from lower economic (and thus academically disadvantaged) areas, automatically decreasing the graduation odds.

But if Cole is right, not one of the 45 freshmen brought in by Henson in a 13-year stretch had what Cole would describe as a negative college experience. Clearly, graduation rates don't tell the whole story.

A lot of headlines screamed "foul" on the subject of graduation rates without analyzing the criteria. Michael Jordan attended North Carolina to set up his future. If he "counts against," there is something wrong with the study.

MAY 19, 1996

If you're looking for silly rules, check the NCAA book of regulations.

CHAMPAIGN — Silly rules?

Hey, the NCAA has some beauties. No wonder the public questions the level-headedness of all those educated representatives who set the college rules.

And we're not just talking about the awful impropriety of buying some prospective athlete a Coke.

— While it is permissible to send out football media guides (with schedules printed in them) to high school prospects, it has not been permissible to mail pocket-size schedule cards to the athletes. In a stunning turnaround, the NCAA has lifted that restriction next year.

— If a local Marching Band or Future Farmers of America group asked for the donation of an autographed basketball from former Illini coach Lou Henson to use in a fund raiser, he could not comply because, in theory, he might be gaining an unfair advantage with a recruit. Yet Henson gave basketballs to all his athletes in his summer camps.

— As a cost containment move a few years back, the NCAA banned three-color athletic department letterheads ... then a year later, after reams of letterheads had been thrown out, voted to permit three-color material again.

— Athletes receive all sorts of mailings, and Lou Tepper sends hand-written notes, but it isn't permissible for a college coach to leave a note for transmission by the prep coach after watching the athlete compete. That is considered "bothering the athlete."

— College coaches are not permitted to talk to any media member about a prospect's ability until the signing is final, but can discuss the athlete with prep coaches and scouts, who are free to relay what the college coach thinks. Many college coaches talk openly about prospects, and writers find ways to get the information to the public without directly quoting them.

— If a college recruiter bumps into a prospect while visiting a high school, he is advised to self-report the "violation." Some judgment must be used because the number of "bumps" can be astronomical when seven members of each university's football staff stroll the halls, offices and gyms of more than 100 high schools apiece during May alone.

Failure to self-report a significant "bump" is what started the winter uproar over Louisiana's All-American football prospect Eric Jefferson.

Months after the alleged event, Illini coach O'Neill Gilbert was accused by LSU head coach Gerry DiNardo of turning a bump into a full-scale meeting. Gilbert and Jefferson denied it, and the high school coach and athletic director indicated they weren't aware of any inappropriate meeting.

"It is always better to report yourself because it removes the opportunity for somebody else to do it," said Rick Allen, named full-time Illini compliance officer by John Mackovic in the wake of the NCAA basketball investigation of the early 1990s.

"These so-called bumps can be tricky. You take the case of Lou Holtz at Notre Dame. If he visits a high school, all the athletes want to go to the coaches' office to see him. We had some of that when Greg Landry joined our staff from the Bears. Landry had been in the NFL a long time, and we worked real hard to familiarize Landry with NCAA rules."

Allen added:

"The uncomfortable aspect of my job is that I feel like I'm perceived by the coaches as saying no all the time.

"I constantly emphasize keeping good records. If your activities are well-documented, at least you have verify where you've been."

Once upon a time, when T.J. Wheeler was being recruited, I had to file a letter with the NCAA because, unbeknownst to both myself and Lou Henson, Wheeler's dad picked us up at the airport. We drove to a restaurant before we knew who he was. Really.

MARCH 18, 1992

Enthusiasm wanes during the post-White and post-Stoner years.

CHAMPAIGN — Will central Illinoisans pour out Friday afternoon to see All-American guard Richard Keene?

A Collinsville sports writer phoned Wednesday to ask if the Kahok guard's appearance in the Elite Eight Friday (12:15 p.m. vs.

Proviso East) will draw a core of Illini fans to the Assembly Hall? That's an excellent question.

Or we might phrase it from a different perspective. Is there anyone short of Garth Brooks capable of lifting grumpy Illini fans out of doldrums?

In case you haven't noticed, general enthusiasm for the UI athletic program has been draining steadily since Mike White and Neale Stoner went flying back to California.

Their firings offended their friends and their followers. And it didn't help when the ensuing years were spent under cloudy community perception that leading UI administrators weren't wholly supportive of Deon Thomas and his wrongly accused basketball coaches.

Said an insider who asks to be anonymous:

"It's very noticeable. It's everywhere I go. Support, both financial and otherwise, has become increasingly shaky. The football team was 6-6 and the basketball team was 13-15. It's like everybody is waiting for something good to happen."

This is a phenomenon worthy of study. John Mackovic had a bang-up four years as football coach but left with no tears on either side, and without ever really capturing the hearts of the fandom. The 1991 attendance average, with super draws Michigan, Ohio State and Houston here, barely squeezed over 60,000. A paltry following accompanied the Illini team to the John Hancock Bowl.

All those close basketball triumphs a year ago allowed Lou Henson's program to hang on a year longer than it figured to. It wasn't until the current quintet lost to Northwestern, and we were reminded of how many times Northwestern has thumped Illinois in a variety of men's sports, that the full realization set in.

The program hit a plateau as it entered the 1990s, and the slippage is undeniable. The Illini basketball team, which reached the Final Four just four years ago, had one sellout all season, and the actual attendance was far below whatever sales figures they reported. A bunch of loyal folks didn't use their tickets.

To the west, Iowa fans remain fanatical about a basketball program that, in addition to Bruce Pearl's disgraceful recruiting practices, has tended to fade at the end of each season. The Hawkeyes lost four of their last six games in 1989, finished 4-15 in 1990, lost nine of the concluding 17 in 1991, and recently finished on a 5-5 non-roll with perhaps the poorest performance in the final game at Michigan State. Still, they bring down the roof at Carver-Hawkeye Arena.

To the east, Indiana basketball followers handle the hills and valleys, not to mention the public cruelties to their athletes, without losing faith in their religion ... and the Purdue program is propelled along by fiercely loyal backing.

In 1990, when nearby Indianapolis had a player like Keene coming to town — his name was Damon Bailey — excitement reached a boiling point.

Fans filled the 41,000-seat Hoosier Dome to the rafters, and demand was such that they could have filled it twice over. If there had been 100,000 good seats, they would have sold them all.

This Class AA tournament doesn't even keep pace with the state's talent-shy Class A event. Attendance for the Friday afternoon Class AA quarterfinal session the last six years has ranged from 8,300 and 9,400. Since 1986, the big-school Saturday night finals, featuring some of the nation's premier high school teams, have ranged between 9,800 and 13,000.

The eight-game Class A show outdrew its Class AA counterpart by 9,000 in 1990 and by 12,000 in 1989, and has outdrawn the big-school event every year since 1985.

So, you ask, will Illinoisans who don't normally attend the state tournament come flying forth to see Lou Henson's new prizes, Keene and Bradley-Bourbonnais' Chris Gandy?

Well, you'd think it would be a fun idea, one that would catch on.

Champaign-Urbana's growing lack of interest in the Class AA tournament led to the basketball tournament moving to Peoria, even though the facility there in no way compares to the Assembly Hall. Interest in the Big U has hurt the high school turnout locally.

AUGUST 31, 2007

The sports world has undergone dramatic change over the years.

CHAMPAIGN — When the Illini football team reported 40 autumns ago following marginal summer training, the staff received on-field coaching help from fifth-year seniors.

Unlike Nebraska, Oklahoma and other powerhouses, the Big Ten did not permit redshirting. As they finished classes toward graduation, these fifth-year students picked up a few bucks assisting on the field.

In the day, leaders of the major conferences agreed that freshmen should serve a year's apprenticeship before playing with the big boys, and mini-schedules of freshman games were played. The stodgy Big Ten went a step further by setting up stiff academic transfer rules to discourage junior college transfers.

And, until 1975, just one Big Ten team could attend postseason play — Rose Bowl only — and for many years a repeat conference champion could not succeed itself in Pasadena.

It became the Big Two-Little Eight with Ohio State and Michigan dominating until the conference was freed for multiple bowl opportunities. Just as the wild-card concept has kept 16 Major League baseball teams in strong playoff contention into late August, today's multiple bowl system makes nearly all November football games critical where once they weren't ... bringing greater depth, incentive and balance to the Big Ten.

In the day, well ... you wouldn't recognize it. The only 300-pounders were viewed as obese. Today, Illinois has 19 squadmen weighing between 290 and 320. At 240, Dick Butkus would be an average-sized linebacker today.

Guard Ron Guenther, Illini MVP in 1966, was listed at 5-foot-9 and 204 after spending his summer as a carpenter. Summer weight training was encouraged but not required. Coaches were slow to accept the idea of water breaks at practice because their own coaches, years before, didn't believe in it. Nor had it become a "requirement" for entire squads to spend their summers training on campus.

You could burn your leaves, smoke in a restaurant and drive without a seat belt. Some of us left our doors unlocked. Men felt undressed without a hat, and donned suits and ties where none are worn today. The common fear was global freezing.

There were no cell phones, much less the Internet, and television viewing was limited to the three major networks. The great John Wooden, who won 10 NCAA basketball crowns at UCLA through 1975, never saw his coaching salary reach $35,000 a year. Some college coaches sold insurance in the summer to make ends meet. Penn State was a happy independent, and Rush Limbaugh would be fired a couple of times before finding his niche. For those who missed Cary Grant in "Gunga Din," Halloween brought out the only "terrorists" we knew about ... pint-sized window soapers.

News-Gazette and Courier sports writers waited two or three days for the mailman to deliver out-of-town newspapers with stories about other Big Ten teams. Long-distance costs restricted our telephone calls. A blog was presumed to be some sort of heavy smog (it still is), and sports call-in shows hadn't yet clogged the radio airwaves.

Football road trips in the 1960s sometimes required traveling reporters to locate a Western Union office that would take typewritten pages and transmit an all-caps article for the newspaper's proof reader to correct and the Linotype operator to produce in hot metal. Sunday columns seldom had fewer than a dozen mistakes.

Yep, those were the good old days.

Practices were open and Pete Elliott, Illini football coach from 1960 through 1966, conducted post-practice interviews informally in a small locker room while he and his assistants showered and dressed. Nobody played "gotcha" in those days.

That would inevitably change, as did a wrong-minded attitude permeating the community's business leaders that, for those in the know, for those who understood what was happening elsewhere, Illini football and basketball really couldn't be expected to succeed without stretching the rules.

An Illini "slush fund" providing monthly stipends for athletes ran through the Butkus-Grabowski and Jones-Dunlap eras until assistant director Mel Brewer, keeper of the illegal books, turned them over to the university president in December 1966. That prevented Elliott from being named athletic director, caused coaches and players to be severed, and sent Illinois careening toward several subsequent run-ins with Big Ten and NCAA investigators.

Guenther and his compliance officers now make concerted efforts to keep the contributors happy without letting them get too close to the athletes. And the continuing flow of alumni contributions has led to an astonishing buildup of facilities on the south campus.

Memorial Stadium, constructed for less than $2 million in donations during the Roaring '20s when few women attended games, was later found to have too few restrooms for the ladies. And no stadium builder thought far enough ahead to construct suites to take advantage of lucrative corporate interests ... those suites, restrooms and other amenities now going up at a cost of $120 million for full stadium renovation. Imagine! It takes $120 million to improve a structure built for less than $2 million.

For many years, football fields were covered with grass. Those fields hadn't yet been named after anyone and often became badly worn and sometimes muddy during the course of the season.

Long before artificial surfaces became popular, Julie Rykovich intercepted an Ohio State pass and tiptoed from the mud to the grassy sideline for a 98-yard return that beat the Buckeyes 16-7 in the UI's first Rose Bowl season of 1946. And who in attendance can forget when Tommy O'Connell squinted through a driving snowstorm and found an unguarded Rex Smith in the slop to edge Michigan 7-0 in

1951? Or 15 years later when Bruce Sullivan matched Rykovich's 98-yarder and dove into a snowbank with the clinching score in Ann Arbor?

Michigan was always tough but didn't carry the same fear factor in those days. Illinois beat the Wolverines seven of 10 in the 1950s. That's just one of many, many changes.

If there is anything to add, it may be that the newspaper business is undergoing a dramatic change with the growth of computers and the Internet. I wonder how most readers will obtain their news in the next half-century.

FEBRUARY 1, 1999

Fans weigh in as Notre Dame considers Big Ten offer.

CHAMPAIGN — That groundswell of complaint you don't hear is an unworried alumni clan skipping along, confident in the belief Notre Dame will not give up its independence and join the Big Ten.

Cup your ear, and the Irish battle cry is clear: "Oh, no, let's don't go!"

For Notre Dame to do otherwise, the Rev. Edward Malloy and his inner circle must make a what's-best decision that would be challenged at every level ... by voting trustees who are overwhelmingly against the idea ... by oft-arrogant alumni traditionalists who support the university with their dollars ... by a student body that revels in Notre Dame's independent football status.

Yes, the faculty senate, recognizing the great advantages of joining the Committee for Institutional Cooperation, voted 25-4 in favor of the Big Ten. But this merely shows the chasm between faculty thinking and the overemphasized importance of football, a chasm that exists on many campuses.

But don't knock football. ND's reputation is football-based. Except for football, ND would be a medium-sized Roman Catholic university on a comparable Midwestern level with DePaul, Creighton, Marquette and Xavier.

Football is the only real reason the Big Ten wants to make Notre Dame the 12th conference member, and football is the only real reason for Irish resistance to joining. Remember, the Big Ten already has denied Notre Dame's desire to be admitted in all sports except football.

If Notre Dame makes sense geographically and competitively, it is a distinct mismatch academically. On one hand, the Irish don't want to lose their identity as an independent (there's that word again) Catholic university with strong religious teachings. On the other, the CIC wouldn't exactly be enhanced by taking in a member with such a small and unimpressive postgraduate program.

It's a complicated question, one that requires foresight. Consider the changes that might occur when Irish football games count in the Big Ten in 2006. Consider how coalitions and agreements might change the bowl picture in the next seven years.

Though the subway alumni are thinking in terms of today, Malloy must think long-range. Where does Notre Dame want to be in 2010?

If he wishes to investigate further and carry the Big Ten issue into the April board meeting, he must be prepared to wage holy war with his vast constituency ... a constituency that will overflow with anti-Big Ten feelings if the debate isn't squelched Friday.

This isn't a money fuss. Notre Dame football will make it financially either way. This is a matter of control, of, yes, independence. The parochial institution spent the 20th century using its religion-based advantages to build an unmatched national reputation in football ... and ultimately a network television contract with NBC. In that regard, Notre Dame is distinct. Or, in constituency thinking, superior. If you disagree, how do you explain the fact no other university has its own network?

And, remember, if all else is equal, Notre Dame will get the nod in bowl selections. Many think if Ohio State had reached the "title game" in Tempe, Ariz., and if Notre Dame had beaten Southern Cal, the Rose Bowl quickly would have forgotten a half-century of relations with the Big Ten to take the Irish over Wisconsin. It's almost impossible to calculate Notre Dame's influence in matters like that.

Knowing they're in the catbird's seat, knowing they have the NBC deal, knowing they have the freedom to build a schedule around the likes of Army, Navy and Boston College, would the Irish rather embark on a century of facing Penn State, Ohio State and Michigan in a league that just hit new heights with a 5-0 bowl record?

And more to the point in insider thinking, do they have the football leader in Bob Davie to take on such a challenge? When Penn State made its momentous move, two factors weighed in heavily: (1) the secrecy of the negotiations and (2) the overseeing presence of Joe Paterno. When the folks from Pennsylvania got caught by surprise, they turned to Paterno, and Paterno calmed them by pointing to league affiliation as a smart, rewarding move.

There is no Paterno at Notre Dame. And this in-the-open issue has become high controversy. Take a poll within the ranks, and you'd get a number similar to Memorial Stadium fans voting for Chief Illiniwek. They know what they want, and they don't want change.

It is the overwhelming desire of Notre Dame's football people to remain independent, regardless of logic and benefits to academia and other sports. Football trumps everything else.

JANUARY 16, 1998

The expansion landscape is confusing as the Big Ten goes forward with 11 schools.

CHAMPAIGN — The secret in bringing Penn State into the Big Ten Conference was secrecy itself.

It was accomplished in darkness, in high-level, presidential meetings and without the disrupting involvement of newspaper editorials, talk shows or any kind of referendum. Opponents didn't have time to stock a pile of rocks to throw.

The idea was so farfetched to the Nittany Lions' fandom that it barely occurred to them. Then suddenly, guided by the vision of then-UI president Stan Ikenberry, it happened.

From here on, all such endeavors will be out in the open. Syracuse couldn't join Penn State as its "eastern partner" without a full, open discussion, without a whirlwind of controversial Internet exchanges, and without the vote of its Board of Trustees.

Syracuse is mentioned because, with Notre Dame repulsing Big Ten overtures and Texas too locked into the new Big 12, the prestigious Orangemen offer the best football-basketball package with all those New York television homes.

"This has been a hot topic, and we've been exploring it," said Don Webb of the Syracuse Newspapers Inc. "I don't think conference shuffling is done yet.

"Some people like the idea (of Syracuse moving) because they see the Big East as a sinking ship. The Big East desperately needs Miami to recover in football, and that may take awhile. And people here would like to see the rivalry with Penn State renewed.

"But it's a mixed bag. Others feel differently. With its contracts, the Big East is financially set into the next century. And Syracuse is very much an eastern-oriented school. From that standpoint, there would be a lot of resistance."

Syracuse athletic director Jake Crouthamel said he's "given it no thought" because he's had no reason to.

"If an offer of that nature came, it would certainly be considered," he said. "But our roots are eastern, and it would be a controversial issue. It would be inappropriate for me to speculate what the trustees might do."

OK, so what about Missouri?

The Tigers are a geographical fit. They're building a new basketball arena, and the football program appears to be bouncing back.

The public position, as it must be, is that Mizzou is happy with its new position in the Big 12. But there are hints of frustration in a conference that focuses so much on Texas.

The school was interested in being No. 12 when Penn State came in, but the Big Ten passed. Now, the question is: Assuming Syracuse won't come or is considered too distant, might the revamped leadership in the Big Ten and at Missouri view the landscape in a different manner than before?

"There is no question that Missouri would look at an overture from the Big Ten," a Missouri source said.

"Potentially, the revenue might be better. Big Ten schools draw well here. The Ohio State football game (Sept. 27) drew our biggest crowd in 15 years. And the basketball game with Illinois in St. Louis is a major attraction.

"I always thought Missouri would be a good fit in the Big Ten. The school has one of the highest entrance requirements in the Big 12."

Before expanding, Big Ten athletic directors would want to know the financial benefits.

Would Missouri, for example, add money to the pot? Or would it reduce the TV pie and the bowl split by taking up one more share?

Note how Penn State boosted everyone's coffers by reaching the football alliance a year ago.

Continuing with 11 schools is a workable option, even if it means one football team is idle each week during league play in October and November. The odd number hardly affects basketball because the quintets play virtually any day, including Sunday.

But most leagues operate with even numbers, and there are seven 12-team leagues in Division I basketball this winter, all divided in one way or another (the Big 12 has one league standings, but pairs its league tournament by divisions).

If the Big Ten had two six- team divisions, it would be possible to set up a lucrative football playoff game, just as the Big 12 and Southeastern Conference have done. With TV contracts set for years, a Big Ten basketball tournament just weeks away, and the Rose Bowl joining the alliance next year, consideration of a 12th team and the conference football playoff is the next major item on the Big Ten agenda.

The Big Ten declined to make an offer to Missouri and appears headed for a lengthy period as an 11-school conference. With Notre Dame out of the mix, there appears to be no logical geographical fit.

MARCH 5, 1995

Tradition no factor in decision to move the state basketball tournament.

CHAMPAIGN — IHSA executive director Dave Fry's announcement Tuesday came as a kick in the stomach to thousands of basketball traditionalists.

The Assembly Hall was the dream, the goal, the obsession of every Illinois youngster who bounced a dribble off his foot in the family driveway, of every teen-ager pretending he was Kenny Battle or Kendall Gill competing in the Elite Eight.

For many, it has become basketball's Holy Grail ... where Lawrenceville gained its fame ... where Thornridge and Quincy and East St. Louis Lincoln celebrated majestic championships ... where Pinckneyville regained its pride.

This isn't Assembly Hall. That's in Indiana. This is THE Assembly Hall and there is a difference. It sets here on the prairie, a cross between a giant mushroom and a flying saucer come to rest. It is wondrous in its setting, an architectural marvel. No one forgets his first interior view. It is what memories are made of.

Since 1963, when Chicago Carver guard Anthony Smedley made a game-winning basket that Cazzie Russell couldn't get the year before, and since 1972 when two quintets were crowned, a state overflowing with basketball desire has watched as its most important championships were decided here.

That's why Tuesday's decision sending the boys' Elite Eight events to Peoria is such a staggering blow.

But this decision isn't about tradition, or about what the state's coaches and athletes overwhelmingly prefer. Three basic reasons led to the move.

— Fry and IHSA leaders visualize a tourney concept that would use Peoria's spacious Civic Center convention hall for associated "opportunities" ... clinics, reunions, leadership conferences, sports exhibitions ... a carnival atmosphere. If Peoria has fewer seats and less parking, the space available "under one roof" is vastly superior.

— Peoria's community-led financial bid is better and will allow a reduction in ticket prices. Peoria has made an intelligent "investment" and has purchased an event that will bring untold new dollars and publicity to the city.

— Folks here took it for granted too long. IHSA officials have grumbled for decades over an Assembly Hall concessions split that they considered inequitable, and harbored grudges over their belief that fans were being gouged by hotels and restaurants.

If the latter problem was corrected in the latest proposal, why couldn't it have been done before the gun was put to their head? It is hard to dispute those saying Champaign-Urbana was waylaid by its own greed.

Ron Guenther, Illini athletic director, has fought this same losing battle (over unreasonable rates) related to football Saturdays. The perception is that "everybody tries to get rich" on a few special weekends.

"The athletic department had no role in these negotiations," said Guenther. "We expressed great desire to keep it, but it was out of our hands."

Will the change hurt UI basketball recruiting? At first glance, you would think so. It worked favorably in attracting Jerry Gee, Richard Keene and Kiwane Garris, who played here as preps. But, then, perhaps not.

"It can work both ways," said UI coach Lou Henson. "If a player has a bad experience here, it can have an adverse effect. In any case, most of the seniors have already made their decisions prior to the tournament."

So, where do C-U and the Assembly Hall go from here?

If it's important, they will study Peoria's scheme and develop stronger leadership for the next go-round after Peoria has had its three-year run.

C-U got caught with its pants down this trip, and didn't really get the team ball rolling until Jim Turpin began calling city leaders from his WDWS office. This came just a few weeks prior to the bid deadline, after the IHSA's Jim Flynn warned Turpin about the seriousness of the situation.

"The disadvantage in being the incumbent is that they can ask why we didn't make the needed changes prior to this bid," said Turpin.

Now the incumbent will be Peoria, which fizzled horribly in taking the Prairie State Games from C-U, and might be less attractive in 1998 after thousands of fans who could otherwise see the tournament are turned away ... and a few inevitable horror stories emerge from the riverboat casino.

Dating to Huff Gym, there was always something special about the high school tournament being held at the site of the state university. And the Assembly Hall made it doubly special. But Peoria outbid Champaign-Urbana for the event and, now that it is a four-division tournament, it is doubtful it ever returns.

AUGUST 14, 2002

It's not easy to pull off, but it pays to redshirt.

"Why should I redshirt somebody for the next coach?"
— Coach George Anonymous

CHAMPAIGN — Having redshirted in 1990, a 22-year-old Dana Howard won the prestigious Butkus Trophy in 1994, a fete that Kevin Hardy repeated in 1995.

Without an extra year, neither linebacker would have been so honored ... and so productive for the Illini. Fact is, you'd be hard-pressed to name ANYBODY who wasn't better at 22 than at 18.

But it remains a touchy subject. To pronounce here that all but a tiny few freshmen should be redshirted is to place that opinion in direct conflict with virtually all of the UI's head football and basketball coaches.

The top players want to play, and the coaches want to play them ... but seldom is it to the long-term benefit of the university.

Fragile egos dominate the hardcourt. Said former Illini coach Lou Henson, who once lost Springfield's Ed Horton by merely breaching the redshirt subject: "In basketball, it's the players. Most don't want to sit out. It's hard to sell."

For prep stars, it's embarrassing enough not to enter the pro draft. To sit out a year is unthinkable. Still, look what it did for Chris Gandy and Brian Johnson. Think what a fifth season meant to Doug Altenberger, Larry Smith, Deon Thomas, Kenny Battle and Jerry Hester. Redshirted Quinn Richardson was vital to the UI's Elite Eight run in 1984.

And consider that the 14-18 dropoff in 1999 could have been avoided if, somehow, Jarrod Gee, Matt Heldman and/or Kevin Turner had been redshirted. Consider further that the anticipated dropoff in 2003 could have been minimized by holding out Robert Archibald, Damir Krupalija and/or Lucas Johnson along the way.

Point is, if Gee and Turner had been available in 1999, Lon Kruger wouldn't have needed Archibald and Johnson then. The process has a cumulative effect. And the advantage of employing 22- and 23-year-olds over 18- and 19-year-olds is overwhelming.

To move onto Ron Turner's good side ... temporarily ... we have positive news that Illini receivers have reversed field and become a vastly improved area during this term. Brandon Lloyd, Dwayne Smith, Walter Young, Aaron Moorehead, Greg Lewis and Eric McCoey have all been redshirted and there isn't a senior in the bunch.

Because of their glue-fingered showing in early drills, there is no reason to play highly impressive freshman Kendrick Jones. But Illinois is thin at outside linebacker, requiring use of raw freshman. Coach Ron Turner calls it "scary." But Turner could have eased that crisis by redshirting Mon Long in 1997, when the green Sarasota plebe managed two solo tackles.

There are other linebacker examples. Eric Guenther entered nine games in 1995, spending eligibility he could have used in 1999. Guenther's presence would have allowed Turner to redshirt Jerry Schumacher, which would be crucial in 2003. Chris Hoffman was employed in 1996, and was therefore unavailable last season when Turner felt obliged to use Joe Bevis and Brad Haywood on special teams. Again, the carryover impact.

And do we dare bring up the QB? Next year, with so many playmakers back, they'll need a leader. And just imagine, the key piece to the 2002 puzzle, Kurt Kittner, would be eligible if he hadn't played part-time in the "lost" 3-8 season of 1998.

You can't redshirt Dee Brown or Deron Williams. I understand that. But it is almost always preferable to withhold marginal freshmen who barely see action. Most recently, the misfortunes of the 2008 basketball season could have been softened if Warren Carter and Rich McBride were still around. There are examples too numerous to mention.